Herbert Marcuse

D1564175

Modern European Thinkers

Series Editors: Anne Beech and David Castle

Over the past few decades, Anglo-American social science and humanities have experienced an unprecedented interrogation, revision and strengthening of their methodologies and theoretical underpinnings through the influence of highly innovative scholarship from continental Europe. In the fields of philosophy, post-structuralism, psychoanalysis, critical theory and beyond, the works of a succession of pioneering writers have had revolutionary effects on Anglo-American academia. However, much of this work is extremely challenging, and some is hard or impossible to obtain in English translation. This series provides clear and concise introductions to the ideas and work of key European thinkers.

As well as being comprehensive, accessible introductory texts, the titles in the 'Modern European Thinkers' series retain Pluto's characteristic radical political slant, and critically evaluate leading theorists in terms of their contribution to genuinely radical and progressive intellectual endeavour. And while the series does explore the leading lights, it also looks beyond the big names that have dominated theoretical debates to highlight the contribution of extremely important but less well-known figures.

Also available

Hannah Arendt
Finn Bowring

Alain Badiou
Jason Barker

Georges Bataille
Benjamin Noys

Jean Baudrillard
Mike Gane

Walter Benjamin
Esther Leslie

Pierre Bourdieu
Jeremy F. Lane

Gilles Deleuze
John Marks

André Gorz
Conrad Lodziak and Jeremy Tatman

Félix Guattari
Gary Genosko

Jürgen Habermas
Luke Goode

Guy Hocquenghem
Bill Marshall

Slavoj Žižek
Ian Parker

HERBERT MARCUSE

An Aesthetics of Liberation

Malcolm Miles

PlutoPress
www.plutobooks.com

First published 2012 by Pluto Press
345 Archway Road, London N6 5AA

www.plutobooks.com

Distributed in the United States of America exclusively by
Palgrave Macmillan, a division of St. Martin's Press LLC,
175 Fifth Avenue, New York, NY 10010

British Library Cataloguing in Publication Data
A catalogue record for this book is available from the British Library

ISBN   978 0 7453 3039 6   Hardback
ISBN   978 0 7453 3038 9   Paperback

Library of Congress Cataloging in Publication Data applied for

This book is printed on paper suitable for recycling and made from fully managed
and sustained forest sources. Logging, pulping and manufacturing processes are
expected to conform to the environmental standards of the country of origin.

10   9   8   7   6   5   4   3   2   1

Designed and produced for Pluto Press by Chase Publishing Services Ltd
Typeset from disk by Stanford DTP Services, Northampton, England
Simultaneously printed digitally by CPI Antony Rowe, Chippenham, UK and
Edwards Bros in the United States of America

Contents

Introduction   1

1 Aesthetics and the Reconstruction of Society   10

2 The Artist and Social Theory   27

3 Affirmations   46

4 A Literature of Intimacy   65

5 Society as a Work of Art   86

6 The End of Utopia   106

7 The Aesthetic Dimension   126

8 Legacies and Practices   145

Notes   165
Index   191

Introduction

In this Introduction I set out my aims in writing the book, its scope, and why I think that Herbert Marcuse's writing is of interest today. I explain why I address his work on aesthetics rather than the wider project for a critical theory of society, sketch the book's organisation, and finally say a little of the background from which I wrote it.

AIMS AND SCOPE

My aim is to increase interest in Marcuse's writing on aesthetics. Although there has been a proliferation of commentary on the work of Walter Benjamin and Theodor W. Adorno – his contemporaries in the development of critical theory, both of whom also emphasised aesthetics – less has been published on Marcuse's work. Benjamin's essay on the work of art[1] has been used almost to exhaustion in courses on photography and media arts, and Adorno is seen as a more philosophically weighty contributor. Yet in the 1960s, when it seemed society might change, Marcuse's writing reached a wider readership and evoked a more immediate engagement with the problems and potential benefits of a cultural revolt.

Marcuse died in 1979, after which a few books on his work were published.[2] But his theories then fell into neglect until publication of the *Collected Papers* began in 1998,[3] followed by a further few critical titles.[4] Yet the *Collected Papers*, edited by Douglas Kellner in collaboration with Peter Marcuse, show the depth of Marcuse's insights into culture, and the consistency of his pursuit of an understanding of social change. At the time of writing, five of the planned six volumes are in print, and have been a key source for my re-reading of Marcuse's work. Organised thematically, the *Collected Papers* juxtapose both well-known and hitherto unpublished material. But the *Collected Papers* will appeal to readers already interested in Marcuse's work. I make no claim to compete with Kellner's scholarly introductions to each volume, and aim instead to offer an introductory commentary relating specifically to Marcuse's aesthetic theories.

An increasing tendency towards interdisciplinary work since the 1970s suggests that Marcuse's effort to integrate social, cultural, political and psychoanalytic insights will be of methodological interest, too, across the arts, humanities and social sciences. His willingness to present seemingly opposed polarities – such as art's social and aesthetic dimensions – as potentially creative tensions, is also interesting, in a period when both education and politics seem driven increasingly by a need for solutions. For the most part, Marcuse's writing was work in progress, developed in the 1960s from one paper to the next as he spoke at student gatherings as well as academic conferences; ideas migrated, and questions were kept open. Andrew Feenberg, a colleague in the 1960s, recalls that Marcuse did not predict the revolution but elaborated 'the conditions of its possibility'.[5] I read this as the necessary ground for an imaginative reconstruction of society, and the beginning of a longer project of realisation.

To introduce Marcuse's writing on aesthetics is less difficult than, say, to comment on Adorno's work with its long sentences and aversion to paragraph breaks, or to explain Ernst Bloch's unrestricted eclecticism. When an interviewer suggested to him that his writing was 'difficult to understand', Marcuse replied that he regretted such difficulty, adding (in his German accent) 'I try to write clearer' and that he took comfort in the fact 'that a few people do and did understand it'.[6] In fact, his most important texts are remarkably succinct: *An Essay on Liberation*[7] and *The Aesthetic Dimension*[8] are each less than a hundred pages long, and accessible. Marcuse's philosophical and literary references are evidently drawn from the German philosophical tradition, and may now appear to be dated, but they are not intentionally obscure or obstructive. To me, what permeates a re-reading of Marcuse now is how radical and refreshing his ideas appear despite the lapse of time since their first publication.

I am, then, confident that this book will engage the interest of second- and third-year undergraduates in the arts, humanities and social sciences; and graduates in areas such as cultural policy, radical philosophy, and research between culture and the political sciences. It may also be relevant to the professional practices of artists, planners and policy makers seeking to look beyond a society governed by the notion that there is no alternative to the way things are. New social movements have proclaimed that a new society is possible; Marcuse's theories link the possibility to a careful reordering of the implicit values of the existing society, and a robust indication of its contradictions.

WHY READ MARCUSE NOW?

Marcuse's aesthetic theories were contextualised by the political realities of the 1930s (the rise of fascism), the 1960s (the counter-culture), and the 1970s (the aftermath of the failed revolt of 1968). Marcuse did not think that history repeated itself; yet if freedom was only a dream in the 1930s, against totalitarianism, and became a dream again in the 1970s (as now) in face of the rise of globalised capitalism, it is appropriate to recall the interlude of hope which occurred between these dire outlooks. Marcuse wrote in 1972 that, 'In its extreme manifestations, it [the capitalist system] practices the horrors of the Nazi regime.'[9] William Robinson writes that 'Transnational capital and its political agents are attempting ... a vast shift in the balance of class and social forces worldwide to consolidate the neo-liberal counterrevolution of the 1980s.'[10] I do not equate advanced capitalism and the Nazi state, but the extent to which neo-liberalism and earlier forms of totalitarianism seek total control of society – now by the soft forces of consumerism and culture – implies that a common form of analysis is needed. But does this include aesthetics? Marcuse argued in *The Aesthetic Dimension* that a concern with aesthetics is justified when political change appears remote. Today, the sporadic growth of new political formations in single-issue campaigning and activism inspires hope, but this is too easily marginalised. Now is an appropriate time, then, for a critical reconsideration of the optimism of the 1960s which Marcuse reflected in his writing. The prospect of a new society was (and might still be) electrifying and contagious, a force to interrupt – and rout – the notion that world history has a single, given course.

For Marcuse, as for Bloch, to imagine another form of society is to begin the process of its realisation. Encouraged by the counter-culture and the New Left, Marcuse argued that art negated the dominant society, reintroducing the emphasis on sensuality of Marx's early writings. Marcuse writes of beauty as a non-repressive order, of society as a work of art, and of the reclamation of verbal language to express new values – in the context of a continuing and vital revision of Marxism for the conditions of the twentieth century. New frameworks arose in feminism, post-colonialism, and environmentalism, from the 1970s to the 1990s, but I argue that Marcuse's work contributes to an imaginative reconstruction of the social order alongside these frameworks, and that they are not incompatible.

As was said above, Marcuse's writing is a development of ideas in progress rather than a resolution of issues which would close debate. His aesthetic theory undergoes various shifts, mainly in line with the three periods identified above (the 1930s, the 1960s and the 1970s). In his early work, art affirms the value-structures of bourgeois society by displacing freedom to a realm of daydream. In his late work he insists on art's capacity to interrupt and to question the normative categories and codes through which the world is apprehended. To re-read Marcuse's aesthetic texts today prompts thought on both the *aesthetic* deficit inherited from Marxism, and the *critical* deficit in the rhetoric of the creative industries in the late twentieth century (which was the dominant narrative of urban redevelopment, evident in the cultural quarters and museums of contemporary art which were inserted in city after city). In place of culture as either dream or cure-all, Marcuse proposes culture as the location of a break in the historical pattern in which past tyrannies are reproduced in future revolutions.

I do not claim, however, that aesthetics was Marcuse's core concern. As Kellner writes in his Introduction to *Art and Liberation* (volume 4 of the *Collected Papers*): 'Herbert Marcuse produced a unique combination of critical social theory, radical aesthetics, psychoanalysis, and a philosophy of liberation and revolution.'[11] Marcuse's work on aesthetics was nonetheless significant. Charles Reitz argues in *Art, Alienation, and the Humanities* that Marcuse sets art-as-alienation against art-against-alienation in a potentially creative axis of tension and offers 'a qualitatively different kind of social criticism than that of classical Marxism'.[12] Kellner, too, writes that while 'aesthetics is not the key, primary, or central element in his thought', it was 'an important part of Marcuse's project that has not yet been properly appraised'.[13]

Within Marcuse's aesthetics there is an element of joy as the expression of a latent sense of pleasure evoked in art. I want – modestly – to complement Kellner's project by taking the promise of happiness as the content of art which is also the source for society's re-imagination. I emphasise Marcuse's optimism in the 1960s, but read this as in part prefigured in his writing in the 1940s on French literature, where he argues that love poems are the last resort of freedom in conditions of extreme oppression. Freedom is then encountered in a literature of intimacy, not in political literature or propaganda. In the 1960s, when the political fuses with personal life, this does not seem a strange idea. I suggest that, together with Marcuse's identification of a young intelligentsia (rather than the working class) as the driving force of change within an affluent society, this may be one of his more lasting legacies. Not everyone will agree on either of these points.

In his most optimistic period, still, Marcuse conjectured on a society as a work of art, as an aestheticisation of politics. This could mean that freedom is displaced to dreamland, and suffering is rendered beautiful, in an aestheticisation of the dominant society. But it can also mean an aesthetic transformation of politics in the production of a qualitatively different society, and the transformation of work into play, and social life into erotic encounter. In the 1930s, fascism garbed itself in the new sublimity of an architecture of searchlights – a culturally acceptable form of tyranny. But the idea of a society as a work of art is more than a dream, and becomes an imaginative re-visioning of society. As such, it re-introduces a utopian aim of ending scarcity, of introducing a life of ease beyond class divisions. Is this fanciful? Is utopia inevitably unrealistic? Looking back, and knowing that the revolt of 1968 failed, rather than discounting Marcuse's papers from the time as wild thinking, I argue that they are a repository of hope vital to any present or future imaginative reconstruction of society. In such a project, a new consciousness defines the historical break, while art's social and aesthetic dimensions are polarities between which critical work is done.

In my view, there is today an even greater need for Marcuse's utopianism than there was in the 1970s. This is confirmed by Angela Davies in an essay on Marcuse's legacy:

Marcuse's life-long insistence on the radical potential of art is linked to this obstinate insistence on the utopian dimension. On the one hand, art criticises and negates the existing social order by the power of its form, which in turn creates another universe, thus hinting at the possibility of building a new social order. But this relationship is highly mediated, as Marcuse continually emphasised ... On the other hand, emancipatory possibilities reside in the very forces that are responsible for the obscene expansion of an increasingly exploitative and repressive order. It seems to me that the overarching themes of Marcuse's thought are as relevant today ... as they were when his scholarship and political interventions were most widely celebrated.[14]

I agree. Marcuse's analyses of culture and society need to be read again, and some of his insights occur in comparable but different ways in more recent post-structuralist analyses of power. Both there and in Marcuse's work we glimpse a future which has more reality than either daydream or the fantasy of consumerism. As Davies says, the forces in charge of the present ordering of society also produce resistance to their dominance. Art questions the ways in which realities are apprehended, reasserting plurality. And art might lend visibility to how those realities are experienced. Part of my purpose towards the end of this book is, then, to speculate on how the ideas put forward by Marcuse remain valid as a framework through which to understand some of today's radical cultural production.

THE ORGANISATION OF THE BOOK

I refer to a range of Marcuse's writings from the 1930s to the 1970s, drawing on books published in his lifetime and texts newly published in the *Collected Papers*. This book, like the *Collected Papers*, is organised thematically, though I incorporate a chronology as well. I begin with early work, move through the optimism of the middle period, and end with the aestheticism of the late work. In the process, I examine strands of art-and-society, the promise of a happy life, and the paradoxical relations which occur between key concepts.

The book is arranged in eight chapters. Each chapter is fully referenced but I do not use notes to qualify what I have said (having used them in the past extensively, I now consider that method as splitting a text between two levels of reading, and at the expense of clarity).[15] The book is not separated into sections, but Chapters 1 to 3 offer some background to Marcuse's writing; Chapters 4 to 6 are the utopian core of the book; Chapter 7 deals with Marcuse's work in the 1970s; and Chapter 8 takes the arguments towards the present via art practice.

I begin Chapter 1, 'Aesthetics and the Reconstruction of Society', by citing Marcuse's last work, not (I hope) to be clever or perverse but as a means of engaging the reader with Marcuse's consistent validation of aesthetics. From that point of departure I address the aesthetic deficit in Marxism, the terrain which Marcuse always occupies. In Chapter 2, 'The Artist and Social Theory', I reconsider Marcuse's doctoral research on the German artist novel – of which Thomas Mann's *Death in Venice* is an example – before situating Marcuse within the Frankfurt Institute for Social Research, where he was employed from 1932, and noting his larger project of a critical theory of society. In Chapter 3, 'Affirmations', I deal with

Marcuse's 1937 essay on the affirmative character of bourgeois culture and the charge that it was complicit in the rise of fascism.

In the next chapter, 'A Literature of Intimacy', I turn to Marcuse's essay on French literature during the German occupation, written in 1945 (or slightly before), which argues that in such conditions freedom is glimpsed not in overtly political texts but in love poems and romantic novels. Chapters 5 and 6, 'Society as a Work of Art', and 'The End of Utopia', deal with Marcuse's most optimistic writing in the late 1960s. I review Marcuse's papers from 1967, given in New York, Berlin, London and Salzburg, in the context of student protest, the counter-culture and the possibility, as it then seemed, that a new society might be about to emerge. In Chapter 6, its title borrowed from a lecture in Berlin, I ask how Marcuse interrogated the process of radical social change; I identify problems in his theory, and ask whether his reliance on a new sensibility was (or is) viable, looking also at Marcuse's book *An Essay on Liberation* (written mainly in 1967 but revised in 1968) as perhaps representing a retrenchment after 1968.

In Chapter 7, 'The Aesthetic Dimension', I cite *Counter-Revolution and Revolt* and *The Aesthetic Dimension* to ask what critical and aesthetic legacy Marcuse leaves for today. In Chapter 8, 'Legacies and Practices', I question his aesthetic theory in relation to the contemporary art world. I look at art outside the norms of museum and gallery presentation in cases of contemporary art. I offer no Conclusion, saying only that the problem of art's relation to miserable social and political realms is not without hope. But I am aware too, of course, that to express hope can be a denial, from fear, of a pessimism too dark to contemplate.

BEFORE BEGINNING

As a painting student at Chelsea School of Art, London, from 1967 to 1971, I felt the optimism of the late 1960s at first hand. The art school was a few yards from the Kings Road, where an English version of the counter-culture blossomed. I wore frilled and flower-patterned shirts and chiffon scarves. Sometime in those years (which are rather vague in my memory) I read Marcuse's *Eros and Civilisation*,[16] his more immediate and accessible *Essay on Liberation*, and, finding a second-hand copy at a bookshop in Bristol, Norman O. Brown's *Life Against Death*.[17] I still have all three. Like Marcuse, Brown revised the work of Freud, if differently. Both writers attracted student readers to an integration of psychoanalysis and social theory (or of the personal and the political). I did not understand much in either book, but I suppose that the freedom to drift between categories meant something to me (I have spent my entire academic career drifting between disciplines). Later, I read Brown's enigmatic work *Love's Body*.[18] It ends, 'Everything is only a metaphor; there is only poetry' followed by a long quotation from a book of Tibetan mysticism. In retrospect that sounds very 1960s, drawing on Eastern religions and mind-changing substances in equal measure. Marcuse smoked cigars not marijuana, however, and occupied another part of the radical-alternative terrain. He was concerned with realities and rationalities, not mind-blowing experiences, yet the non-instrumental rationality he proposed was more mind-blowing (and history-reversing) than smoking funny cigarettes. And if I understood *An Essay on Liberation* as licensing my own desire for liberation from the conditions in which I had spent my suburban adolescence, that, too, had a wider implication that protest was not in vain.

I had been active in the peace movement since 1966, but was not at the Roundhouse when Marcuse spoke there, at the Dialectics of Liberation Congress in July 1967. I might have appreciated it had I been a year or two older, less socially inept, nervous, and what I took to be innately lonely. As it was I simply did not know about the event, in the gap between grammar school and art school. I remember going to a free concert on Parliament Hill Fields, and that, in my first weeks as an art student, a song about going to San Francisco and wearing flowers in your hair was on the radio all the time. Meanwhile the subtler strains of Nico and the Velvet Underground were played more or less constantly in the art school studio. I had shoulder-length hair and wore a string of orange wooden beads given to me by a girl I met while taking part in a free school organised by Bristol Free University in the summer of 1968. I remember the students who occupied Hornsey School of Art coming to Chelsea, too. But my critical thought really began when I started teaching in 1972. In a remarkably inter-disciplinary and creative environment at Farnham, I contributed to courses on alienation, symbolism and modernism for studio-based art and craft students.

It was then that I started to grapple with Marcuse's writing, trying to explain it in pub conversations as much as in lectures. Then, around 1980, after the publication of *The Aesthetic Dimension*, I had conversations with the critic Peter Fuller on how reading the book had changed the direction of his work. For Fuller, it was a catalyst for his abandonment of Marx – eventually for Ruskin (but that is another story). I was too vague a Marxist to be able to abandon it, but I noted Marcuse's insistence on revising, not relinquishing, Marxism. Later, in the 1990s, by which time I had begun to have writing published in the London-based magazine *Art Monthly*, I was able to introduce Marcuse's work to post-graduate students in art criticism at City University, London; and then taught a course on Marcuse's aesthetics at the University of Portsmouth. Embarking subsequently on doctoral research (late in my wayward career), I was able to revisit some of Marcuse's questions in open-ended conversations with my anarchistic supervisor, David Reason at the University of Kent. My main focus was Ernst Bloch's utopianism, employed as a way to look at contemporary art. Now I find Bloch too eclectic, except in his millenarianism. Marcuse's voice seems more measured.

This enabled me to reflect on Marcuse's radicalism, and his refusal of a system of knowledge affirming the status quo. How, then, might a new society emerge? Can it be within the dominant society: a revolution before the revolution? How does revolt avoid the reproduction of tyranny? Does art have agency? In a society which is a work of art, as Marcuse projected in 1967, there is no need for art as a specialist profession; but that is not the situation in which I find myself. A continuing concern for aesthetic theory is therefore necessary, and I am grateful to Pluto Press for the opportunity to re-read Marcuse's writing, and to regain something of the spark of hope which pervaded his work in the 1960s and coloured my time at art school and in the peace movement. Those experiences gave me a new horizon: a hope for liberation, for a life of joy which is not over the rainbow but is really possible. And I see it now, not through dark glasses or rose-tinted spectacles, but in protest which begins again against a capitalism now obviously, wildly incoherent and irrational. 'The horizon of history is still open.'[19]

1
Aesthetics and the Reconstruction of Society

In the opening words of *The Aesthetic Dimension*, first published in German in 1977 and in English in 1978, Herbert Marcuse admits a note of despair:

> In a situation where the miserable reality can be changed only through radical political praxis, the concern with aesthetics demands justification. It would be senseless to deny the element of despair inherent in this concern: a retreat into a world of fiction where existing conditions are changed and overcome only in the realm of the imagination.[1]

A number of ideas are fused here. There is an assertion of dark times which I read as the miserable reality of the 1970s, when the optimism of the 1960s faded into history. Yet there is a continuity between Marcuse's work from the 1960s and the 1970s. In the 1960s he looks to a new sensibility as prerequisite for a new society; and in the 1970s he argues that, while art cannot change the world, it contributes to an awareness from which appropriately informed political action – praxis – changes the conditions which produce (and reproduce) the miserable reality. The term praxis is a key concept in Marxism, and means more than the fusion of theory and practice. One definition would be the gaining of appropriate insights into past and present conditions in order to imagine future possibilities for change. By invoking the notion of 'radical political praxis' Marcuse confirms his position within successive re-groupings of the Left since the 1960s, and within a re-visioned Marxism. So, if at first reading the passage above implies that aesthetics is a substitute for politics in a period of despair, I think that Marcuse argues, on the contrary, that aesthetics *is* politics, taking a world of fiction – or imagined reality – as an oblique route to real change. In later parts of the book he argues that art has a potential to rupture the codes and categories of how the world is seen, to imagine the world not as it is but as it might be. There is an alternative to the way things are. It begins in imagination; the problem is how imagined worlds become material reality.

DREAMING SOCIAL CHANGE

Dreaming is involuntary and daydreaming is only vaguely intentional, but aesthetics involves consciousness and judgement. It introduces an *imaginative reconstruction of society* (a phrase I borrow from Ruth Levitas),[2] which I locate at the core of Marcuse's project for a critical theory of society. Hence the theory articulated in *The Aesthetic Dimension* is not defeatist but presents a viable strategy in the circumstances of the 1970s. I would argue that it remains viable today, though the frameworks through which the conditions of unfreedom need to be analysed have changed, following feminism and post-colonialism, and the interrogation of power in post-structuralism. Marcuse was aware of feminism, and often alluded to struggles for national identity in ex-colonial countries; he planned a series of essays on Marxism, feminism and the failure of the Left, some of which were published in German.[3] But the English edition planned for Beacon Press in Boston never appeared; instead Marcuse completed the essay which became *The Aesthetic Dimension*, describing it in a letter to the publisher as 'a very responsible text, not a lecture, but a larger essay'.[4]

Douglas Kellner, introducing the fourth volume of Marcuse's Collected Papers, *Art and Liberation*, argues against some reviews of the book which took it to mark an inward turn after a life of political engagement. Kellner accepts that 'Marcuse never developed his aesthetic theory into a comprehensive volume such as is found in the works of Adorno, Lukács, and in more fragmentary form in Sartre, Goldmann, and Benjamin.'[5] He notes that Marcuse's insights on the writers Louis Aragon and Paul Éluard, contained in his essay on French literature under the German occupation, were not included in *The Aesthetic Dimension*. Kellner concludes that perhaps Marcuse was 'too old to put in the sustained work to finish his aesthetic'.[6] But he also notes that Marcuse remained politically and philosophically engaged, giving a lecture in 1979 in which he stated that 'art can enter, *as regulative idea*, the political struggle to change the world'.[7] Marcuse contends that art acts against consumerism, and re-presents humanity as freed from alienation while enshrining a past remembrance of a utopian realm as a precondition for liberation.

I think Kellner is accurate when he writes that 'Marcuse's work on art and aesthetics is best contextualised in the trajectory of his critical philosophy, social theory, and radical politics.'[8] The political, social and aesthetic intersect in *The Aesthetic Dimension*, but in such a way that art is not treated as ideological illustration or the representation of a political stance – as was the case with Socialist Realism (the officially sanctioned art of the Soviet Union). Kellner reads this as consistent with Marcuse's work since 'he began seriously writing about art in the 1960s'.[9] For example, he says, '*The Aesthetic Dimension* is a sustained attack on reductive Marxist aesthetics, criticizing notions that revolutionary art should be proletarian art.'[10] That engagement began, I would say, in the 1930s with Marcuse's essay on affirmative culture (see Chapter 2). The point remains that there is a continuity throughout his work ensuring that the later work is not a recantation, more a consolidation of his earlier thoughts on culture modified only to reflect a shift in the conditions in which he wrote.

In the opening section of *The Aesthetic Dimension*, Marcuse lists six points from a conventional Marxist aesthetic, such as the link between art and class, and that a class in decline – the bourgeoisie in a Marxist trajectory – produces only decadent art. He questions what he reads as a no-longer tenable split between the material base of a society and the social and cultural structures built, as it were, upon it, arguing that to relegate culture to the margins is to miss the point (central to Marx) that 'radical change must be rooted in the subjectivity of individuals themselves, in their intelligence and their passions'.[11] Without the subjective factor of human imagination (as in the imagination of another world), there is no prospect for radical political change even when objective factors (such as are provided by technology) are present. This means that art has an indirect agency for change, which is not distracting but involves the occupation of a liminal zone of criticality, a positive dreaming. The circle which needs to be squared is one in which critical distance relates to intervention within the conditions analysed.

There is one further point I would like to make here: although Kellner writes that the insights from Marcuse's essay on Aragon are omitted from *The Aesthetic Dimension*, they do resurface in the final sentence of the Preface to the English edition: 'there may be more subversive potential in the poetry of Baudelaire than in the didactic plays of Brecht'.[12] At the time – 1978 – this may have sounded extraordinary, given Brecht's status among the Left, his association with the German Marxist milieu of which Marcuse was a member in the 1930s, and Walter Benjamin's comment that Brecht articulated a revolution of the relations of production in literature.[13] Almost a throw-away line at the end of the book, not included in the German edition a year earlier, this sentence reaffirms that art carries the latent memory of freedom – and does so almost regardless of other factors, as if inherently, as if beauty itself is a protest against an unfree world.

   This passing remark nonetheless locates Marcuse as a revisionist in a Marxist realm. In keeping with the project of critical theory, he reconstructs Marxist theory from within. Marxist theory was never strong on art, and part of Marcuse's aim was to address its aesthetic deficit – which is my focus in this chapter, contextualised by a brief outline of the model of dialectical materialism in which Marcuse's Marxian aesthetics fit.

ART IN ACTUALLY EXISTING SOCIALISM?

Marcuse gives a succinct expression of his aesthetic theory in a book which is seldom read today: *Soviet Marxism: A Critical Analysis* (first published in 1958). Before the optimism of the 1960s, and as a philosophy professor at the University of California at San Diego, Marcuse gave a detailed critical account of the socio-political formation in which art had the function of representing 'the established social reality as the final framework for the artistic content, transcending it neither in style nor in substance'.[14] That is, if the Soviet Union was the state produced by actually existing socialism, then Soviet art had no further need to be critical (as in the bourgeois era) but could instead convey that actuality as it was, in straightforward representations. The approved style for this was Realism, which Marcuse notes could be 'a highly critical and progressive form of art, confronting reality "as it is" with its ideological and idealized representations'.[15] He does not mention French Realism in the 1840s – the work of Gustave Courbet in particular – but it would exemplify this. He does mention Brecht – then working in the German Democratic Republic (GDR) – as producing a literature which implements state policy carefully. But Marcuse's main objection to the culture of the Eastern bloc is that the actually existing socialism claimed for it did not actually exist, so that art's role remains, in theory, to negate that reality. He writes, 'But art as a political force is art only in so far as it preserves the images of liberation', and hence, in a society which disallows this by classifying it as dissidence, art preserves a memory of freedom only by negation.[16] Art is the 'refusal of everything that has been made part and parcel of reality'.[17]

The same, I would add, is the case in the affluent society called the West. To say this is obviously polemical, and involves a stark separation of art from life that contrasts with Friedrich Engels' assertion in *The Dialectics of Nature* that the great artists of the Renaissance were engaged in other areas of production: 'Leonardo da Vinci was not only a great painter but also a great mathematician, mechanician and engineer', and 'Albrecht Dürer ... invented a system of fortifications.'[18] In the 1930s, Benjamin had argued that the committed writer must situate writing within the relations of production, so that writers would become readers, readers would write for publication (as in the Soviet press), and the division between writers as specialists and readers as passive consumers would be collapsed.[19] Benjamin cites the Soviet writer Sergey Tretyakov, who joined the Communist Lighthouse collective farm to spend his time, as a writer still,

> calling mass meetings; collecting funds for down-payments on tractors; persuading private farmers to join the collective farm; inspecting reading-rooms; launching wall newspapers and directing the collective farm newspaper; reporting to Moscow newspapers; introducing radio, travelling film shows, etc.[20]

This was not the art Marcuse had in mind. If it was consistent with Engels's idea that art 'is based on economic development'[21] the image of the writer ordering tractor parts could be read as too literal an engagement, and reliant on exactly the division between economic and cultural life which Marcuse rejects.

The issue is complex. For Marx, art is part of the superstructure constructed over the base of economic life. It does not answer basic human needs such as those for clothing, food and shelter, but art still reflects the base from which it is produced even if it answers higher needs. In actually existing socialism it reflects the realised utopia of a classless society. But art does not change reality, though changes to the base cause changes in the superstructure, hence in art. In revising Marxism, Marcuse sets aside the division of base and superstructure. Informed by modernist art – the art of the early twentieth century, such as German Expressionism, which draws back from representing reality in order to present an imagined reality – Marcuse reasserts a divide between a not yet existing utopia and an art which exposes that non-realisation in the non-realism of its images (contrary to the realism required in Soviet art). For Marcuse, Soviet Marxism asserts a link between social progress and the yet to occur 'obsolescence of art'[22] in the state of actually existing socialism. Without the tension of an imagined freedom and a real unfreedom, however, art for Marcuse has no more than a residual function of representing reality. This is inadequate in Marcuse's view. He argues that 'the Soviet treatment of art is not simply an outburst of boundless authoritarianism',[23] in that it requires a reliance on art's cognitive function – its representation of reality in images which can be read as data – and a claim to the objective truths of science.

Critical theory refutes that claim; even scientific theory is produced, not given, just as critical theory itself re-presents the conditions of its own production in social research and theoretical abstraction.[24] This enables critical theory to intervene in, not merely record, its social situation. Following from that, and before looking at the aesthetic deficit in Marxism as Marcuse perceived it, it is helpful to note that critical theory in the 1930s, and Marcuse's writing in the post-war period when he remained in North America, are contextualised by the rise of modern art and abstraction.

For many of those employed by the Frankfurt Institute for Social Research – and in the re-convened International Institute for Social Research at Columbia University, New York after 1934 – art was peripheral. For some of its associates, notably Benjamin and Bloch, it was central; and Marcuse stands out among the Frankfurt Institute's staff in making detailed studies of literature and art. His main interest was always literature, but modernist art had a pervasive presence even if its significance was beginning to be questioned from new perspectives in feminism, post-colonialism and analyses of mass culture by the 1970s. Recalling her time as a student in San Diego, art historian Carol Becker writes: 'I thought Marcuse was trapped in modernism, unaware of how times had changed. The imagination ... was now virtually oppressed by the effects of mass media.'[25] Continuing, though, Becker sees Marcuse as having been correct to insist on the resistant capacity of art: 'Within the creative process *is* resistance.'[26] In the 1960s, or even the 1950s, abstract art in the West resisted an unfree reality through images on the edge of nothingness. For some this was a freedom to be quiet. For others it was the near-silence which is the last gasp on the edge of terror – a terror sedimented in the work which refracts it, redirecting attention critically to the conditions in which a gasp is all that can be uttered.

Marcuse rejects Socialist Realism, then, as a device for social control; the possibility for art is to rupture such mechanisms. Although there is no direct link, his position follows exchanges on German Expressionism in the 1930s between Bloch and Lukács.[27] For Bloch, the medium of montage carried the content of a time of flux, while abstraction (in Expressionism the adaptation rather than erasure of images as it became in post-war Abstract Expressionism) enabled a latent hope to be shaped within a movement towards a utopian future denied by fascism. In *The Principle of Hope*,[28] Bloch sought to establish hope's semi-scientific status, equivalent to a Freudian drive; this is, however, not viable, and Bloch's eclectic cultural history does not always help his case. Marcuse's more limited focus (and shorter text) is more open to reconsideration now. He cites Greek tragedy in passing in *The Aesthetic Dimension*, but writes of art abstractly, as if in a perpetual present. Marcuse indirectly echoes Bloch, however, when he writes that 'artistic images have preserved the determinate negation of the established reality – ultimate freedom'.[29] This was not a case of art's obsolescence, but of its continuing necessity. Vincent Geoghegan argues that Marcuse followed Marx's early writing by insisting on 'the necessity of non-conceptual cognition in critical theory'.[30]

I think a parallel can be drawn between Marcuse's rejection of Socialist Realism and the prevailing art criticism of the time in the West, notably that of Clement Greenberg (which remained influential in the 1960s). Without any documented link, Greenberg's essay 'Avant-Garde and Kitsch'[31] – written in 1939 in the aftermath of the Hitler-Stalin Pact – is a helpful comparative text to place beside Marcuse's remarks on art in his book on Soviet Marxism. Greenberg argues that the purpose of avant-garde art – or modernism – is to keep art moving, thereby avoiding the stagnation of kitsch, regardless of the wide divide which tends to open up between new art and a mass public. This leads Greenberg to argue later for a formalist art; hence he champions the painters Pablo Picasso, Henri Matisse and Paul Klee for a 'pure preoccupation with the invention and arrangement of spaces'.[32] Kitsch, or mass culture, seems to have the same place for Greenberg as Socialist Realism does for Marcuse: as a non-authentic culture. Greenberg aligns his view of Socialist Realism to kitsch but mistakenly cites the example of the nineteenth-century artist Ilya Repin, a popular Russian artist who depicted historical scenes, as a precedent for Socialist Realism but not an example of it. Leaving that anachronism aside, what Greenberg and Marcuse have in common is the identification of resistant art with the avant-garde. Citing Marcuse's essay 'Philosophy and Critical Theory',[33] Geoghegan remarks that Marcuse used a concept from the Western tradition in which 'imagination enables one to transcend the given by cognitively creating the future'.[34] This is the imaginative reconstruction of society proposed by Levitas; and the justification for writing about aesthetics when political change is remote.

THE AESTHETIC DEFICIT OF MARXISM

Marcuse wrote of the Soviet Union in the 1950s that 'It wants art that is not art, and it gets what it asks for.'[35] In the West, Soviet art tended to be seen as the residue which occurs if more advanced tendencies such as abstraction are banned. But in terms of Soviet cultural policy (before a liberalisation in the 1960s),[36] abstract art was deemed to undermine the supposed reality of actually existing socialism because abstraction was seen as a product of mental disturbance, of a kind that cannot exist in really existing socialism.

Indeed, the distortion of the image called abstraction (in German Expressionism) is a product of disturbances produced by capitalism. And in fact the breadth of styles allowed under the term Socialist Realism was diverse, sometimes bordering on abstraction – as in the work of Alexander Deineka.[37] In art and architecture there were national variations; the Soviet Union comprised many constituent national republics whose cultures were incorporated into a wider Soviet culture.[38]

There was an easing of Soviet cultural policy after Nikita Khrushchev's denunciation of Stalin, but it would not have been evident in the West when Marcuse's book on Soviet Marxism appeared. Marcuse cites Khrushchev as maintaining a 'late Stalinist policy' on economics,[39] and makes no mention either of a cultural shift in the early 1950s. In 1951, for instance, still in Stalin's time, Alexander Gerasimov, painter of Socialist Realist portraits of Stalin, was criticised at the Artists' Union in Moscow. In 1954 he was asked, and then required, to step down as president of the Fine Art Academy: 'That night he sat up, drank a whole bottle of vodka and had a heart attack. He never recovered his health.'[40] Marcuse's view of Soviet art is restricted, then, and in any case a more pressing question is whether the critique he outlines, and his aesthetic theory in general, is consistent with Marxism. Did Marcuse 'go beyond traditional Marxist categories' to come to terms with a cultural landscape that departs from that of Marxist analysis, as Stuart Sim argues?[41] Or is Marx's theory sufficiently robust to be extended for new modes of cultural production?

Marx and Engels wrote in *The Communist Manifesto* that the bourgeoisie had 'converted the physician, the lawyer, the priest, the poet, the man [*sic*] of science, into its paid wage-labourers'.[42] Setting aside the use of a universal masculine, Marx implies a world in which science and culture were once not at the service of money but were instead the means to human fulfilment. The appeal to a golden age in a suitably remote past was a standard strategy in Enlightenment thought, as in Jean-Jacques Rousseau's concept of a noble savage embodying a pure humanity, isolated in far-away sites such as Polynesia (then discovered by French sailors) from European corruption in the form of the arts and sciences. Setting aside the issue of whether such a world ever existed, and of the impact of colonisation upon it (not least in the transmission of sexual diseases, a taste for alcohol), the German Idealism which formed the background to Marx's early work implied a trajectory in which humanity rose, by design, to a high point of realisation: reason as freedom, the end of history. This is implicit, too, in classical Marxism. And Marx draws on German Idealism's concept of a better world beyond the present in his model of a social pyramid in which the base (the working class) supersedes the strata above (the aristocracy and the bourgeoisie). It makes little difference to the argument whether the imagined better world is a past recovered or a future not-yet-attained, even if Marxism looks to the latter, because one is a projection of the other: utopia is Arcadia regained. In so far as he writes at all on art, Marx sets it apart from the conditions of ordinary reality. In the passage from *The Communist Manifesto* cited above, art is presumed to have been originally a non-alienating vocation, not mere toil but the work of craft for the craft-worker's benefit and satisfaction. The crime, as it were, of capital is to reduce poetry to toil within a decline which the Marxist image of the future will reverse. This is not a social theory of art, however, but an assertion that the character of art differs in a qualitative way from that of the production of, say, ditches. The poet dreams. The ditch digger digs for wages. This is a romantic position which omits the fact that artists have always had contracts and sought to be paid, as have lawyers and physicians. But this formulation reflects the philosophical condition in which it was produced, and it denotes a creative tension between Idealism and Romanticism, which Marx seeks to reconcile.

Marx never developed a theory of art, but to the extent that he deals with it his ideas were informed by his training in art history in Prussia in the 1830s, and the conflicting philosophical and religious currents of the time. German art criticism and German art were held by two contesting polarities: the language of classical antiquity and that of the Christian (post-classical) art of a group of German painters called the Nazarenes, forebears of the English pre-Raphaelites of the 1850s. The writer Heinrich Heine, who influenced Marx in the 1830s and 1840s, saw the Nazarenes as mystifying, and thus evading reality, using a backward-looking technique and an outdated subject-matter to present a gloomy, doom-laden view of life. Classicism, in contrast, offers an empathy with material objects while realigning how they are perceived according to over-arching laws of form in service of an idealised view of life. Margaret Rose reports in *Marx's Lost Aesthetic* that Heine described the paintings of the leading Nazarene Peter Cornelius as 'so mournful that they looked as if they had been painted on Good Friday'.[43] The Nazarenes' idyll was located in a mythical Christian past too remote for historical accuracy, but that temporal distance was no barrier to visits by several artists and writers to the Holy Land – the Pre-Raphaelite Holman Hunt, for instance, painted by the Dead Sea with a rifle on his lap to fend off bandits, producing *The Scapegoat*, as mournful and doom-laden a picture as can be found anywhere. But, still, the Christian world of the Nazarenes was represented in the non-classical visual language of Italian early Renaissance art (if leaning sometimes towards a more florid high Renaissance style), as a refusal of the pagan, pantheistic associations of the classical world. It is stylistically distanced from Prussia in the 1830s, too, because it seeks a reformation of ordinary life on the divine model – the imitation of Christ. This is no less a regained paradise than that of classical Arcadia projected onto a utopian future, but it is a specifically Christian (and Western Christian) vision grounded in human piety and modesty.

Piety informs the images of the Nazarenes, displacing the promise of a better world to a religious dimension, a pictured hereafter. Piety was, too, the culture favoured by the then monarch, Friedrich Wilhelm IV, who gave Cornelius a commission in Berlin in 1841. He also tightened an already strict Prussian press censorship. Marx was employed as a journalist, and reacted against both the censorship and the art style of the state. Rose notes that Marx took press censorship to be 'a betrayal of the Enlightenment State to which Prussia aspired under Frederick the Great'.[44] Against this background, a group of young Hegelians sought a renewal of cultural and philosophical rationality. Hegel favoured Romantic art but among his younger followers Bruno Bauer developed an aesthetics drawn from classical rather than either Romantic or Christian precedents – a Hellenic position specifically in opposition to the Nazarenes.

Bauer set out this aesthetic in his thesis 'Hegel's Teaching on Religion and Art Judged from the Standpoint of Faith'. Marx was to have contributed a section on Hegel's aesthetics but did not complete it. Rose summarises that for Bauer, Hegel saw Greek art as 'limited through the sensuous character of its depiction of the beautiful in Nature to a depiction of the material world', while Bauer himself asserted that Hegel had not sought to deny a sensuous quality in classical art.[45] Bauer's hypothesis drew Marx towards a Hellenic sense of empathy, which was not-pietism, and not-Romantic other-worldliness. While Marx later developed a social theory in scientific terms, his aesthetic theory remained incipient, hence open to future extension and interpretation. The deficit in Marxist aesthetics, then, is one of non-completion. Unlike Heine, Marx was not attracted to the idea of an avant-garde. Rose quotes the French utopian philosopher Claude Henri de Saint-Simon:

> They [the artists, the men (*sic*) of imagination] will lead the way in that great undertaking; they will proclaim the future of mankind; they will bring back the golden age from the past to enrich future generations; they will inspire society with enthusiasm for the increase of its well-being by laying before it a tempting picture of a new prosperity; by making it feel that all members of society will soon share in enjoyments which, up to now, have been the prerogative of a very small class; they will hymn the benefits of civilization and they will employ all other resources of fine arts, eloquence, poetry, painting, music, to attain their goal; in short, they will develop the poetic aspects of the new system.[46]

Saint-Simon lends the artist the equivalent of a priestly function, leading society to the renewed golden age by representing it (implying a foreknowledge of it), developing a cultural programme for the new social order. There are a number of difficulties here, not least that the privileged insight of the artist reproduces an elite status in what is to be, otherwise, an egalitarian society. The utopian future is a projection of a supposedly golden past, which has the advantage that the future is already validated; but it has the disadvantage that there is no evidence that the envisioned past existed, or is more than a compensatory daydream revealing what the present lacks. This is the posturing which Marx rejects when he maintains an allegiance to classical art.

Leaving aside art's priestly function, for which Marx has no time, the artist and the poet would be liberated along with other types of worker. Rose summarises:

> To valorise art as a form of escapist illusionism and as an alternative to production would have been (and, in fact, clearly was) for Marx, to revive the type of art and artistic politics practised by the German Nazarenes and protected by Friedrich Wilhelm IV in his time, as also to eliminate one possible way to the reformation of the alienating elements in production under which art itself might be made to suffer.[47]

Rose adds that Marx did not resolve the question of how art could be both part of alienating toil and a means to its ending, though the idea of art as non-alienating labour in which the artist follows a vocation, and remains in charge of the means of production, has often been proposed. But Marx looks only to production, and offers little in the way of reception theory. What he said was that art contains evidence of the conditions of its production so that, for instance, Greek art is attractive to a museum audience because it sheds light on those conditions. But Greek art was not the product of a fully realised social harmony. It carried, as Rose says, 'the perception of a reflection of our childhood, as also of the processes of historical change themselves'.[48] And, Rose adds, for Marx art is 'the victim of exploitation under industrial capitalism'.[49]

For Heine, though, Saint-Simon's case was more persuasive. Heine was an exile from Prussian censorship in Paris in the 1830s, both his writing and Saint-Simon's being banned. Throughout, there seems to be an element of counteracting a despised stance by looking to its opposite: from pietism to classicism, from Prussia to France, and so on. Marx took on this dynamic, and if his model of dialectical materialism (which I discuss below) resolves the opposition in a new way, he did not extend this to art and its theoretical construction as either a means to envision rational freedom or a model of non-alienating work. The former risks association with the rejected pietist model of salvation, and the latter lacks evidence. This does not mean that Marx made no further reference to art or to aesthetics. He does, in the *Grundrisse*, but only in terms of what can be learned by looking at past art and its vicissitudes. He writes:

'In the case of the arts it is well known that certain periods of their flowering are out of all proportion to the general development of society.'[50] He cites Greek epic poetry, which he says is no longer viable because Greek poetry reflected Greek mythology's characterisation and apprehension of the natural world in a historically specific way which cannot be reproduced in different conditions. Myth reworks natural reality unconsciously in the popular imagination, to be re-worked again consciously in art. It illustrates an uneven socio-economic development when conditions are what Marx calls unripe;[51] hence art remains attractive as an illumination of human history like a memento. And yet the British art critic Peter Fuller commented in 1980 that, 'if the ideological, political, social and economic mediations of a work are *so* important', he could not see how it was that he could 'walk into the Victoria and Albert Museum, look at a piece of sculpture from an ancient Indian civilization ... and still enjoy it'.[52]

Perhaps the aesthetic deficit of Marx's theory is that the contradictions inherent in the avant-garde position argued by Saint-Simon are not worked through. For Marx, the division of labour in capitalism means that art is an occupation reserved to those trained in it. Sub-divisions and specialisms appear, such as painting and sculpture, while 'In a communist society there are no painters but at most people who engage in painting among other activities.'[53] What is missing is the idea that art offers sensuous enjoyment. After the 1917 Bolshevik Revolution, artists in Russia formed collectives for the production of creative but functional items, as in Varvara Stepanova's designs for workers' clothes, and Vladimir Tatlin's *Monument to the Third International* (1919–20), a design (never built) to equal the Eiffel Tower. Coincidentally, Eiffel, whose tower commemorated the centenary of the 1789 French Revolution, was a Saint-Simonian. Stepanova and Tatlin exemplify a path whereby artists engage in art among other activities, and daily life becomes creative. But I am left wondering what a Marxist theory of art might have been. Does 'human-sensuous activity'[54] (as Marx says in his Theses on Feuerbach) denote a transition from imagination to action, from contemplating beauty to enacting it? This suggests Charles Fourier's idea of work as libidinal social activity – erotic play.[55] Fuller turned to psychoanalysis, and his reading of *The Aesthetic Dimension* was a catalyst to a more developed critique in which the question of art's perennial appeal was a driving force.[56] But he rejected Marxism wholesale. Marcuse remained a Marxist, seeking appropriate ways in which to revise and extend a virtually unwritten theory.

For Marcuse, art stands as non-repressive order, a non-alienated means to critically reveal alienation in the wider society. Art could also affirm repression, normalising it as a kind of escapism or mere decoration – as I discuss in Chapter 3. But Rose makes an interesting point when she says that Marcuse ignores Marx's insistence on art as a form of production. But I leave that there, and need now to outline the key insight of dialectical materialism as glimpsed by Marx in 1845, which I assume as a basis for Marcuse's work.

INFORMED PRACTICE: PRAXIS

In his eleventh thesis on Feuerbach, Marx wrote that the philosophers have interpreted the world in various ways but that the point is to change it.[57] This was the foundation of dialectical materialism. The Theses on Feuerbach are very short, despite their daunting title: the longest has 14 lines in the 1888 edition, the shortest two. Marx wrote them in longhand in a notebook while in Brussels in 1845. The theses outline his reflections on Materialism and Idealism. Including them in his study of Feuerbach, Engels 'ferreted out and looked over the old manuscript of 1845–46', finding the section on Feuerbach 'incomplete'.[58]

In his account, Engels divides philosophers into two camps: those who give primacy to spirit and those who assign it to nature: Idealists, and Materialists for whom nature is 'the sole reality' while for Hegelians nature is the realm in which the absolute idea is alienated from its fullness.[59] Feuerbach's *Essence of Christianity* is cited: 'With one blow it pulverised the contradiction ... it placed materialism on the throne again.'[60] It did this by insisting that nature is independent of philosophy: it exists anyway. Engels summarises: 'It is the foundation upon which we human beings, ourselves products of nature, have grown up. Nothing exists outside nature and man [*sic*], and the higher beings our religious fantasies have created are only the fantastic reflection of our own essence.'[61] Engels adds that Hegelianism was not disposed of so easily. Bruno Bauer (noted above) and his brothers Edgar and Heinrich continued to develop it in one way, and David Strauss in another – though both factions were close politically. Engels describes Feuerbach as breaking through the axis of rival Hegelianisms; but it might be more helpful, in retrospect, to say that the breakthrough belonged to Marx.

For Feuerbach, people are conditioned by their environment – materially (by nature, the need for shelter, and so forth) and culturally (as in education). Changes to the environment produce changes in human development, implying the idea that intervention in, for example, education can be organised to produce a more liberated human. Unlike Idealism, Materialism offers no informing over-spirit driving the process forward as if inevitably. It emphasises human endeavour in seeking an exit from the conditions of repression. In relation to miserable reality (to use Marcuse's term), Materialism has no forward plan or path. But Marx goes beyond Feuerbach by asserting the primacy of human society over the abstract civil society implied in Feuerbach's conditioning of life through institutions such as educational structures.

The call for 'a practical, human-sensuous activity'[62] in the fifth thesis is a proposal for intervention. Marx brings the progressive aspect of Idealism into Materialism's emphasis on conditions, to produce a reflexive and critical Materialism: dialectical materialism. Ernst Fischer puts it succinctly: Marx 'transfers the active, creative principle from the systems of Idealist philosophy into materialism: reality as process ... and *social reality* as the *interaction* of objective and subjective factors, of *objective* circumstances and *human activity*'.[63] By objective factors are meant material conditions; and by subjective, human consciousness (a dualism which infuses Marcuse's theories in terms of his idea of a new sensibility, or human consciousness). Fischer adds that the philosophy of practice avoids blind action, seeking to understand what people do, why they do it, and 'for what purpose and under what compulsion ... it learns from practice so as to teach practice to become *self-cognitive*'.[64]

Dialectical materialism, from Marx's early writing onwards, is a philosophy of practice. The human subject intervenes in the conditions by which she or he is shaped, informed by critical analysis. This is the basis, too, for critical theory. In his essay 'Philosophy and Critical Theory', Marcuse does not cite Marx; nevertheless, as Kellner remarks, 'Marx is the founder of the critical theory referred to ... the positions enunciated in the essay are the basic positions of Marxism.'[65] And Marcuse sets the beginning of critical theory in the 1830s and 1840s, coincident with Marx's early writing, reiterating the philosophy of practice by arguing that freedom is not abstract:

> human freedom is no phantom or arbitrary inwardness that leaves everything in the external world as it was. Rather, freedom here means a real potentiality, a social relationship on whose realization

human destiny depends. At the given stage of development, the constructive character of critical theory emerges anew. From the beginning it did more than simply register and systematize facts. Its impulse came from the force with which it spoke against the facts ... Like philosophy, it opposes making reality into a criterion ... [as in positivism]. But unlike philosophy, it always derives its goals only from present tendencies of the social process. Therefore it has no fear of the utopia that the new order is denounced as being. ... the utopian element was long the only progressive element in philosophy.[66]

Marcuse reasons that, in a bourgeois period, philosophy separates its vision of a future social form from actuality by universalising the values of truth and beauty which that vision reflects, while valorising individuality for economic reasons so that 'it is the emancipated, self-reliant individual who thinks'.[67] But for Marcuse, echoing early Marx, a radical shift in social organisation requires a shift in consciousness at both the social and the individual scale. The ideas of community and individual thus constitute polarities. Bourgeois philosophy makes them incompatible: 'The subject thinks within a horizon of untruth that bars the door to real emancipation.'[68] Hence,

in every act of cognition the individual must once again re-enact the 'production of the world' and the categorical organization of experience. However, the process never gets any further because the restriction of 'productive' cognition to the transcendental sphere makes any new form of the world impossible.[69]

Yet the universal values of truth, goodness and beauty persist for Marcuse to reveal a consciousness of potential emancipation which is thwarted but not destroyed by the mechanisms of bourgeois society. It is not a matter of universal truths revealed in a trajectory of realisation (as in Idealism); but nor is it a matter of immutable conditions moulding the subject (as in Materialism). In the impasse produced when Idealism's trajectory collides with Materialism's unbending nature, Marcuse inserts the concept of imagination:

the abyss between rational and present reality cannot be bridged by conceptual thought. In order to retain what is not yet present as a goal in the present, phantasy is required. The essential connection of phantasy with philosophy is evident from the function attributed to it ... under the title of 'imagination.' Owing to its unique capacity to 'intuit' an object ... imagination denotes a considerable degree of independence from the given, of freedom amid a world of unfreedom.[70]

There are difficulties: imagination can become fantasy in the colloquial sense of the compensatory daydream – or as Marcuse puts it, as the property of children and fools. And there is the problem, to which Marx alludes, of what happens to the work of imagination in a free society. But in the miserable reality of the 1970s, being able to worry over the problem of art in a free society was a luxury – champagne tomorrow when the problem was how to deal with ditch-water today.

2
The Artist and Social Theory

In this chapter I discuss Marcuse's thesis on the German artist novel (*künstlerroman*), which he completed in October 1922. I situate his early work on aesthetics within the project of the Frankfurt Institute for Social Research in the 1930s, and conclude by arguing that insights developed in Marcuse's later work derive from this early period. In this context, aesthetics is not tangential to social theory. The artist novel is a social novel as well as a study of what might be called the artistic personality; and Marcuse's contribution to the work of the Frankfurt Institute concerned, among other things, the role of bourgeois culture in the rise of fascism. I accept Douglas Kellner's argument that aesthetics was not Marcuse's 'key, primary or central' concern, even though he made 'a sustained attempt to reflect on the connection of art and politics'.[1] In this chapter I examine one example of that connection, which continues to inform Marcuse's work in the 1930s (see Chapter 3) and after.

I begin by sketching the context for Marcuse's early work in the failure of the German revolution in 1918–19, after which he resumed his studies of philosophy in Freiburg – away, that is, from the turmoil of Berlin. Marcuse was haunted by this failure and by the subsequent rise of fascism. This helps explain an emphasis on the problems more than the possibilities of culture in his early work. Marcuse was personally involved in the events of 1918–19, at one point carrying a rifle in Alexanderplatz. Max Weber wrote of 'the enormous collapse … customarily called the Revolution'.[2] Barry Katz writes that although 'possibilities for organized political action on the left remained', the outlook for success 'came to look only more distant',[3] and Kellner sees Marcuse as 'too young and inexperienced to pursue the career of a professional revolutionary'.[4] It is not surprising, then, that he returned to the abstractions of academic philosophy; nor is it surprising that his philosophical investigations are suffused throughout his life by a determination to redress the balance of failure in 1919.

Marcuse and his family fled Germany in 1932, going to the Frankfurt Institute's office in Geneva before moving to the United

States. The project for a critical theory of society was thus informed by the memory of 1919 and the 1930s, and the project for an aesthetics of liberation within that was similarly a reclamation of a failed past. Yet it went much further, extending from the utopian tradition to speak amid the conditions of a society of unprecedented affluence in North America in the 1960s.

REVOLUTION IN GERMANY?

The failure of the German revolution raised two immediate questions, the more obvious one being why it failed – why political organisation was inadequate; why social democrats had collaborated with the Right; and why the Weimar Republic established as the outcome of these events may have been inherently unstable. For Marcuse, however, there was a second type of question relevant to Marxism: why was it that revolution succeeded in the relatively backward conditions of Russia in 1917, yet failed in Germany, by then an advanced industrial power? For Marx, the objective conditions for revolution were those of advanced industrial states where the organised working class were the driving force of social change. Marx established this in his early work, but the position was confirmed later by Friedrich Engels. In the Preface to the German edition of *The Communist Manifesto* published in 1890, Engels writes that it had 'never occurred' to Marx or himself to repudiate the slogan, 'Working men [*sic*] of all countries unite!', nor that history would see other than 'the working men of all countries' united in the struggle.[5] Engels presents the call to mobilisation as self-evident. In Germany 30 years later, a workers' revolution failed amid the after-effects of Germany's defeat in the 1914–18 war. Not only was the old regime completely destabilised, as a military regime in charge of a lost war, but the Bolshevik revolution in Russia ended the war on the Eastern front, restoring communications between revolutionary groups in both countries. Why, then, did revolution not spread to Germany (or even begin there)?

It would be mistaken to say that Russia was not an industrialised state, however, or that it lacked a history of organised protest. Tzar Alexander II had introduced a series of constitutional reforms before his assassination in 1881, and serfdom was officially abolished (though conditions in the vast rural areas remained primitive). In the cities, workers were organised in factory groups, and intellectuals had a public role (if often at the cost of imprisonment and always despite censorship). A return to autocracy on the part of Nicholas

II produced increasingly militant opposition in the early twentieth century, so that the revolution of 1917 was not the first attempt to end his power. In an attempted revolution in 1905, 400,000 workers took strike action across Russia while the professional unions were organised on a national scale for the first time, joined by a Women's Union seeking female suffrage. Semi-professionals – railway workers and pharmacists, for instance – affiliated to the Union of Unions. Through it intellectuals found a channel of communication to workers' organisations while the far-Left parties – the Bolsheviks and Mensheviks, which were to be instrumental in the events of 1917 – grew in strength: membership rose from around 10,000 prior to the events of 1905 to around 40,000 in 1906.[6] Marx's writings were available in Russia, including to the Bolsheviks imprisoned in the Peter and Paul fortress, St Petersburg. Despite obvious privations, prisoners in the fortress were able to undertake considerable reading and creative activity: Dostoevsky's *The Little Hero*, Gorky's *The Children of the Sun* and Chernyshevsky's *What Is To Be Done?* were written in its cells.[7] The latter title was borrowed by Lenin for his political tract of 1902.

The situation in Germany in 1917–18 was not entirely dissimilar to that in Russia: the military command was the effective government from 1916, just as the Tsar had assumed personal control of the war effort. Yet while the workers of a Moscow iron-rolling plant announced to the owners in 1917: 'Your cards are on the table. Your time is up',[8] such political action as occurred in Germany was less coherent and less united. Conditions appeared ripe for revolt in Germany in 1916, however, when the prospect of losing the war emerged, together with severe food shortages. Strikes and food riots occurred across Germany in August that year and were the pretext for the military command's assumption of complete charge of the state. Disquiet grew over the war's conduct, but also over the grounds for its original justification. Left factions which had backed the war in 1914 in return for promises of political reform withdrew their support as those promises seemed increasingly unlikely to be kept. Katz observes that a 'hitherto dormant socialist opposition was finally stirred into activity' around critics of the war including the militant radicals Karl Liebknecht and Rosa Luxemburg.[9] By 1917 there were two groupings on the far Left, beyond the Social Democratic Party (SPD): the Independent Social Democratic Party (USPD) and the Spartacus League, 'a militantly anti-war and internationalist group' founded in July 1916 as a faction within (or break-away group from) the USPD.[10] Luxemburg and Liebknecht were both active in the League, which became the German Communist Party (KPD) in 1918.

These were sudden developments in a nation-state unified only in the second half of the nineteenth century. While there was a history of Idealism, there was no build up of revolutionary forces equivalent to that in Russia, nor any systematic consideration of tactics by the far-Left parties. A German revolution did nonetheless begin, and echoed aspects of the situation in Russia. As John Willett writes:

> The German revolution of November 1918 came almost exactly a year after the Russian and resulted largely from a similar disillusionment with the war.... Accordingly for some years the Bolshevik leaders expected it to go through the same stages as their own....
>
> Outwardly the pattern seemed to be repeating itself: the revolutionary sailors, the red flags, the taking over of public buildings, above all the formation of Workers' and Soldiers' Councils, or Soviets.[11]

The working class was most militant in Berlin where the revolutionary shop stewards organised a general strike in January 1918, before the end of the war.[12] Parallel to the political process, a number of cultural groups proclaimed radical Left messages, such as the Novembergruppe in Berlin – whose members included the artist Otto Dix and the architect Erich Mendelsohn. As well as organising an Expressionist exhibition, the group sought to contribute to state policies in areas such as town planning, museums and art education. Coincidentally, perhaps from similar roots, Marcuse also looked to the integration of culture, education and politics. Charles Reitz notes that 'Marcuse sought a new theory of art and culture that could act as a countermovement to culture and education that affirm the status quo.'[13] A more radical Arbeitsrat für Kunst (Work Council for Art) established an architectural committee headed by the utopian Bruno Taut. These groups were, however, eclipsed by the establishment of the Constituent Assembly in Weimar in December 1918, which adopted a moderate position. In an effort to separate Germany from the revolutionary currents of Russia, Soviet representatives who sought to address the Assembly were expelled, although Karl Radek, a friend of Rosa Luxemburg, made brief contact.[14] Where was Marcuse in all this?

Marcuse was drafted for military training in 1916, aged 18, and sent to a military camp at Darmstadt. Having poor eyesight, he was transferred to the Zeppelin Reserves in Potsdam instead of being sent to the front. The Reserves were an elite group with far better conditions than those of regular units. Not only was he not at the front, where the rate of casualties was high, Marcuse also 'enjoyed the wartime luxury of being able to concern himself with matters other than bare survival',[15] still attending lectures in Berlin.[16] He became radicalised by the pointless violence of the war and an erosion of civil liberties by the military regime, and joined the SPD. In 1918, he was elected to represent the Soldatenrat (Soldiers' Council) for the working-class Berlin district of Reinickendorf. As Katz notes, 'Marcuse's political education was acquired abruptly, imposed on him by circumstances.'[17] Marcuse was from a bourgeois background, and Katz writes of his 'secure and comfortable Berlin childhood, sheltered by a close-knit nuclear family, money, spacious homes, servants, European holidays, and summer excursions to the country.'[18] But Marcuse was aware of experimental culture, and, more to the point here, was sent (as a representative of the Soldatenrat) to defend the new Republic in Alexanderplatz, against sniper fire from armed gangs from the far-Right. He later reflected, 'I must have been crazy!'[19] But these events foreshadowed those of 1933 (when the Nazis assumed power): the SPD saw the growth of far-Left groups as more threatening than the Right, reinforcing its own position by making an alliance with the discredited but still active military command. Then in January 1919, amid street fighting when armed gangs from all factions roamed Berlin, Luxemburg and Liebknecht were murdered. After more strikes and demonstrations, 1,200 people were killed in a final insurgency in March 1919, including 'a perfectly innocuous detachment of thirty revolutionary sailors ... collecting their pay' who were in the wrong place at the wrong time.[20]

Marcuse's sympathies were never with the SPD, however, nor with the KPD, but with a more intellectual USPD faction led by the poet Kurt Eisner. Along with Left intellectuals including Ernst Toller and Gustav Landauer, Eisner sought an alternative government. He was assassinated in February 1918, but the outpouring of popular sympathy which followed enabled the Bavarian Workers' Council to proclaim a Socialist Republic, re-formed as a Soviet Republic in Munich in April 1919. It lasted a week. Armed gangs kidnapped and killed its leaders. The poet Rainer Maria Rilke, who had no political affiliation, had his apartment searched simply 'because he was a poet'.[21] Katz notes:

Their attempt to transform revolutionary politics into an ethic and an aesthetic ended in murder, prison, and ridicule, but Marcuse nevertheless regarded the specifically 'aesthetic' dimension of Eisner's political movement with admiration, and always considered it to have represented one of the most progressive tendencies of the German revolution.[22]

But the German revolution was over. The manner of its failure prefigured events in the 1930s when gangs of far-Right thugs again marched through German cities. Even in 1919, in Weimar, the Right complained of the Spartacist and Jewish tendencies of the newly established Bauhaus.[23] There was an obvious continuity when, in 1933, the Frankfurt Institute was closed by the Nazis, and its members, largely Jewish Marxists, were under threat.

Writing this in a quiet town in Devon in 2011, I have to make a big historical adjustment to understand that critical theory emerged in conditions in which the lives, and not just employment prospects, of those who contributed to it were radically insecure.

THE GERMAN ARTIST NOVEL

In 1919, Marcuse resumed his research in German Studies (*Germanistik*) at Humboldt University, Berlin. When Humboldt's Rektor publicly applauded the restoration of the military to power in 1920, Marcuse moved to Albert-Ludwig University in Freiburg to study German literature, with philosophy and political economy as second subjects. It was in Freiburg that Marcuse researched the German artist novel for his doctorate and, after a period back in Berlin, studied with Martin Heidegger from 1928 to 1932.

His topic, the artist novel (*künstlerroman*), is a subdivision of the genre of the novel, which Marcuse took as the major literary form of bourgeois society in the nineteenth and early twentieth centuries. It stands beside the education novel (*Bildungsroman*) in which the protagonist gains integration into society through increasing self-awareness (the journey of self-education in society). In the artist novel, in which the artist may be a writer, the story unfolds as a journey of experience post-innocence, and the emergence of a renewed and more aware self. This reflects the plot of the education novel, but the artist novel revolves around the artist's alienation from the wider society, and his or her efforts to either become integrated into it or to live with the alienation. As Katz says, 'The artist thus appears set against a non-artistic environment and its modes of life, which are themselves alien and antagonistic to the artistic experience: the goal of the artist's life ... becomes the solution or resolution of this alienation.'[24] This suggests that the two polarities – art and society – are antagonistic but open to adaptation in a new synthesis. Kellner reads a Hegelian structure in Marcuse's thesis:

> in each chapter, after sympathetically examining and portraying a type of artist novel and artistic life, Marcuse discloses the contradictions and deficiencies in the novels and writers under consideration. He then shows how the problems with various forms and types of the novel give rise to competing positions ... Marcuse especially valorizes the syntheses of Johann Wolfgang Goethe, Gottfried Keller, and Thomas Mann for their ability to overcome the tensions and contradictions within the problematic of the German artist novel.[25]

Marcuse identifies two types of artist novel: the romantic and the realistic-objective.[26] But he prefaces his discussion by aligning the form of the artist novel in general with that of epic poetry. The epic (as in archaic Greece) states a unity of the individual and the community, almost an antediluvian image, and, as Marcuse writes, a unity, too, of 'is and ought, reality and form of life'.[27] This is possible because in the conditions in which the epic was produced, the ego is not yet aware of a potential for free existence: 'It senses itself only as a member of the community and is absorbed into the community's form of life.'[28]

The epic carries a collective but not an individual self-awareness; in the epic poem it is figured in a stream of episodes as a protagonist moves from situation to situation in which an over-arching narrative unfolds sequentially. The novel extends this form but instead of unity it offers only the 'longing and striving' for unity which is all that is possible in bourgeois life, when that unity is a distant memory.[29] Marcuse continues:

> The rupture, the cleft, between what is and what could be, the ideal and the reality, has demolished the original wholeness. The progressive differentiation and diffusion of the nation into estates and classes, the expansion of social and cultural life, do not fit any longer into one strictly closed artistic form. The novel adapts itself to the social estates, accompanies their development, is compelled

more and more to present 'excerpts' from life ... In this manner, the novel presupposes a 'reality that has already become *prose*.'[30]

The potentially creative tension between individual and society is evident, then, in the novel as an articulation of bourgeois society's division of labour and class distinctions. It is more evident in the artist novel, where the artist or writer is especially outside social norms – a position assumed since Baudelaire and the Romantic generation of the early to mid nineteenth century. Similarly, just as the novel structures its narrative around a protagonist, so the artist novel is built around the character-forming experiences of the artist or writer.

This could be read as romanticising the epic and the society it represents, such as in the obvious case of archaic Greece, and romanticising the artist as a person set apart from broader social currents. I need to be careful, also, not to project onto Marcuse's model of the artist as antagonist a 1950s notion of the artist as the one who plumbs those psychic depths which lesser mortals fear to probe (as attributed to post-war New York artists such as Jackson Pollock).[31] Marcuse takes the Greek epic on the terms ascribed to it in German aesthetic discourse, as both a precondition of narrative before the novel and a projected foil to the novel's representation of individualism in bourgeois society. That is, the novel extends and departs from the epic. This dynamic of literary forms seems to echo that of the artist or writer who departs from, but remains bound to, the society of which she or he is a product. The artist novel affirms artistic alienation but does so as a product, like its bourgeois readers, of that society. Whether this perception was (or is) perpetuated by artists, or by readers and the market, is another question. I think, though, it is interesting that Katz remarks that Marcuse 'reveals the first signs of the sensitivity to the "underside" of the respectable bourgeois tradition of European thought and culture'.[32] Hence, straining against the surfaces of bourgeois life, as Baudelaire had done, the artist forges an identity out of negation, while the validity of that negation as art still requires negotiation of bourgeois society's institutions. Two alternatives are constructed as exits from the dilemma: conformity and erasure.

Of more interest to Marcuse in 1922 was the Hegelian dimension to the thesis: that is, the idea that the artist's work is integral to society only when society has reached a specific point in its development, such that idea and reality converge. In bourgeois Germany in the 1920s, the artist novel denotes the division of individuals from society, as epitomised in the isolation of the artist, not a future unity. But a vision of unity may yet pervade the discussion of a literature denoting its absence:

> Only when the artist stands in such a fusion can he [*sic*] gratify himself as a part of the community, absorbed in the form and life of the whole. Only when the very environment itself expresses a perfect unity of thought and form, intelligence and sensuousness, essence and appearance, does the artist find the appropriate and needed way of life.[33]

Odd as it might seem now, Marcuse then asserts that such a fusion, as the condition for epic culture, existed at the beginning of German culture in the Viking way of life as evident in the Norse saga. Appeals to the fabled origins of German culture might in retrospect be tainted after their misappropriation by fascism, but in the 1920s the idea was contextualised by a broader search for national identity in a Teutonic revival. This relates to affirmative culture and I will discuss it in terms of public monuments in Chapter 3. Here, I read Marcuse's allusion to the Vikings as coloured by conditions in German cultural and educational institutions at the time. Marcuse was, in any case, concerned with literary form, not with cultural memory. The saga and the epic have something in common, which Marcuse identifies as non-personal narrative. So, in modern literature dealing with social disunity, 'in the event that the artist does become a particular personality, the representative of his own type of life that he fundamentally does not share with those around him, he may become the "hero" of the novel'.[34]

Another fabled reference occurs when Marcuse looks to the travelling singers of medieval Germany. Kellner summarises: 'There is anticipation too of his position in which alienated outsiders ... are important forces of opposition.'[35] He then cites an extract from Marcuse's thesis:

> travelling bands of theatre folk and mimes, especially the young clerics and students, broke free from the 'strict discipline of the cloister school and cell and charged out into a life of laughter ...'.
> ... but all in all they were exiles and outsiders, for whom there was no space in the surrounding world's form of life.[36]

This could be compared to a passage in *An Essay on Liberation* where Marcuse remembers the role of radical imagination in the events of May 1968:

> It has been the great, real, transcending force ... in the first powerful rebellion against the whole of the existing society ... The graffiti of the '*jeunesse en colère*' joined Karl Marx and André Breton ... the piano with the jazz player stood well between the barricades; the red flag well fitted the statue of the author of *Les Misérables*; the striking students in Toulouse demanded the revival of the language of the Troubadours, the Albigensians.[37]

The supposed original state of unity in which art and life were fused requires life to enact spirit (Idea in a Hegelian sense). But in bourgeois society, even in the late middle ages, 'the spirit had to sense its incarnation as a divergence and a diminution, and seek to present itself purely as untethered to reality – and in opposition to it. Now life is no longer the material and the form of art: it is in itself without art, without thought, it has become a "problem".'[38] With the growth of towns, the artist strives to be 'a decent citizen who is absorbed in the type of life of the bourgeoisie'.[39] In the seventeenth century, the Thirty Years War tore life apart: 'The subject viewed with disgust the completely debased, immiserated, raw, and hostile social environment that allowed no fulfillment.'[40] Marcuse takes the novel *Simplizissimus* as 'the greatest novel of the century' with its feelings of 'terrible disillusionment'.[41] In the protagonist's abjection, Marcuse reads the awakening of the self in a new, authentic consciousness. If this involves projections onto a misty past, literature remains a perpetual store of insight, so that when Marcuse writes of an emerging German culture and an authentic voice in the folksong of the period, when the main artists of the day stood apart from life as 'academics, armchair poets',[42] he in effect reiterates the question of engagement as it emerged in 1918 and 1919. This is interesting because the model presented in Marcuse's reflections on the literature of the seventeenth century positions the established writers of the time as remote from the popular struggle taken up by folk singers. In 1919 Marcuse opted for an academic career which separated him from political engagement, yet the thesis brings back the prospect of engagement in a dissident literary form.

In the seventeenth century, there was no concept of Germany as a nation-state, only a German language. Perhaps, then, there is a parallel between Marcuse's references to Nordic saga as Germanic culture, and art historian Wilhelm Wörringer's theory (in his doctoral thesis of 1908) that decorative or distorting abstractions in northern European art denote a specifically northern sensibility. Wörringer's ideas informed the German Expressionists, especially Paul Klee and Wassily Kandinsky – notably in the latter's treatise on abstraction, *Concerning the Spiritual in Art*.[43]

Marcuse identifies two strands in German literary culture: a pietism which valorised inner life (as for the Nazarenes – see Chapter 1), and an Enlightenment rationality which saw a possibility to intervene in the conditions of society. The latter sets the scene for the artist who intervenes in the conditions of alienation:

> Here is where the artist novel sets itself to work. Here the artist seeks somehow to come to grips with his painful twoness ... Somehow a solution, a new unity, must be found, because this contradiction is so painful that in the long run it is unbearable without destroying the artist and humanity. As a human being, the artist is placed in the middle of the real world's forms of life. ... The artist must overcome this twoness: he must be able to configure a type of life that can bind together what has been torn asunder, that pulls together the contradictions between spirit and sensuality, art and life, artists' values and those of the surrounding world.[44]

This is the plot of the artist novel. In its romantic form the artist flees reality; in its realist form the artist seeks to change reality and renew the self. When the artist novel represents engagement, 'the currently prevailing historical movements and forms of culture will exert a strong influence'.[45] Yet, Kellner observes, Marcuse prefigures his later aesthetic theory when he argues that the artist-protagonist can intervene via 'revelations of utopian images of fulfillment and happiness' to counter 'an oppressive and alienated world'.[46] The non-integrated artist can imagine a world that is integrated and transformed, resolving the split between the artist's sensibility and the philistine world. Among the writers whom Marcuse praises are Goethe, Keller and Mann. Mann wrote novellas – stories structured around a single episode. An example is *Death in Venice*, in which the protagonist Gustav von Aschenbach (who acquires his aristocratic title on his fiftieth birthday) lives a bourgeois life but has a vision of convulsive beauty in the person of a blond Swedish boy at the Venice lido. In Goethe's *Wilhelm Meisters Lehrjahre*, the writer-protagonist achieves integration in society, but Mann dwells on the impossibility of resolution between the sense of beauty and the norms of bourgeois life. Werther, the protagonist of Goethe's *The Sorrows of the Young Werther*, was also trapped in his subjectivity, hence unable to 'transcend the split between idea and reality'.[47] Aschenbach is bound by the conventions of a successful professional life in contradiction of the irrational energies which led him first to travel and then to admit feelings which destroy his mental stability. So he dies.

For Katz, Marcuse conveys a sympathy with 'the plight of art and the self-conscious artist confined by a narrowly materialistic society, a sympathy whose standard is the poetic world of the beautiful'.[48] This implies, he adds, 'the struggle of the German people for a new community'.[49] I think there is a twist: Aschenbach's work as a bourgeois, upwardly mobile professional resolves his relation to bourgeois society at the price of controlling his sensibility, which is his creativity. This states an inherent, which means a not-negotiable, opposition between a Dionysian energy and the social order. Katz quotes from the last part of Marcuse's thesis: 'He belonged to a different order of humanity, to a different world, and in the face of the Dionysian forces which have their roots in that humanity and that world, no heroism or determination could protect him.'[50] In the 1920s, this indicated a Nietzschean influence in German philosophy. And in *Eros and Civilization* Marcuse writes of the survival of the erotic in the philosophy of Friedrich Nietzsche as a counter-trend to bourgeois repression. In the context of this chapter, the description of Mann's novella offers a theory of art as a fracturing of the dominant society's mind-set, in a consciousness of beauty.

Beauty, as Marcuse elaborates in his essay on affirmative culture, is linked in Greek thought to truth and goodness, above the concerns of ordinary life. In *Death in Venice*, an awareness of beauty unannounced ruptures the perceptions and the moral codes of bourgeois life – which, in the person of the protagonist, fall into dereliction. But this is literature, not real life.

INTERRUPTIONS

Yet political life was falling into dereliction all around. In March 1920, when Marcuse was in Berlin, a Rightist putsch provoked a workers' general strike, passive resistance in the civil service, and armed resistance in the Ruhr (in Essen – see Chapter 8), and in Thuringia, where nine workers were killed in fighting in Weimar.

Bauhaus students painted banners for their funerals.[51] In June 1920, the Berlin Dada Fair (*Dada-Messe*) exhibited the work of radical artists for whom art in innovative, anti-aesthetic forms was a refusal of the bourgeois values seen as taken to a new height (or irrationality) by the Right. By attacking art's institutions, such as the norms of representation, Dada struck at bourgeois society itself. But as Willett records, 'Nobody greeted this show with much enthusiasm'[52] and the KPD newspaper warned its readers against Dada. In literature there was little evidence of a surge, though Franz Jung's *The Red Week* (*Die Rote Woche*) related a rising in Mansfeld in March 1921. Jung joined the Communist Workers' Party (KAPD), a break-away fraction of the KPD, commandeered a ship to take him to Russia to affiliate the KAPD to the Third International, and argued for a proletarian culture.[53]

In contrast, Marcuse's analysis of the artist novel locates a direct and fracturing effect in the plots in which a qualitatively different sensibility emerges. For Kellner, Marcuse's thesis articulates dilemmas he felt in his own life between the cultivation of aesthetic understanding and everyday life. Mann enacts a resolution of the dilemma: a bourgeois writer concerned with professionalism and creativity: 'If the writer can become an educator and ethical force within bourgeois society, he [*sic*] has overcome his alienation and is once more an integrated member of society. Then he can quell his "demonic Eros".'[54] Kellner concludes that Marcuse reads *Death in Venice* as Mann's catharsis, as an attempt to 'free himself from the demonic powers and artistic alienation so often portrayed in his early work' to gain an '"objective epic" style of "Homeric mania and beauty"'.[55] Leaving aside the allusion to Greek culture, the point remains that the perceived beauty is other-worldly – necessarily so in terms of bourgeois society's lack of sensitivity to beauty (as it is, not as it is mediated in the harmonies of art).

In 1920, prior to adopting an overtly Marxist critique based on the representation of class struggle in actually existing socialism, Georg Lukács warned against attempt to regain the unity of Greek society:

> any resurrection of the Greek world is a more or less conscious hypostasy of aesthetics into metaphysics – a violence done to the essence of everything that lies outside the sphere of art, and a desire to destroy it; an attempt to forget that art is only one sphere among many, and that the very disintegration and inadequacy of the world is the precondition for the existence of art and its becoming conscious. ... a totality that can be simply accepted is

no longer given to the forms of art: therefore they must either narrow down and volatilise whatever has to be given form ... or else they must show polemically the impossibility of achieving their necessary object ... in this case they carry the fragmentary nature of the world's structure into the world of forms.[56]

Adorno's aesthetic theory is not in disagreement with the last sentence above; nearly 50 years later he sees the absurdity of the administered world mirrored in the plays of Samuel Beckett.[57]

In 1920, Lukács differentiated the representation of specific instances of a world in flux from the reproduction of fragmentation in fragmentary art (Expressionism). In the 1930s he adopted a view of avant-gardism as a 'dissolution of realism'.[58] In a published disagreement with Ernst Bloch he quotes Marx: 'The relations of production of every society form a whole.'[59] He continues that when capitalism is in crisis, 'the experience of disintegration becomes firmly entrenched ... in broad sectors of the population'.[60] For literature, this means an imperative to be 'an authentic realist' – as an example of which he cites Mann in contrast to the Surrealism of Joyce. This was a response to Bloch's attack on Realism,[61] but where Lukács cites Mann as an authentic realist Marcuse saw Mann as resolving the divide between the writer and a society in crisis metaphorically. Marcuse is closer to Lukács' earlier theory in which the novel renews the function of the epic (expressing totality) in a divided society; and Katz sees Lukács' adaptation of Hegel as underpinning Marcuse's thesis.[62] What emerges is the significance of art for Marcuse, not merely as a profession but as a vehicle for negation of unfreedom when political conditions are not open to radical change. Mann's integration in society is the means by which he offers society a critique of its own condition, distanced in the form of literature. This is not to say that Mann himself felt an attack of convulsive beauty at the Venice lido – it is a literary trope on which to hang the plot of a novella. But the term demonic Eros (used above) relates to Marcuse's later *Eros and Civilization*, in which he foresees a liberation of Eros as a playful, joyful force. This colours the jazz player's stance at the barricades, and is the *promesse du bonheur* in French literature during the occupation (see Chapter 4). His mention of Breton (in the same passage, cited above) is significant in that Surrealism emphasises exactly the convulsive beauty by which bourgeois norms are fractured – the carrying of a fragmentary reality in Lukács' 1920 critique (above) – and stretches language unconventionally. Marcuse withdrew from politics to resume his studies of German literature, but as a means towards the critique which was his own resolution of the situation he was in. Marcuse writes in 1972 that, 'In the last analysis, the struggle for an expansion of the world of beauty, nonviolence and serenity is a political struggle.'[63]

MARCUSE AND THE FRANKFURT SCHOOL

Returning from Freiburg to Berlin, Marcuse briefly co-edited a radical arts journal, *Das Dreieck*, described by Katz as 'an eclectic review that ranged freely between cultural and political criticism, original mythopoeic verse and prose, and polemical reviews and commentaries'.[64] In 1928 he returned to Freiburg to study with Martin Heidegger. With his friend Alfred Seidemann, Marcuse read Heidegger's *Being and Time*, announcing that it achieved a transformation of philosophy at 'the point where bourgeois philosophy transcends itself from within, and opens the way to a new, "concrete" science'.[65] In normal times he would have expected to complete a second thesis (*Habilitationsschrift*) to qualify for an academic career. His major text during this period was *Hegel's Ontology and the Theory of Historicity* (1932),[66] which draws from Hegel a sense of humanity that Marcuse read as a basis for Marx's early writing. This marked a departure from Heidegger's ontology in what John Abromeit summarises as 'a distinction between a critical, immanent, action-oriented current in Hegel's early works, which culminates in the *Phenomenology of Spirit*, and an affirmative, transcendent, passive, epistemological current, which gains the upper hand in *Logic* and dominates Hegel's late philosophy'.[67] It was, Abromeit explains, no coincidence that Marcuse located the high point of Hegel's philosophy in *Phenomenology of Spirit*, 'the work that Marx considered "the true point of origin and the secret of the Hegelian philosophy"'.[68] Marcuse's text was completed as the Frankfurt Institute published Marx's early writings, the *Economic and Philosophical Manuscripts of 1844*. Looking back, Marcuse describes reading these texts as the discovery of 'a new practical and theoretical Marxism. ... Heidegger versus Marx was no longer a problem for me'.[69]

Kellner argues that Marcuse 'developed a synthesis of phenomenology, existentialism, and Marxism', anticipating existentialist and phenomenological Marxists such as Jean-Paul Sartre and Maurice Merleau-Ponty.[70] Reitz reads him as linking 'the testimony of art' to understandings of 'the historical human condition'.[71] Kellner agrees with Reitz in grounding Marcuse's work on art in Marxism, if not with his reading of 'moments of an idealist aesthetics' which contradict his sociological view of art.[72] For Kellner, Marcuse's aesthetic theory emerges from the project for a critical theory of society. For Reitz, Marcuse moves from a Marxist analysis of alienation to the dimension of human life in 'sensuousness, historicity, and art'.[73] Reitz cites Marcuse's 'The Foundation of Historical Materialism' as engaging with a theory of revolution in relation to Marx's early writing. But this is also a shift towards culture:

> Marcuse's theory of the subjectively historical character of the human essence must be philosophically distinguished from that of the materialist conception of history embodied in classical Marxism. The latter stresses natural history and biologic evolution ... Marcuse explicitly interprets the historical character of the human essence in terms of the philosophy ... stressing the technical notion of 'historicity' (*Geschichtlichkeit*).[74]

The term 'human essence' might not be used today; however, the argument remains that Marcuse does not dwell on scientific Marxism's analysis of objective conditions, but looks instead to the transformational possibilities of subjective conditions and human artifice. At this point, Heidegger's emphasis on abstract being becomes less important to Marcuse. It was this departure – evident in his critique of Hegel – which attracted the attention of scholars at the Institute, such as Theodor W. Adorno.[75] This coincided with the end of Marcuse's hopes for an academic career. Although his second thesis was accepted for publication, 'At the end of 1932 it was perfectly clear that I would never be able to qualify for a professorship under the Nazi regime.'[76] Heidegger joined the Nazi party in the Spring of 1933; the Nazis had 230 deputies in the Reichstag, and thousands of brown shirts on the streets,[77] and Marcuse was desperate to join the Institute.

The Frankfurt Institute for Social Research was founded in 1923, attached to the University of Frankfurt-am-Main. It was financially supported by a wealthy Jewish businessman whose son, Felix Weil, organised the First Marxist Work Week – an intensive workshop for Marxist intellectuals – in 1922. Among the Institute's staff were Max Horkheimer, Leo Löwenthal, and Friedrich Pollock, as well as Adorno. It was the first Marxist-oriented research centre in Germany,[78] and undertook economic and social research. This included a survey of skilled and unskilled workers in the Rhineland and Westphalia which exposed the extent of an authoritarian mindset. With Horkheimer's appointment as Director in 1930, the Institute adopted a theoretical approach alongside its empirical work.[79] From 1932 onwards, the Institute's papers were published in the *Journal for Social Research* (*Zeitschrift für Sozialforschung*).

It was a diverse but tightly-knit group of researchers and thinkers; 'committed to Critical Theory [they] fluctuated constantly between hope and desperation, and when Horkheimer and Adorno painted the gloomiest of pictures, Walter Benjamin responded with his messianic philosophy of history'.[80] Benjamin's philosophy of history is gloomy, too, as it happens, stating that 'The tradition of the oppressed teaches us that the "state of emergency" in which we live is not the exception but the rule.'[81] But the aim of critical theory was, while producing critical insights on social formation conducive to a theoretical reconstruction of society, to be critical, too, of its own historically specific production. For Horkheimer and Adorno this was emphatically not a path to activism. Angela Davies recalls that when she was studying in Frankfurt in the 1960s, Adorno (who had returned there after the war) told her that 'my desire to work directly in the radical movements of that period was akin to a media studies scholar deciding to become a radio technician'.[82] Davies worked later with Marcuse.

With the coming to power of the Nazi regime, the Institute's offices were searched by the police on 13 March 1933; in July it was formally closed for anti-state activities, and its assets seized. Most of its members had already fled, though Adorno stayed in Germany for another year. Marcuse was employed by the Institute late in 1931 after being interviewed by Löwenthal, moving with his wife and son to its satellite office in Geneva. He worked with Horkheimer on the definition of critical theory,[83] then joined the US intelligence services during the Second World War, and worked for the de-nazification programme from 1945 to 1951 (see Chapter 4).[84]

In New York, the Institute's funds were diminished, and Horkheimer began to steer it away from an overt Marxism towards a position more in keeping with the situation in the US. This caused tension between, for instance, Adorno and Benjamin (in Paris) over the extent to which Marxist positions should or could be included in material for publication – notably in Benjamin's essay on the work of art in a period of technical reproducibility.[85] The Institute's coverage extended to material in social psychology and mass culture, which suited Marcuse. Kellner notes that Horkheimer, Adorno and

Marcuse were all 'professional philosophers who argued for the importance of philosophy in social theory'.[86] And they were haunted by the rise of fascism, needing to understand how this occurred; the idea of an authoritarian personality type seemed to fuse insights from empirical research and cultural theory and to offer some kind of answer. Marcuse contributed to the project by investigating the function of culture. Kellner summarises the basis for this research, which was also the basis for Marcuse's essay on the affirmative character of bourgeois culture (see Chapter 3):

> They perceived the roots of fascism in: (a) socioeconomic crises that were given a totalitarian solution in order to protect the capitalist relations of production and to secure the control of the ruling class; (b) institutions such as the bourgeois family and repressive socialization processes which created authoritarian personalities who conformed to and accepted socially imposed domination; (c) culture and ideologies that defended, or transfigured, the existing society while mystifying social relations of domination; and (d) a totalitarian state which imposed its rule on the entire economic, social, political, and cultural system.[87]

These themes were to inform Marcuse's work in the 1960s when the counter-culture appeared to interrupt the conditions of the bourgeois family and the liberal-authoritarian state. In the 1930s, away from the Germany of the literary and philosophic traditions in which he had evolved intellectually, Marcuse developed a critical view of culture which combined an analysis of authoritarianism with recognition of the liberatory aspects of art – even if the latter are obscured by compromise. Kellner puts it succinctly, saying that Marcuse 'is concerned at once to preserve what he regards as emancipatory elements in the bourgeois tradition, while criticizing tendencies which he concludes serve the interests of repression and domination'.[88] The revolutionary ideals of bourgeois society hint at liberation, while ideals of human rights, democracy and the primacy of human needs remain important in critical social theory. But there was still a need to understand the catastrophe which had enabled the Nazis to take power in the country of Hegel, Marx and Goethe. For Marcuse and Horkheimer, fascism, or the authoritarian attitude it exemplified, was implicit in the contradictions of bourgeois society: 'Hence the love of freedom and reason in Enlightenment is', Kellner writes, '"from the outset a contradiction"' within bourgeois civilization.[89] One outcome of the decline is social atomism, leading to a 'gangster state'[90] in conditions of monopoly rather than market capitalism. To understand this requires inter-disciplinary research drawing on culture, economic theory, law and political philosophy. Within that, the link between culture and the rise of fascism is the subject matter of Marcuse's 1937 essay on affirmative culture, discussed in the next chapter.

3
Affirmations

In this chapter I discuss Marcuse's 1937 essay 'The Affirmative Character of Culture'. I situate the essay in terms of different views on how it relates to Marcuse's work to this date; set out the essay's main argument, noting Marcuse's sources and links to his later work; and comment briefly on cultural currents in Germany in the 1930s. While Marcuse left Germany in 1932, and so remained outside these currents, issues arise in relation to Nazi popular culture and the resistant tendency of German Expressionism which I think are part of the essay's context. So, I selectively introduce material from Ernst Bloch's critique of Nazi culture and the 1937 Munich exhibition of Expressionism (classed as degenerate art). In passing, this becomes a foil to issues to be raised in Chapter 4 on the location of freedom in a literature of intimacy, not in overt contests with the regime. I realise, of course, that the essay on affirmative culture was written more than 70 years ago, and that it relates to specific historical developments: in terms of its writing, to the rise of fascism; in terms of its content, to the development of bourgeois culture, primarily literature. In both cases, the histories are now encapsulated in a past distant by two generations. So I begin with a justification for re-reading it now.

For Marcuse, fascist culture was 'the product of an irrational social organization'.[1] It was necessary to understand culture's contribution to the rise of fascism in Germany in the 1930s – when art was pressed into 'service of national defence and of labour and military discipline' and was 'marked by its social function of organizing the whole society in the interests of a few economically powerful groups and their hangers-on'[2] – in order to understand how it might never be allowed to recur. Was the tendency towards inwardness and other-worldliness in bourgeois art a factor? Did that inward-looking tendency arise from alienation, to lend currency to Nazi culture's revival of old myths in its cult of blood and soil? If bourgeois art is characterised by displacement of the idea (or the ideal) of freedom to an inner realm; that is, to an aesthetic dimension acting, in effect, as a dreamland, then the idea of a free society is a beautiful illusion by which not only are the dominant society's mechanisms of social and economic ordering untroubled, but also the un-beautiful illusion of the myth of blood and soil reigns unchallenged. In Germany in the 1930s this culture, devoid of its primary content, was brought into the project of Nazism as a reaction against bourgeois decadence, playing on insecurity on a social scale to construct an illusory collective of an apocalyptic kind. Understanding affirmative culture, then, is a way to understand the conditions in which fascism grew. For Marcuse, Nazi culture and the Nazi regime were extensions of capitalism – a view coincidentally shared by artists such as John Heartfield, George Grosz and Otto Dix.

But while Marcuse's analysis was philosophical, their intervention was practical. The gap between Marcuse's position and theirs is more than the physical separation of the Atlantic, and raises questions as to art's function as reflexive critique or activism. To me this issue remains important today, when artists claim variously to offer critical positions within art's institutions, or to act politically in more direct engagement. The extent to which almost any art can now be subsumed by the mainstream (see Chapter 8) suggests that the choice is more limited than it appears, and that affirmative culture has not gone away.

SITUATING THE ESSAY

Douglas Kellner, introducing *Art and Liberation*, Volume 4 of Marcuse's *Collected Papers*, writes that the essay on affirmative culture should be read in the context of the wider aim to construct a critical theory of society. As I said in the Introduction, I agree that this was Marcuse's central project and that his work on aesthetics is framed by it. But what constituted his point of departure into aesthetics? And, in particular, was this an affirmation of the transcendental quality of art, or a recognition of art's autonomy?

Before re-reading the text, I need to situate it in relation to readings of Marcuse's wider project as a critical thinker. First, as an employee of the International Institute for Social Research, based at Columbia University, Marcuse reflects the reconstituted Institute's move away from the social research which had formed its core activity in Germany. The essay is discursive, calling on the evidence not of empirical data but of argument in the theoretical discourses which precede it. Second, within that, the essay revolves around different forms of art's separation from ordinary life. Transcendence – the cultural quality of Idealism – tends to universalism, in contrast to a realist analysis of art's production and reception in historically specific circumstances (in which an image is read only in terms of its social context). Transcendence can be situated in a Kantian aesthetic in which the beauty apprehended in art – by a suitably educated spectator – is distanced from material realities. But between 1800 and 1900, apart from the rise and fall of realism, there is in European art a shift from a concern with beauty to a claim for autonomy. Art's autonomy relies on universal laws of form distanced from everyday appearances in perception, and has that in common with transcendence.

But autonomy – as the principal claim of modern art since the 1880s – also offers a metaphorical space of criticality. Art's autonomy is a recurrent theme in Marcuse's writing, and in this early essay it overlaps with art's relation to the social conditions in which it is produced. The question is whether art mirrors those conditions, transcends them, or critiques them – in its time, or across times. But these are my own glosses on the essay's detailed content; for two different ways to situate that content in relation to Marcuse's theoretical development I turn now to Kellner and Barry Katz.

Kellner disagrees with Katz's view that Marcuse's period of study with Heidegger from 1927 to 1933 imbued his aesthetic theories with a transcendentalism by which art is deemed to be outside temporality.[3] For Kellner, Marcuse's theory is a form of Marxist aesthetics, based in dialectical materialism – art rooted in, and able to engage with, the circumstances of its production – even if this was not elaborated by Marx (see Chapter 1). For Kellner, then, Marcuse's writing on art is 'grounded in very specific historical environments' as part of a critical theory of society, providing analysis of a given society yet looking for the radical transformation of that society.[4] Because cultural forms are produced, not given by a predetermined order, they are open to intervention, like social forms. This does not presuppose an essential human nature, an essential aesthetic impulse, nor imply the separation of a superstructure (in which culture figures) from a material base. Rather, it implies a dialectical relation between the materialities of art and everyday existence.

Katz, by contrast, argues that Marcuse embarks on a radical ontology – or a philosophy of being integrating Marxism and Heidegger's phenomenology – citing Marcuse's paper 'Contributions to a Phenomenology of Historical Materialism' (1928) as evidence.[5] I cannot go into that paper here, but cite Katz to summarise its argument:

In identifying two planes or dimensions of human existence – the 'essential structure' uncovered by phenomenology and in its 'concrete forms and configurations' as analysed by historical materialism – Marcuse had outlined the intellectual project that would occupy him in varying forms throughout the rest of his career: the effective integration of an essential standard of criticism with its material, historical objects.[6]

This effort, Katz continues, is first evident in Marcuse's doctoral thesis (see Chapter 2), and Marcuse maintained a concern for ontology, seeking to 'penetrate beyond the abstractness of the existential framework constructed by Heidegger'.[7] Heidegger provided a basis for the project, arriving in his book *Being and Time* at the proposition that to be human is to exist in time. But I think Kellner may be right: Marcuse rejects the essentialism of Heidegger's work, maintaining a materialist view:

> The idealist, utopian, and ontological moments of Marcuse's analysis should thus be read in the framework of the critical theory of society that informed his work from the 1930s until his death. Interestingly, in his first major publication on art and culture ... Marcuse focuses on the ideological and mystifying aspects of art in the contemporary era.[8]

Kellner adds that 'The Affirmative Character of Culture' is 'one of Marcuse's enduring theoretical masterpieces' which 'radiates with illuminating ideas and is a paradigm of dialectical thought'.[9] The essay begins by citing Greek culture, but is as much a reflection of the period in which it was written as a reflection on a past philosophical tradition. The Greek culture it cites, that is, is evidenced in a surviving literature, but I suggest it is read in the present of the 1930s. I move now to a re-reading of the essay.

AFFIRMATIVE CULTURE

Marcuse concluded his doctoral thesis with praise for Thomas Mann, seeing Mann's professional life and writing as evidence of an integration in society which allowed a critique of its values as well. But there were questions. If an artist sought integration, did the individualism of bourgeois society inhibit or prevent it? And to what extent did an artist's intervention, even if beginning as withdrawal, change that? Marcuse writes that community is not given, 'but given up and something to strive for ... Beyond the literary historical problem, a piece of human history is visible: the struggle of the German people for a new community.'[10] When he wrote that in 1922, the idea of the German people, rather than the German language, was relatively new, after German unification in the 1860s. In the 1930s it took on a new meaning in the rhetoric of one people, one empire and one leader – a terrifying parody of the concept of community. It seems important, then, to take Marcuse's idea of community in context, and I will return to the development of a nationalist culture in Germany (evident in a proliferation of public monuments) later in the chapter. At this point I would say only that Marcuse's main concerns in the 1937 essay revolve around a different periodisation, from Greek classicism to bourgeois culture and its mainly nineteenth-century forms. As Kellner summarises: 'The concept of "affirmative culture" ... refers to the culture of the bourgeois epoch. Affirmative culture projected its spiritual realm as a higher, more sublime, and valuable realm than the everyday world and claimed its values were crucial to the individual's well-being.'[11]

Two ideas are stated here: first, the separation of high values from low life; second, the centrality of the individual in bourgeois society, as if separated from the social. In a way, the artistic withdrawal of the 1890s – in the Secession movements of Berlin, Munich and Vienna, and in French symbolism – could be read as both a rejection of bourgeois society's market values, and, at the same time, as a reflection of a bourgeois individualist withdrawal from common life (as both low life and shared norms).

The essay was first published in *Zeitschrift für Sozialforschung* in 1937, three years after the closure of the Frankfurt Institute for Social Research, the dismissal of 1,600 Jewish and leftist German academics under the Act for Reform of the Civil Service (7 April 1933), and Marcuse's departure for Geneva, and later the United States. It is not surprising that Marcuse's aim in the essay is to examine bourgeois culture's role in creating the conditions under which the blood-and-soil culture of the 1930s became credible. Just as culture was not Marcuse's core concern then, neither was it a primary interest in the Institute, though Marcuse and Leo Löwenthal both worked on literature. Yet the understanding of culture as a form of evidence of social attitudes, such as the willingness to bow to authoritarianism, was part of the project of understanding how a society could turn in the direction taken by German society in the 1930s. To examine bourgeois culture was to examine the conditions in which a terrifying irrationality had been produced. Again, it is important to remember that in the critical theory of society which was Marcuse's core project, culture's forms are not essential (in the sense of given by nature) but specific. Yet they communicate beyond the conditions of their production. In an interview published posthumously (cited by Kellner), Marcuse uses the term trans-historical to refute a claim that *The Aesthetic Dimension* (1978) stated a transcendental aesthetic: 'Transhistorical means transcending every and any *particular* stage of the historical process', but, he adds emphatically, does not mean transcending the historical process itself.[12] A work of art may speak outside of its own time, but not outside of time (eternally). In *The Aesthetic Dimension* (see Chapter 7 below), this becomes even more central to the justification of aesthetics. In the 1937 essay it allows consideration of specific art works outside of the circumstances in which they were made, but does not attribute to art a quality of standing above or beyond the time or the circumstances in which it is later received.

As in his thesis on the artist novel, Marcuse begins with disintegration. If the 'doctrine that all human knowledge is oriented toward practice belonged to the ancient nucleus of philosophy', he writes in its opening sentence,[13] unity becomes duality in the Greek separation of knowledge of the good, true and beautiful from that of ordinary life and work. This supposes an original unity (located in early Greek culture), which I take as a point of departure necessary to begin the argument, or an assumption for the sake of argument, rather than a reading of history. Otherwise it would suggest a pre-historical Eden or Arcadia, which would be an Idealist projection. Leaving that aside, Marcuse glosses from Aristotle that the world of ordinary life is insecure, driven by necessity, and hence unfree. There, the location of certainty lies in the higher reflection offered by beauty, goodness and truth as if against practicality. These are abstract concepts, their pursuit open to those whose lives are not governed by toil (which requires skill). So, 'ancient theory is precisely at the point where idealism retreats in the face of social contradictions'.[14] Since thought is not-work it is distanced from ordinary life, yet has a capacity to critically re-imagine that life. That, in fact, is the central and abiding lesson of all Marcuse's aesthetic theory.

In Platonic philosophy, and in German Idealism, 'the authentic, basic demand of idealism is that this material world be transformed and improved in accordance with the truths yielded by knowledge of the Ideas'.[15] The separation of thought as a higher realm from ordinary life as a lower realm is its exoneration, just as a separation of the Idea from sensuality is potentially redemptive. But as a Marxist, Marcuse does not see Idealism as complete; he follows Marx in integrating its imaginative element with an emphasis on materiality and the conditions of production. In dialectical materialism, this enables a concept of agency – the human capacity for intervention in those conditions by which the human actor is shaped. In bourgeois society, for Marcuse, the balance of these possibilities is unsettled:

> In the bourgeois epoch the theory of the relationship between necessity and beauty ... underwent decisive changes. First, the view that concern with the highest values is appropriated as a profession by particular social strata disappears. In its place emerges the thesis of the universality and universal validity of 'culture'.... By their very nature the truth of a philosophical judgement, the goodness of a moral action, and the beauty of a work of art should appeal to everyone, relate to everyone, be binding upon everyone.[16]

Beauty is removed from the social process by means of a definition of culture: not, as 'the totality of social life in a given situation' but as an entity 'lifted out of its social context' so that it brings a false unity to projects such as the construction of national culture.[17] This resembles the split between the anthropological meaning of culture as the articulation of shared values in everyday life, and its specialist meaning as the arts.[18] Tangentially, I note, in today's debates on the cultural industries (or the culture industry)[19] there is a tendency to attribute universal value to culture as the arts, while relegating local cultures, which entail ways of dwelling and the products of creative work in such lives, to a marginal status.[20]

For Marcuse, bourgeois culture generates popular forms such as the novel, but it uses them to offer a picture of life as it might be which is confined to an aesthetic realm. In this scenario, art is separated from the life-world in which its content might otherwise have agency. Bourgeois art displaces dreams of freedom to an immaterial realm where they do not threaten the existing social order. Culture's criticality is diminished and its agency erased. Affirmative culture affirms the status quo. Marcuse writes:

> By affirmative culture is meant that culture of the bourgeois epoch which led in the course of its own development to the segregation from civilization of the mental and spiritual world as an independent realm of value that is also considered superior

to civilization. Its decisive characteristic is the assertion of a universally obligatory, eternally better and more valuable world that must be unconditionally affirmed: a world essentially different from the factual world of the daily struggle for existence, yet realizable by every individual for himself [*sic*] 'from within,' yet without any transformation of the state of fact. It is only in this culture that cultural activities and objects gain that value which elevates them above the everyday sphere. Their reception becomes an act of celebration and exaltation.[21]

It might be added that only in that context does art have a market as an object of high social status and conspicuous consumption.

After the ancient world's assumption of joy as the quality of a beautiful life when the individual and society are united, bourgeois society posits an individual who becomes a separate entity and, outside common bonds, must seek its own purpose in life. Bourgeois life liberates individuals from the binding ties of feudalism, 'But the universality of this happiness is immediately cancelled, since the abstract equality ... realizes itself in capitalist production as concrete inequality.'[22] Conversely utopia – as happiness – is cancelled in ordinary life and allowed instead in art. Kellner comments: 'In fascinating anticipations of his later aesthetic theory, Marcuse claims that in the medium of beauty, possibilities of sensual happiness are expressed, although bodily pleasure is sublimated into aesthetic contemplation.'[23] A sublimated sensuality retains, however, a memory of joy which is art's promise of happiness and is not necessarily confined to an aesthetic realm but can be taken as a promise of a yet to be realised society of ease. That becomes part of Marcuse's interpretation of French literature (see Chapter 4); here I suggest that one implication is that political change may begin in the glimpse of joy encountered in art. But can a representation of freedom displaced through art remind the spectator of a really possible freedom? I leave the question open.

As Marcuse argues, the relation between beauty and happiness underwent a significant change in the bourgeois period. The concern for the absolutes of beauty, goodness and truth is democratised for the bourgeois class; but the bourgeoisie replace them with a single, universal cultural value devoid of the concepts' original content. So, bourgeois culture and bourgeois thought sell the doctrine of universal freedom in the guise of an individualism which is inherently un-free, and in a society where the mechanisms of production and exchange are designed to ensure inequality. The bourgeois revolutions of the eighteenth century in North America and France proclaimed liberty, but this did not mean freedom, it meant progress – the value of the rising commercial class. Or, as Marcuse puts it:

> To accusing questions the bourgeoisie gave a decisive answer: affirmative culture. The latter is fundamentally idealist. To the need of the isolated individual it responds with general humanity, to bodily misery with the beauty of the soul, to external bondage with internal freedom, to brutal egoism with the duty of the realm of virtue.[24]

It is as if a doctor prescribed, not medicine, but a picture of a pill; or, as Adorno put it, the diners in a restaurant should make do with eating menus. But that is not the whole story. A genuine longing for a better world is the implicit content of bourgeois culture but cannot be its explicit content because that would contradict the bourgeois economic imperative involved in the division of social classes and labour: 'By making suffering and sorrow into eternal, universal forces, great bourgeois art has continually shattered in the hearts of men the facile resignation of everyday life.'[25]

Kellner notes that a critical aesthetic recovers 'the positive emancipatory and utopian features of cultural phenomena that can advance the cause of human liberation'.[26] For Charles Reitz, too, Marcuse was 'aware of the paradoxical circumstance in which the aesthetic treatment of social realities could actually lead to an *anesthetic* "tranquilization" of perception and thought'.[27] Art carries a memory of the desire to be free, but in bourgeois culture the memory of freedom is decorative. Reitz cites the recapitulation of part of the argument from 'The Affirmative Character of Culture' in Marcuse's *Counter-Revolution and Revolt* (1972). Marcuse writes:

> The affirmative character of art was grounded not so much in its divorce from reality as in the ease with which it could be reconciled with the given reality, used as its décor, taught and experienced as uncommitting but rewarding value, the possession of which distinguished the 'higher' order of society, the educated, from the masses. But the affirmative power of art is also the power which denies this affirmation.... art retains that alienation from the established reality which is at the origin of art. It is a second alienation, by virtue of which the artist dissociates himself [sic] methodically from the alienated society

and creates the unreal, 'illusory' universe in which art alone has, and communicates, its truth.[28]

As a general principle, this explains art's agency for repression while resting equally on its utopian content. The question of whether the utopian content is taken as a foundational aspect or an original (as if pre-historical) quality can be set aside. Either way, art has a dual character, its liberating side is diminished as its repressive side becomes enhanced in bourgeois culture. In the 1937 essay, Marcuse writes of art's treatment of love that, in a society of isolated individuals, it transmutes from a setting aside of individuality to a reproduction of duty when its representation becomes tragic:

> The individual has the character of an independent, self-sufficient monad. His relation to the (human and non-human) world is either abstractly immediate ... or abstractly mediated.... In neither case is the monadic isolation of the individual overcome....
>
> The idea of love ... requires that the individual overcome nomadic isolation and find fulfilment through the surrender of individuality in the unconditional solidarity of two persons.[29]

Marcuse adds that in a society based on individualism the complete surrender of individuality occurs only in death, which 'eliminates all of the external conditions that destroy permanent solidarity'.[30] Art turns to pathos. He goes on: 'While in art love is elevated to tragedy, it threatens to become mere duty and habit.... Love contains the individualistic principle of the new society: it demands exclusiveness.'[31] In this way, affirmative culture renders beauty a means to displace a dream of freedom, or of solidarity, and a means to safely internalise the unreality of freedom. The moment at which beauty becomes convulsive, of course, blows this out of the water (but may also shipwreck the spectator), which is another story.

Marcuse does, however, see a counter-possibility in a prospect of a convulsive beauty: 'But even beauty has been affirmed with good conscience only in the ideal of art, for it contains a dangerous violence that threatens the given form of existence.'[32] He draws here on Surrealism, but the shock-wave effect of beauty was recognised by poets such as Verlaine and Rimbaud,[33] and in the 1970s by the singer-writer Patti Smith quoting Rimbaud on an album cover. Marcuse cites Friedrich Nietzsche – for whom 'beauty reawakens an "aphrodisiac bliss"'[34] – as an anti-Kantian source. Then, citing Goethe's *Faust*, Marcuse pronounces that 'Beauty is fundamentally shameless'.[35] But in bourgeois society beauty can be enjoyed only in certain ways, under certain conditions, as either relaxation or dissipation. Bringing the argument back to the framework of dialectical materialism, Marcuse continues:

> Bourgeois society has liberated individuals, but as persons who are to keep themselves in check. From the beginning, the prohibition of pleasure was a condition of freedom. A society split into classes can afford to make man [sic] into a means of pleasure only in the form of bondage and exploitation. Since in the new order the regulated classes rendered services not immediately, with their person, but only mediated by the production of surplus value for the market, it was considered inhuman to exploit an underling's body as a source of pleasure ... On the other hand, harnessing their bodies and intelligence for profit was considered a natural activation of freedom. Correspondingly, for the poor, hiring oneself out to work in a factory became a moral duty, while hiring out one's body as a means to pleasure was depravity and 'prostitution.' Also, in this society, poverty is a condition of profit and power, yet dependence takes place in the medium of abstract freedom.[36]

He adds, however, that even under conditions of servitude an 'anticipatory memory' of a sensual beauty remains. And in *Counter-Revolution and Revolt* he argues that if bourgeois culture uses the sublime to erase meaning by substituting art for reality, it may be that classical art retains an unsettling dimension in which 'extreme qualities' appear as an '*un*sublimated' expression of passion and pain, against which affirmative culture offers shame.[37] Then, 'Perhaps we can no longer cope with this *pathos* which drives to the limits of social restraint.'[38]

The similarities between arguments rehearsed in *Counter-Revolution and Revolt* in 1972 and in the 1937 essay denote a continuity in Marcuse's aesthetics; and, although this would be easy to overlook, the above passage clarifies the working through of his Marxist framework in terms of aesthetics. The mention of class division reminds the reader that bourgeois society is an economic and political mechanism designed to ensure the advantages of the owners of capital. Affirmative culture validates that division, and denies the owners of capital encounters with a beauty which is shameless and hence, in a repressive society, convulsive. The shock effect of beauty counters the reassuring beauty of bourgeois art.

That is, in its agency for social rupture, it 'displays what may not be promised openly and what is denied the majority'.[39] Then, since art is not-life, 'Unlike the truth of beauty, the beauty of art is compatible with the bad present.'[40]

Citing Schiller's idea that a better society is produced by aesthetic education, Marcuse adapts the idea for a society in which joy 'is compressed into a momentary episode'.[41] Rather than being a path to freedom, beauty is allowed 'in spiritualized, ideal form' while idealisation annuls 'the meaning of happiness'.[42] Beauty is then no more than consolation, separated from the content of 'gratification in the present'[43] – which is sensual and political. This shift takes place through the internalisation of moral censorship in which the subject denies a prospect of freedom in favour of its representation in a distanced, no longer really possible form. In his study of authority, published a year before 'The Affirmative Character of Culture', Marcuse locates the beginning of such coercion in Kant's philosophy:

> Kant had introduced the antagonism between freedom and coercion into the idea of freedom itself: there is only freedom under the (coercive) law. The supersession of this antagonism was sought in the unification of the individual and the general community. In the sphere of social action this appeared as the voluntary all-round self-limitation of the united individuals through which social existence as a world of free individuals or as 'bourgeois society' became possible for the first time.[44]

Later, in *The Aesthetic Dimension*, Marcuse links art to deception: it cannot represent extreme suffering, rendering it as acceptable images. Citing Auschwitz and Mai Lai (a massacre of Vietnamese civilians by US soldiers), Marcuse states: 'Art draws away from this reality, because it cannot represent this suffering without subjecting it to aesthetic form, and thereby to the mitigating catharsis, to enjoyment. Art is inexorably infested with this guilt.'[45] In the next sentence he argues that art retains a necessity to recall that which survives even in extreme conditions: 'the need to create images of the possible "other".'[46] But in the 1937 essay the point is that culture's displacement of that dimension is internalised relates to Marcuse's efforts to understand the rise of fascism from the soil of Idealism. Perhaps that is the difficulty: Idealism introduces the sublime, a non-reality above reality which it identifies with an ultimate, universal beauty and truth. As abstraction, such ideal beauty materially denies human solidarity in favour of an inwardly pursued and individually experienced truth. Near the end of the essay on affirmative culture Marcuse echoes his argument in the essay on authority when he says of Germany in the 1930s that 'Affirmative culture had cancelled social antagonisms in an abstract internal community.'[47]

To take stock for a moment: Marcuse locates a unity of individual and society in early Greek philosophy, and he sees a separation of the individual, especially the cultured individual or the artist, arise within bourgeois society. Unity becomes the preserve of law and self-coercion. The idea of a lost unity located in pre-classical Greece is a projection of a present lack onto a past that is remote enough to bear it; but, as I said above, I take it only as a point of departure, necessary to set in motion an argument concerning its absence in the present. In face of a real lack of social cohesion, art reproduces its illusion. In Germany in the 1930s, 'The individual is inserted into a false collectivity (race, folk, blood, and soil)',[48] and this externalisation in Nazi culture had the same function as the prior internalisation in bourgeois culture: renunciation and subjection. As Marcuse writes: 'That individuals freed for over four hundred years march with so little trouble in the communal column of the authoritarian state is due in no small measure to affirmative culture.'[49] In a more sober tone, he states,

> The intensive education to inner freedom that has been in progress since Luther is now ... bearing its choicest fruit. While the mind falls prey to hate and contempt, the soul is still cherished.... the festivals and celebrations of the authoritarian state, its parades, its physiognomy, and the speeches of its leaders are all addressed to the soul. They go to the heart, even when their intent is power.[50]

As Reitz observes, Marcuse aimed at an aesthetic theory in which art ceased to affirm coercion, or resisted it. This emerges in his writing in the 1960s, as the counter-culture appeared to take such a direction, and it reappears in his later work as a potential of liberation which art counter-poses to illusion. In between, in the heady optimism of the 1960s, illusion seemed to be broken by an incipient new society verging on a work of art (see Chapter 5). But what of German art in the 1930s?

A NATIONALIST CULTURE

I want to look briefly now at some of the currents running through art in 1930s Germany. This involves three strands: German

Expressionism – as in the work of Wassily Kandinsky, Franz Marc and the Blue Rider group in Munich, for example – which begins in the 1910s but returns to prominence in the 1937 Munich exhibition; the rise of a Nazi culture of blood and soil appealing to the petit-bourgeoisie, trading on illusion and nostalgia; and a countermovement in the form of Berlin Dada, or John Heartfield's montages satirising Nazi politics (published as magazine covers), also predating but continuing through the rise of fascism. The axis between Expressionism and a possible fourth strand represented by Socialist Realism was the subject-matter of papers in literary journals, as in Bloch's defence of Expressionism against Georg Lukács' attacks on it as, in effect, bourgeois art (seen from within the Soviet Union). Expressionism seems in turn to be poised between Idealism and an abstraction which Bloch reads as conveying the utopian content of an art which also reflects the flux of modern society. Utopianism is Bloch's core concern, though there are references to it in Marcuse's 1937 essay, too. First, I cite Bloch's treatment of Nazi culture, because although Marcuse does not review its forms, to take note of them helps to contextualise his 1937 essay (reading it as a counter-blast).

Bloch identifies a superficial dualism in Nazi popular culture, writing of the Nazis' use of the Left's emblematic forms such as the torch-lit parade, or the fanning of popular nostalgia for better days. That nostalgia, arising from a sense of present lack in the turmoil of economic depression and excess inflation in the 1920s, translates into the new sublime of Nazi architecture – buildings for a thousand-year Reich. Bloch sees a false utopianism – a concept allied to false consciousness in Marxism – in fascist art and culture: 'Thus hell mocked right from the beginning with a grotesque mask of salvation, again and again.'[51] He catalogues the Nazi's thefts of the Left's traditional forms from the colour red to the carrying of banners, political posters, and the street parade. He writes, 'they pretended to be merely workers and nothing else, thus distorting boundlessly'.[52] Bloch identifies a specific area of appropriation, too, when 'Goebbels expressly declared the film "Battleship Potemkin" [made in the Soviet Union by Eisentstein] to be a model for the German film', adding, 'so far does the formal consent go, as the crook and thieving perverter imagines it'.[53] In a further text, Bloch writes:

> After all, the Nazi did not even invent the song with which he seduces. Nor even the gunpowder with which he makes his fireworks, nor even the firm in whose name he deceives. The very

term Third Reich has a long history, a genuinely revolutionary one. The Nazi was creative, so to speak, only in the embezzlement at all prices with which he employed revolutionary slogans to the opposite effect.[54]

Nazi culture, then, presents an awkward mix of modernism and medievalism, in some cases fused with a form of classicism. Having been forced, like Marcuse, to flee Nazi Germany in 1933 – his name was on a list of those to be arrested, and his wife was a Communist Party activist and courier – Bloch had cause for venom. But he makes two points relevant to this chapter: first, the use of an emotive popular culture (when the Left relied on sober reasoning); second, its grounding in a revival of old songs, as it were, from a remote tradition. The term Third Reich is itself adapted from the Third Kingdom of millenarianism.[55] That current – the songs of lost crowns in the Rhine, and returning kings – informed some of Richard Wagner's music, and might be read as parodying that unity of the individual and society which Marcuse (who does not cite Wagner) finds in Greek epic theatre. But it also informed, directly, a new tradition of public monuments from the 1870s onwards which, I suggest, are as interesting a part of the context for Marcuse's essay and Bloch's texts as is the romantic and inward-looking medievalism that inspired Wagner. For a recently established state trying to appear old, this public tradition has the attraction of an appeal to nationhood, through an evocation, for instance, of the mythicised return in the hour of need of the Emperor Friedrich Barbarossa, for a state sufficiently insecure in its identity to need such affirmations.

Germany was an imperial power with colonies in Africa, but it was also a recently unified state. It was not Germany but Prussia which had defeated the French at Sedan in 1870. The idea of Germany required establishment in public monuments which, while very new, looked timeless. Most used a Teutonic (that is, anti-classical) language, as had the Nazarenes in the 1830s. To give an example, Joseph-Ernst von Bandel's *Arminius Monument*, completed in 1875 to commemorate a first-century anti-Roman insurgent, adopted a gothic style as a German style, set in the Teutoburger Wald where Arminius had defeated the Roman legions. Arminius was a minor figure historically but, in the monument, is 'rescued from oblivion to become one of the pivotal figures in the creation of German national identity'.[56] Sergiusz Michalski notes a continuity in the development of a new German national style in opposition to the classicism more predominant in France, the epitome of which is the

Kyffhäuser Monument designed by Bruno Schmitz for a remote site
in the Harz mountains, completed in 1896. The crown of the Reich
is placed on top of a stone tower; Emperor Friedrich Barbarossa
sits at its base; in front of him is a forecourt separated from the
spectator, who has already climbed a mountain road, by a rocky
chasm. The chasm was engineered by removing stone used in the
construction of the monument, in an extension of the logic by
which permanent materials such as stone and bronze lend a timeless
quality to public monuments. But here nature is conscripted, too,
as the ultimate repository of timelessness. Below the chasm a fake
Romanesque portico is inserted into the remains of a real medieval
castle. Above Barbarossa is an equine statue of Kaiser Wilhelm I.
Michalski sees it as 'an architectural complex whose very structure
seems to have been determined by successive layers, of both natural
and symbolic character, starting with the primeval rocks'.[57] Bloch
notes the Barbarossa revival, too:

> It cannot be denied that alongside the crudeness there is an
> undercurrent of very old dreams. The strongest is that of the
> 'Third Reich', the very phrase already shrouds the petit bourgeois
> in premonition. Music on the square piano, bands in beer gardens
> sang out to him, when there had already long been a Kaiser: 'A
> crown lies in the deep, deep Rhine'. The Prusso-German Reich
> had long been founded, and the crown of this petit-bourgeois
> music was still hidden ... As Kaiser of the *future*: uniquely today
> a 'future state' is proffered ... by the Kyffhäuser line.[58]

At greater length, this is Marcuse's insertion of the individual
in 'a false collectivity' (cited above). Later, Schmitz designed
the Monument to the Battle of the Nations commemorating the
centenary of Napoleon's defeat near Leipzig in 1813, used as
a meeting place by the Nazis. The vast scale of this monument
informed the design of the parade ground at Nürnberg, and in turn
the architecture of searchlights which was the Nazi new sublime.
Michalski concludes that this genre's perpetrators 'betrayed an
insecure nation whose fight for political and cultural primacy in
Europe ... separated it from Western rationalism'.[59]

Marcuse does not cite any of this, but nevertheless offers a critique
of the society which arose from German nationalism, situating it a
continuity with German Idealism:

The loud pugnacity of the authoritarian state against the 'liberal ideals' of humanity, individuality, and rationality and against idealist art and philosophy cannot conceal that what is occurring is a process of self-abolition. Just as the social reorganization involved in passing from a parliamentary democracy to an authoritarian leadership-state is only a reorganization within the established order, so the cultural reorganization in which liberalism changes into 'heroic realism' takes place within affirmative culture itself.[60]

This is followed by the assertion that affirmative culture explains how a hitherto free people could march for an authoritarian state. They were marching, it seemed then, in a land already framed by a revived grandeur (which never existed), and scripted as the heirs to long-lost traditions which, thus, validated present violence as the continuation of, not the break with, history. How could anyone oppose Barbarossa (or his heirs, as they sang their nostalgic, Aryan songs around their camp fires in the woods)?

DEALING WITH EXPRESSIONISM

But what of the opposition? Was German Expressionism a counter-cultural force to Nazism? In an obvious way it was, when it was declared degenerate (*entartete Kunst*), by the regime in 1937, in an exhibition in Munich which contrasted Expressionism with an art seen by the authorities as more appropriate to a myth of blood and soil, trading on an awkward mix of realism, classicism and aspects of older German art in works by, for instance, Eduard Grützner (1846–1925) and Franz von Defregger (1835–1921).

Bloch is the defender of Expressionism against its degenerate status, as he is against Lukács' attack on it from the position of Socialist Realism. (Bloch was writing in North America in enforced exile, unable to find a post at the Institute due to his lack of English, and his alleged communist sympathies.) But the Nazis closed the Bauhaus in Dessau, a home of modern art, despite also having used a modernist architectural style in functional buildings such as the power station at Essen (the largest in Europe, opened by Hitler). If the Bauhaus, like Russian Constructivism, aimed to 'produce modern environments for quintessentially modern lives',[61] then it might be possible to counter-pose fascist myth and modernist rationality. But such generalisations are unhelpful. For his part, Marcuse links the outward, heroic face of Nazi culture to the inwardness of Idealism in what he calls the 'united front against the mind'.[62] And like Bloch he acknowledges the use of emotive imagery in the Nazi's aestheticised politics: 'The idealist cult of inwardness and the heroic cult of the state serve a fundamentally identical social order to which the individual is now completely sacrificed.'[63] But Expressionism, too, is an art of inwardness, drawing on the psychological rather than material reality. As Wilhelm Wörringer argues in his 1908 thesis, abstraction is not an inept distortion of the appearances of perception, but expresses another sensibility in the decorative motif and strained figuration. After its classification as degenerate it was hard not to see Expressionism as oppositional art (though Emil Nolde, a leading Expressionist painter, was a member of the Nazi party, and still prohibited from painting in the early 1940s). For Kandinsky, art was outside politics; unsettled by the Revolution after his return to Russia in 1914, he moved first to Weimar, then to Paris.[64] In 1967, though, Marcuse cited Marc's statement from 1914: '"We set a No in opposition to entire centuries."'[65] Marc adds: '"We seek the internal, the spiritual side of nature."'[66] By 1967 Marcuse had embarked on a theory of beauty as non-repressive order, and form in art as carrying a necessarily different content from perception: art can both reflect and critique reality while being trans-historical; its negating form can 'shatter the false reality of the status quo'.[67] But I run ahead (see Chapter 5). Here, I will focus on Bloch's comments on Expressionism to ask if the latter can be characterised as an art of refusal.

In 'Jugglers' Fair Beneath the Gallows', Bloch cites Hitler's speech at the opening of the 1937 exhibition as 'the revenge of the rejected art student'.[68] Bloch adds that the Führer recommended a chair in astrology to the Berlin Faculty of Science. Against all that, Marc 'is no match ... in the gentle mystery of his animals'.[69] If the defence of Expressionism appears provoked by its degenerate classification, however, Bloch also defends it against Lukács' attack on it as an art of unrealism. In 'Expressionism Seen Now' Bloch notes that the degenerate pictures gained four times more visitors than those of the official taste in a separate room in the Munich exhibition; but he demarks Expressionism from New Objectivity, too: 'Klee almost alone, the wondrous dreamer, remained true to himself and to his unrefuted visions; he nailed the expressionist colours to the mast, and it is not his fault that they were no longer regarded as a flag.'[70] He traces a pre-history of Expressionism in the work of Paul Gauguin and Vincent van Gogh, whence the artist takes the role of voyaging in the psyche. But for Bloch this is political as well:

'Humanity distinguishes socialism from fascism; reason enough to remember with honour an art which the philistine spits on, an art in which human stars ... have burned or wanted to burn.'[71] This reflects Bloch's case that the Left failed in Germany through a reliance on rationality when fascism used torches and songs to engage the mass public intuitively. He adds: 'But the Expressionists dug out fresh water and fire, wells and wild light.'[72] Bloch's writing is an acquired taste, and if Bloch reproached Lukács for a lack of attention to the specific artists he criticised,[73] he seems to make the same error here in not referring to specific works. Yet there is a sense that Expressionism carries the quality of rupture – a quality which Marcuse later aligns with Surrealism (see Chapter 6). But by the 1930s, this was already dated.

Heartfield's technique of montage, used for direct political satire in the magazine AIZ – Workers' Illustrated Daily (*Arbeiter-illustrierte Zeitung*) – shows a more politicised disruptive agency. Among his covers is a picture of a German family, with a baby in a pram, eating bicycle and munitions parts, captioned 'Hurrah, the butter is all gone!' (*Hurrah, die Butter ist alle!*) from a remark by Herman Goering that the Reich needed no butter or schmaltz, just iron. Nationalism denies the ability to express critique;[74] I end this chapter by stating my own position, that in those conditions, the shock-effect represented by Heartfield was necessary, exposing the contradictions of Nazi rhetoric in ways which were both visually sophisticated and genuinely funny. Expressionism, despite all that Bloch says of it, remains ambivalent; Marc was killed in the war in 1916, but Kandinsky went on to produce a pure abstraction (a non-representational visual language) which he saw as prefiguring a new spiritual age. I find his writing somewhat elitist, however, just as I reject his spiritualism (derived from the spiritualist Madame Blavatsky) as confusing mysticism. For these reasons, it could be argued at a stretch that Expressionism is an off-shoot of, rather than a radical departure from, affirmative culture. But this should be read in conjunction with the next chapter, where another possibility emerges.

4
A Literature of Intimacy

In this chapter I reconsider Marcuse's essay 'Some Remarks on Aragon', written in 1945 (or shortly before) but not published until 1993.[1] The essay's main concern is a literature of intimacy found in the poems of Paul Éluard and a novel by Louis Aragon from the early 1940s, the time of the German occupation of France. Both writers were known for their Left affiliations, and both took part in the Resistance. Their work was published in clandestine editions during the occupation, yet Marcuse sees more than a propaganda value in it, setting it in a literary development he traces back to the poems of Charles Baudelaire in the mid nineteenth century, and which acts as a foil to, or negation of, the realities of the occupation. From the work of Baudelaire, Éluard and Aragon, Marcuse draws out a literary memory of joy, or a promise of happiness (*promesse du bonheur*) which, in face of terror (fascism), is freedom's last resort, the glimpse of it available in those conditions.

The essay represents a number of departures in Marcuse's work. First, it deals with French rather than German literature. Second, it turns from the view of bourgeois culture as complicit in fascism of his 1937 essay (see Chapter 3) towards a more positive image of literature as reinstating joy, and as the sole location of freedom amid a totally repressive actuality. I should emphasise that Marcuse deals with a *literature* of intimacy, not acts of intimacy. Third, while Marcuse's 1937 essay reconstructed broad and abstract tendencies in bourgeois literature, with relatively little close reading of specific cases, his essay on French literature contains many direct quotations, indicating a close reading of the texts (as did his doctoral thesis). Indeed, this essay complements his thesis on the German artist novel. Perhaps there is a commonality in that French love stories and German artist novels involve a journey of self-realisation, or the negotiation of tensions between the protagonist and the conditions in which the narrative is set. There is also a commonality with some of the inward-looking aspects of German Expressionism – the depiction of a subjective world – but in a very different way, in that love is material, real not confined to the mind, and a fulfilment in contrast to the anxiety of Expressionist distortions. This sense of fulfilment also seems to affirm the emphasis on sensual human activity in Marx's Theses on Feuerbach.

In the artist novel the tension is between isolation and social integration. In Aragon's novel *Aurélien* it is between the paths of personal and political awareness, at first in the relative quiet of the inter-war years and then in the immediacy of the invasion in 1940. The agency of the individual, standing for the artist or writer, is questioned. In *Aurélien* there is a sense of a historical tide which overtakes individuals, but also of crevices within conditions in which unexpected meetings can occur. The conditions in which Marcuse wrote his thesis in 1922 and the essay in 1945 differed, however. The thesis was written in the relative safety of a comfortable life in 1920s Freiburg; in the 1940s, in wartime, after fleeing Nazi Germany with his family, Marcuse arrived at a model of internalised agency: only in a literature of intimacy is freedom remembered as the beacon of a future hope. A tension between intimate withdrawal and political life occurs in the essay's sub-title: 'Art and Politics in the Totalitarian Era'. But are the insights gained from investigation of this special case helpful in understanding art's agency in other times and places? My argument is that the essay, while a minor piece, is central to Marcuse's aesthetic theory. I explain why below. Here, I put the chapter's literary material in two contexts. I begin with Marcuse's work for the US government in the 1940s, dealing with propaganda while remaining in contact with other members of the Institute. I then reconsider the 1945 essay's theme and references to French literature, and set it in context of the allied forces' use of that literature – including a poem by Éluard – as air-dropped propaganda. My argument is that Marcuse would have been aware of this at least vaguely, but that he goes beyond propaganda to read in the content of love poetry, as a genre, a memory of a utopian consciousness. I then review Marcuse's summary of Aragon's novel, via my reading of the English edition, and finally explain how I think this essay links to Marcuse's later aesthetic theory.

WARTIME CRITIQUES

The essay 'Some Remarks on Aragon: Art and Politics in the Totalitarian Era' dates from Marcuse's period in US government service. In late 1942 he became a senior analyst in the Office of Strategic Services, after a time at the Intelligence Bureau attached to the Office of War Information. His role was to study propaganda, and to analyse the internal dynamics of the Nazi state. As he recalls:

> My main task was to identify groups in Germany with which one could work towards reconstruction after the war; and to identify groups which were to be taken to task .... Based on exact research, reports, newspaper reading and whatever, lists were made up of those Nazis who were supposed to assume responsibility for their activity.[2]

In 1942 Marcuse went to Los Angeles aiming to collaborate with Max Horkheimer on a study of the authoritarian personality within scientific rationality.[3] This became the book *Dialectic of Enlightenment*,[4] which Horkheimer co-authored with T.W. Adorno. Horkheimer seems to have put potential collaborators in competition with each other after moving to California in 1941 for health reasons, reducing his responsibilities as the Institute's Director to concentrate on philosophical writing. But there were already tensions between the Institute and its host, Columbia University; these may explain Horkheimer's reluctance to allow Marxist content in the Institute's journal, *Zeitschrift für Sozial-forschung*, and to employ Ernst Bloch (whom the US authorities described as a premature anti-fascist – whatever that means).[5] Walter Benjamin's essay 'The Work of Art in a Period of Technical Reproducibility' was also stripped of its Marxist passages before publication – a censorship in which both Horkheimer and Adorno were involved.[6] But I wonder if this is a full explanation.

Cultural criticism in New York was not devoid of leftist elements in the late 1930s. Clement Greenberg's 1939 essay 'Avant-garde and Kitsch' states that 'it becomes necessary to quote Marx word for word'.[7] Greenberg's attack on Socialist Realism in the essay is based on a continued commitment to an avant-gardist position, but was written in the aftermath of the Hitler–Stalin pact in 1937. Left intellectuals were dismayed by this unholy alliance, which allowed comparison of Nazi and Soviet art as representing two totalitarian regimes. Still, Greenberg remained a Left critic. His essay ends: 'we look to socialism *simply* for the preservation of whatever living culture we have right now'.[8] And his essay on the avant-garde was published in the Fall 1939 issue of *Partisan Review*, a journal sympathetic to Trotskyism and world revolution.

Greenberg also reviewed Bertolt Brecht's *The Beggar's Opera* for the Winter 1939 issue of *Partisan Review*, and had earlier translated a German text on Nazism in other countries for a New York publisher.[9] He sought to widen his readership in his essay on the avant-garde, yet his writing in the 1930s and 1940s suggests an acceptance of Left critique in New York intellectual and cultural circles, which included European artists and intellectuals fleeing Hitler's Germany – like Marcuse. But if the readership of *Partisan Review* was confined to a faction of the Left, that of the Institute's journal (still published in German) was also narrow. Still, its persistence in being German can be seen against a background of US isolationism in the pre-war years, and a suspicion of Europe as a zone of troubles. At the same time, perhaps Horkheimer's caution may have reflected a growing conservatism of his own.

Adorno joined Horkheimer in California in 1941 and, as just noted, collaborated with him on *Dialectic of Enlightenment*. In 1955, Adorno received a paper by Marcuse on Freud, which formed a chapter in Marcuse's first major book *Eros and Civilization*. Adorno wrote to Horkheimer that Marcuse's critique of Freud was really theirs, and that they should have been credited for it; they should, he concluded, 'do *absolutely nothing*' in regard to publishing the book in German in the Institute's series.[10] I make no comment. Anyway, membership of the Institute provided Marcuse with an exit from Germany when it became clear in 1931 that as a Jew he would never gain an academic post there. The Institute gave him employment in a research programme, working with other Left thinkers and social researchers, from late 1931 until he took up government service in Washington in 1942. It was a formative period.

At the Institute, Marcuse worked with Franz Neumann on a study of social change,[11] and wrote a study of authority and the family which concluded with a section on the shift from bourgeois authority to totalitarianism.[12] Characteristically, totalitarianism was described as an outcome of, not a departure from, the values of bourgeois society. Marcuse set out a dualism within bourgeois thought, summarised by Douglas Kellner as, on the one hand, 'a progressive heritage of humanist-emancipatory elements', and, on the other, as 'a reactionary heritage of conservative, mystifying, and repressive features'.[13] Marcuse worked with Horkheimer to define the project of critical theory as a future-looking philosophy for liberation, emphasising a utopian vision within an integration of theoretical and empirical methods.[14] Barry Katz sees in it

> a bridge between the concern of empirical social science with the material conditions of life, and the transcendent truths

embedded in the abstractions of idealist philosophy. This implied a thoroughgoing critique of both traditional Cartesian theory and idealist metaphysics, each of which failed to grasp the material conditions of its existence.[15]

In October 1941, as a member of the Institute, Marcuse met Robert Lynd, a sociologist at Columbia, aiming to arrange a series of lectures. Lynd complained at the outset that the Institute had made too little of a great opportunity for its members. Marcuse wrote to Horkheimer after the meeting:

> I had really only wanted to say hello, but he immediately took off on a nearly one-hour speech on the Institute. Basically the same old story: that we had wasted a great opportunity. That we had never achieved a true collaboration ... That our first 'fatal mistake' was to have published the *Zeitschrift* for years in German, and that when we finally published it in English, we failed to change the design and format.[16]

The lectures on fascism were arranged, however. Marcuse spoke in 1942 on the Nazi state as combining lawless irrationality with technological rationalism – a technocracy in which, 'the technical considerations of imperialistic efficiency and rationality' take precedence over 'traditional standards of profitability and general welfare' associated with bourgeois capitalism.[17]

Marcuse's work at the Institute carried over into his government service. In late 1942 he circulated his analysis in a document titled 'The New German Mentality' which he had written earlier that year in California.[18] He sees both pragmatic and mythological aspects in Nazism, the former aligned to efficiency (technological rationalism) and the latter to paganism and racism (lawless irrationality). He suggests 'The two layers are two sides of one and the same phenomenon',[19] and notes that the mass public had by then absorbed a fatalism in which the annihilation of the Nazi state would amount to a destruction of the German nation. Marcuse identifies re-education as a strategy against Nazism, in a reassertion of fact against ideological distortion; then 'the language of recollection or remembrance'[20] might evoke resistance. I quote from this part of the text as a prelude to the 1945 essay on French literature because it established Marcuse's idea that fact and memory are potent forces against terror:

The grip of the past over the present might provide a lever which might help to break up the present. Used as such a lever, remembrance has the function to resurrect images which lighten up the present terror. For the past was not only frustration and misery, but also the promise of freedom.... The German people has not forgotten, neither the traitors nor the martyrs of freedom. Their names are defamed, and loyalty to them is punished by death and torture. But there might be another form of liberating the living memory, namely, the form of art. To lighten up the reality by the promise of freedom and happiness has always been an essential function of art, and in the present struggle, this function might obtain a new significance.[21]

In wartime, the vehicle for long-distance re-education was propaganda. This included aerial drops of literary material, including Éluard's poem 'Liberté'. I do not know if Marcuse knew what literature was dropped over France, but as an intelligence officer working on propaganda it is likely that he was at least aware of the strategy. After the liberation of France in 1945 these matters became public knowledge.

Marcuse left his government reports at the OSS but, Kellner argues, his wartime work in intelligence informed his developing theoretical outlook.[22] In September 1945 the OSS was dissolved following accusations of communist sympathies on the part of its immigrant members (mainly leftists, like Marcuse). It was then reconstructed as the Central Intelligence Agency, under new (American) management. Marcuse moved to the State Department as head of its Central European office, though this provided less scope for research in a diminishing circle of European immigrants in government service. The main programme at the State Department was German reconstruction, followed by a study of world communism at the beginning of the Cold War (when the Soviet state replaced the Nazi state as the object of analysis). Marcuse's contribution to that project was later developed at Columbia and Harvard Universities, to become his published book on Soviet Marxism.[23] I move now to the essay on French literature.

FRENCH LITERATURE UNDER THE OCCUPATION

Marcuse argues that in conditions of terror, the remembrance of freedom is found in a literature of intimacy, such as love poems – not in political writing. As Kellner interprets this, 'an alternative reality completely at odds with an oppressive social reality'[24] is found here. Marcuse describes the despair of the political situation (when northern France was under direct German occupation and southern France formed the Nazi-complicit Vichy Republic). The essay begins: 'Intellectual opposition to the prevailing form of life seems to become increasingly impotent and ineffective.'[25] This prefigures the first words of *The Aesthetic Dimension*: 'In a situation where the miserable reality can be changed only through radical political praxis, the concern with aesthetics demands justification.'[26] (I take that up in Chapter 7.) Marcuse then goes on to say (in the 1945 essay) that the aim is liberation from domination; this is unrealised in advanced capitalist society because there, 'The revolutionary forces which were to bring about freedom are being assimilated to the all-embracing system of monopolistic controls.'[27] This rehearses a later position, found in papers written in 1967[28] and *An Essay on Liberation* in 1969.[29] The view is dark: 'Revolutionary social and political theory remains academic, even when it stipulates the right political action, and this action is either co-ordinated with the powers that be, or crushed by them without resonance.'[30] In culture, too: 'All indictments are easily absorbed by the system which they indict.... Picasso's *Guernica* is a cherished museum piece.'[31] I will take up that reference in Chapter 8, and here mention simply that Picasso's mural-scale painting *Guernica* was exhibited at the Museum of Modern Art in 1939 in a retrospective show of his work. It commemorates the bombing of Basque civilians by German planes in support of Franco's seizure of power from the legitimate Spanish Republican government in 1937.

But Marcuse sees *Guernica* as an 'object of aesthetic contemplation'.[32] This raises the issue of art's transformation of experience as aesthetic reality, a theme also restated in *The Aesthetic Dimension*. But he identifies the painting, too, with a historical moment to which it is tied as an 'extra-artistic means'.[33] Is *Guernica* propaganda? Does the painting defeat its object as a representation of a suffering which it beautifies? Éluard, by contrast, does not represent the conditions in which *Liberté* was written but alludes to them indirectly, presenting freedom in the guise of the object of love.

To return to the opening section of the 1945 essay, Marcuse observes that intellectual opposition to fascist terror meets an obstacle: it cannot 'formulate its task' to break 'the spell of total assimilation'.[34] This follows from art's antagonism – 'its power to remain strange' – while simultaneously being a reservoir of repressed but remembered desires, and its ability to seem 'more real than the reality of normality'.[35]

But normality is mutable. In 1945 it was shifted in an irrevocable way by newsreels of the liberation of the concentration camps, and the devastation caused by bombing of civilian targets (great cities such as Dresden and Hamburg), which might have seemed to a North American public to be images of a far-away place, like an unreal country. Marcuse's remark, 'the exposure of concentration camps ... makes bestsellers or movie hits',[36] is more easily understood in this context, however excessive it might at first seem. The newsreels obviously also outstrip *Guernica* in horror, being photographic documentation, not art.

Art, unlike documentary, assumes an antagonistic role, conveying what is-not. It does this less through subject matter (the objects depicted, which Marcuse calls content) than through what would in German discourse be called the *form* of art. Form, that is, is autonomous, it has its own structures, it does not rely alone on the conditions in which it is produced (though in a Marxist analysis it reflects and critiques them) any more than it relies on the semblances of visual perception. Again, the driving force for art's autonomy is the threat of assimilation. There is a deep pessimism, as if assimilation is inevitable even when art takes forms such as Surrealism. Marcuse writes:

> the solution may be found in the form. Free the form from the hostile content ... by making it the instrument of destruction. Use the word, the colour, the tone, the line in their brute nakedness, as the very contradiction and negation of all content. But this shock, too, was quickly absorbed, and the subconscious which it involved became easily a part of the official consciousness. The surrealistic terror was surpassed by the real terror. The intellectual avant-gardists joined the Communists, split on the issue of Stalinism, fought with the Resistance forces. Now, in France the avant-gardists of the 1920s and early 1930s ... celebrate the severe classical style.[37]

Two points stand out: first, that the shock effect of Surrealism in art and literature in the 1920s and 1930s was overtaken by the shocking irrationality of fascism in the 1930s and early 1940s; and second, that the avant-garde, though once radical, adopted a traditional mode of expression (classicism). The latter refers to the work of Picasso in the 1940s, not to *Guernica* which uses a visual language drawn from Cubism in the 1910s. Although Picasso's work remains figurative, some immigrant European New York painters in the 1940s began to develop non-referential art as an extension of the Surrealist tendency cited by Marcuse. I doubt Marcuse saw such work in 1945, but another use of the term abstraction was current in German cultural criticism from the late 1900s onwards in discussions of German Expressionism (see Chapter 3).

Later, Marcuse constructs a variation of this hypothesis as the idea of beauty as a non-repressive order.[38] In his 1945 essay he remarks: 'The avant-gardistic negation was not negative enough. The destruction of all content was itself not destroyed. The formless form was kept intact';[39] and: 'The work of the Resistance writers represents a new stage of the solution.'[40] It consists in an oblique reflection of the immediate reality in narratives located in the scenes of private life. In the conditions of the Nazi occupation of France, politics was abolished. The political could be conveyed only 'in the way in which the content is shaped and formed'.[41] If everything is subject to total domination, the content of art must be shaped to reveal 'the negative system in its totality ... the absolute necessity of liberation'.[42] This retains an allegiance to Marxist theory:

> This ultimate principle of socialist theory is the sole absolute negation of the capitalist principle in all its forms.... Such freedom is the realization of the fully developed needs, desires and potentialities ... liberation from the all-embracing apparatus of production, distribution and administration which today regiments ... life.[43]

A tension emerges between the real need for liberation and art's distancing from its subject matter, or necessary non-realism. According to Marcuse, 'the reality which it creates is alien and antagonistic to the other, realistic reality which it negates and contradicts – for the sake of the utopia that is to be real'.[44] If liberation requires action, art reflects this indirectly in a re-assertion of sensuality. Marcuse cites Baudelaire,[45] who invites his child, his sister (*Mon enfant, ma soeur*) to dream; he interprets this to mean that Baudelaire refuses the ordering of toil as normality in favour of a realm of sensual desire (*désir*). The point is that art is distanced from – arises within but can resist – the political conditions of the occupation (as, for Baudelaire, the conditions in Paris in the 1850s, amid modernisation and the rise of the bourgeoisie). Hence, sensuality in art 'preserves the goal of political action: liberation'.[46]

Marcuse cites Aragon, who wrote in 1924 that he thought of nothing except love as his continual distraction and reason for existence which eclipses all other ideas (*Il n'y a pour moi pas une idée que l'amour n'éclipse*).[47] And he cites Éluard's '*Les sept poèmes d'amour en guerre*', published in a clandestine edition in 1943. The seven poems form one text prefaced by a remark by Aragon, using the name François la Colère (his Resistance code-name), that he writes in a country where people are stuck in filth and thirst, hunger and silence.

The occupation is evoked as terror – the footsteps heard under the floor, the misery and tiredness of a life reduced beneath mere toil – but a terror in which glimpses of hope appear as a lamp in the night. The poem offers sensual affirmations, as in the name of a mouth kissed, a hope interred. Invoking the imprisoned, the deported and the martyred comrades who refuse obscurity, the poem ends (in an extract not quoted by Marcuse but which denotes the transcendent content he advocates):

> We must drain the anger,
> make the iron rise
> to preserve an image above
> of innocents among the hunted,
> who will overcome everywhere.[48]

Beside love, Marcuse argues, country and liberation 'become artistic contents only in so far as they are preconditions for the fulfilment of the "promesse du bonheur." Love and Liberty are one and the same.'[49]

I think Marcuse treats the idea of love and liberty as an abstraction for which images in the poem stand as reminders, indicating that these are buried desires. It could be argued that Éluard treated these images as depictions reflecting his own emotional life, standing metaphorically for a memory of happier times. Or, perhaps, their ambivalence is the point. Baudelaire's depiction of a life of ease is situated on a mythical isle (like the island of Cythera in three paintings of the *Embarkation for Cythera* by Antione Watteau),[50] as a refusal of the mundane conditions of Paris at the beginning of its industrialisation and remodelling by Baron Haussmann for Napoleon III. Éluard's opening lines in '*Les sept poèmes d'amour en guerre*' similarly evoke another world, either in the past or in another realm entirely:

A ship in your eyes
Masters the wind
Your eyes were the country
One found again in a moment

Your eyes patiently await us

Under the trees of the forest
In the rain of tempests
On snow-covered summits
Between the eyes and the games of children

Your eyes patiently await us

...

Awaiting us to see us
Always
As we counted love
Love's youth
Love's reason
Love's wisdom
Its immortality.[51]

Marcuse quotes the last four lines. The imagery echoes Surrealism's shifting images – eyes, a ship; a landscape, the patiently awaiting gaze; and while it alludes to the anti-image of meagre human seasons (*maigre moissons humaines*) which may denote war, or human alienation, the first section of the poem ends with a repetition of the word love (*l'amour*). Marcuse's gloss reads awkwardly: 'to these political poets and active communists, love appears as the artistic a priori ... the artistic counterblow against the annexation of all political content by monopolistic society'.[52] For Éluard, who was a communist, it might have been a personal expression. The personal and political are, after all, compatible. The memory of one fractures the terror of the other, and may be all that it can do in extreme conditions.

   If love and freedom are coterminous in Marcuse's reading, in Éluard's poem '*Liberté*' this is literal. Structured as a ballad in four-line non-rhyming verses, each verse ends with the poet's writing of a name. But it is an as yet un-named subject's name. It is to be written on everything from copy-books to gilded images, on the night and the day, on the horizon and on birds' wings, even on death's procession. Only right at the end, after 21 verses, is the name revealed as Liberty.[53]

The poem was included in the 1942 collection *Poésie et vérité* (*Poetry and Truth*) and became known as an iconic poem of the French Resistance. Its reception, as Marcuse implies, follows from Éluard's use of a traditional form: 'the classical vocabulary of love, suggesting the well-known, long-practised paraphernalia and rituals'.[54] The poem's force is in its repetition – the word 'On' (*Sur*) is used at the beginning of three of the four lines in most verses – building up a rhythm reminiscent of a roll-call, an epic, or perhaps of banging one's head against a wall. In the fifth verse before the end a shift of tone appears:

> ... well above silence

via references to devastation, and to absence, on death's threshold, it turns:

> On the regained health
> On the danger which has gone
> On the hope which is not remembered
> ...

and then:

> I recommence my life
> I am born to know you
> To say your name[55]

Liberty is finally pronounced. For Marcuse, the poem preserves distance in a classical verse scheme differentiating it from ordinary description, and in images of tenderness which interrupt terror to re-invoke the promise of joy (*promesse du bonheur*), which stands for the world not as it is but as it will become.

I want to make a detour now, however, because I think there is a realist way to read the poem's propaganda role, an awareness of which is a necessary prelude to understanding Marcuse's departure from propaganda.

WAR AND ANTI-FASCIST LITERATURE

French literature played a role in the war effort, supported by the allies (the British and US forces, along with the Free French), through aerial drops over occupied France, Vichy France (in the south, compliant with fascism), and French colonies in North Africa. Its importance to the war effort is indicated by the use of scarce resources to print the materials in special, often high-quality miniature editions, and the making of often dangerous flights over enemy territory to deliver it. Marcuse does not refer to this, but the content of *Liberté* validated it as propaganda without negating its literary status, in the context of the widely known Left affiliation of both Éluard and Aragon in the 1930s.

By the time of the German invasion, Éluard had been active on the Left for many years. He was linked to the French Surrealists, who collectively, if briefly, joined the Communist Party in the 1930s. The Party, however, was suspicious of intellectuals and saw modern art's claims to autonomy as contradicting Socialist Realism. Éluard was expelled in 1933 but he remained committed to the Left. From 1934, in any case, the Party and its trades union organisation joined a broad anti-fascist front. Walter Benjamin's lecture 'The Author as Producer'[56] was given to a meeting of anti-fascist writers organised by the French Communist Party in Paris in April 1934. For Benjamin, as Esther Leslie writes, the writer's task in the conditions of the 1930s was to transform cultural and educational systems by widening participation in the production of writing: readers became writers and writers became organisers. Benjamin followed a line, however, which ceased to be current for the broader Left after 1934. The cultural policy of the Soviet Union (and with it that of the French Communist Party) became more open: 'a popular front, class collaborationist rehabilitation of pre-revolutionary models'.[57] Aragon was as orthodox as Benjamin, however, speaking the following year at a Conference for the Defence of Culture, and changing the name of the journal *Commune*, which he edited, to *Pour la défense de la culture*. Remaining in the Party, Aragon attacked the artist Fernand Léger for using experimental media such as montage.[58]

By 1942, the occupation put such debates in the past. The immediate task, for anyone, was to resist the occupation. Aragon joined the National Writers' Committee (*Comité National des Ecrivans*), and worked in the Resistance in the Vichy Republic. Éluard took part in Resistance work in the occupied zone (the north), and rejoined the party in 1942, also renewing his friendship with Aragon. Thanks to allied propaganda, reading poetry became a potentially subversive act, as did reading cultural reviews written in French but printed in England for aerial distribution. Valerie Holman notes that the literary review *Fontaine* (edited in Algiers by Max-Pol Fouchet) was published in a miniature edition in 1942, printed in England to be 'dropped with arms and medical supplies' to the Maquis (Resistance) in the occupied zone: 'Consisting of eighty pages, printed on Bible paper, fifty lines to a page measuring no more than thirteen by eight centimetres, the copies were extremely small and light so they could more easily be hidden.'[59]

From 1940, French publishers were subject to a self-policed censorship, immediately removing a total of 143 titles from their catalogues. In September 1940, the French Publishers' Association agreed to ban books by Jews, or books which were hostile to Germany. Further prohibitions followed; by 1943 a total of 934 titles had been banned.[60] Some booksellers hid banned books in their shops to sell (often at high prices) to trusted customers.[61] Nevertheless, the censorship system was not very efficient – only 18 readers were appointed by the regime to vet new books, creating a large backlog. Control of the paper supply was a further, indirect means of censorship, however, and by 1944 it had run out.[62] Despite these difficulties, clandestine editions of new literature appeared using whatever materials and equipment were to hand, often in north Africa. Meanwhile the British authorities identified industrial workers, professionals, technicians and intellectuals as their most likely underground allies in France, to be targeted by a form of propaganda which was specifically cultural because this was what they were deemed most likely to be influenced by.[63]

In 1941, after the US entered the war; both countries' propaganda campaigns were placed under the control of the Psychological Warfare Division of the Supreme Headquarters Allied Expeditionary Forces. A large part of British printing capacity was taken up with propaganda, in some cases printing deliberately badly to give the impression of a clandestine output.[64] In other cases, the most advanced printing techniques were used for the sake of quality, quantity and speed.

Éluard's *Liberté* was published in *Fontaine* in May 1942. The journal's editor, Fouchet, worked from Algiers and met Éluard – whom he considered the leading poet of the time – who subsequently sent him the poem, then titled *Une seule pensée* (*A Single Thought*). Fouchet recalls giving the poem to the censor when he first received it. The censor read the first ten verses and said, 'Oh, I see what it's about, it's a love poem – you poets always say the same thing over and over again.'[65] The poem was cleared and published openly. It was then republished under the same title in the fourth edition of *La Revue du Monde Libre* in April 1943, printed in England in a miniature format for aerial drop over France. This represents the poem's clandestine history, and its widest distribution during wartime. The same issue contained an extract from Jean Bruller's novel *Le Silence de la mer*, described as a work by a well-known (un-named) writer already secretly circulated in France (under the author's secret name Vercors).

A nuanced relation between open and clandestine forms of publication in France and Britain emerges, by which the attraction of a work might be linked to its clandestine as well as its conventional literary status. *La Revue du Monde Libre*, for instance, was published monthly from the beginning of 1943, and was in most respects a cultural review not a political or propaganda tool. For the allies who made aerial drops of such material it remained literature, reasserting the values of pre-occupation life in France, in keeping with the strategy identified by Marcuse. For publishers it represented an unprecedented expansion of the market into print runs of over 100,000. As Holman remarks: 'What is significant here is that the RAF enabled literature to be widely distributed like propaganda, and to reach new audiences undreamed of by the publishers themselves, who had been careful to deliver individual [clandestine] copies only to people they knew.'[66]

This was, as Holman elaborates, despite the difficulties of paper supply, the danger of enemy attack for the planes involved, and wind-drift as the bundles of paper fell from altitudes of 6,000 feet or above. The material was treated as classified and the flights identified as being made simply for reconnaissance purposes.[67] Given *Liberté*'s heritage, it is not surprising that, according to Stuart Kendall, French schoolchildren are required to learn it by heart.[68] Again, the point is that a resonant poem has multiple meanings, which are not contradictory.

Marcuse's reading of the poem, as of Aragon's novel, as a politicised withdrawal from political writing is consistent both with this and with its use as propaganda. As Holman writes: 'From 1943 onwards, culture became a central feature of propaganda leaflets, and this not only indicated new political priorities, but also paved the way for reconstruction after the war ended.'[69] This coincides with Marcuse's concern for re-education within the post-war reconstruction programme in Germany. Perhaps taking that into account allows a broader understanding of the significance he placed on Éluard's and Aragon's work, beside its content as a vehicle for the remembered promise of joy. Nevertheless, Marcuse is not concerned with literature as propaganda, but as literature – decidedly other to the world of politics and war. I think it might be that, to whatever extent Marcuse did or did not know that literature was used as propaganda, his essay was an attempt to make a case for a much deeper subversion, not only against terror but by implication against all forms of repression. But I speculate and must return to the text.

THE LOVERS' TRAGEDY

Moving to Marcuse's coverage of Aragon's *Aurélien*, he asserts that it marks a return to classical form as found in nineteenth-century novels, and as a '*roman*' in the genre of the *Gesselschaftsroman*[70] in which a society is depicted as a whole, reflected in the specific narrative of the protagonist's progress through it. The *roman* is a key cultural form of the bourgeois period, telling stories about individuals to individual readers. That Marcuse read a social purpose into the artist novel in his thesis contextualises his use of the romance as a vehicle for a memory of liberation, and *Aurélien* certainly offers a broad-brush picture of intellectual and cultural (as well as aspects of bourgeois) life in Paris in the inter-war period. Marcuse describes the plot selectively:

> A young petty-bourgeois wife from the provinces [Bérénice] comes to Paris, is caught in the glittering, decadent, immoral life of the metropolis, falls in love with a formidable playboy [Aurélien], feels betrayed by him, escapes with an avant-gardistic inhabitant of Montmartre, eventually returns to her husband in the provinces, meets, after twenty years, her true love again, and dies in his arms from the bullets of the German invaders.[71]

The novel is the third in the trilogy *Le Monde Réel*, and, for Marcuse, takes the series to the heights of a love-tragedy which absorbs the protagonists' entire life and 'makes them incapable of any solution'.[72] But much of it is concerned with the luxurious and a-moral life of a group of artistic acquaintances in Paris, among whom Bérénice is an outsider. She is not beautiful, and is married to a one-armed chemist in the provinces. Aurélien is an insider, a veteran of the 1914–18 war esteemed by his ex-comrades and in receipt of an income from family sources. Only at the end of the main story does he find himself forced to take a factory job. But it is not a story of class, more a romance entwined with the mutable world of Parisian society.

To resume the plot: Bérénice decides to leave her husband, and goes to the apartment in the Isle Saint Louis where she had met Aurélien. But he is not there. She spends the night in a chair on the landing. In the morning he returns, having spent the night with a prostitute (whom she already suspected of being his lover). The dream disintegrates.

> After that they both paused, meditating the depths of the silence and the irrevocable catastrophe, the ruin, the appalling thing that had befallen them. Bérénice's eyes still reflected that long night of waiting and dismay, and, at last, exhaustion. They did not know that there had been an instant in the night that was gone when their thoughts had crossed, as they had crossed at midnight.[73]

This is a love story in which the protagonists' love is never consummated. After the fateful night, Bérénice leaves Paris, decides not to return to her husband, and begins a relationship with Paul, a young associate of the same Paris literary group. They live in rented rooms in a mill near Claude Monet's garden at Giverny. Bérénice has sex with him but does not love him. There are moments of a remembered bliss, nonetheless:

> By now the whole countryside was filled with spring. In these parts of Normandy, spring did not come with the same suddenness as it did in R. [her husband's home town] nor was it the same as in Provence [her childhood home], where sometimes there is no transition and one wakes up one morning to find oneself in full summer. Nor was it the same as in Paris, where it lights up, one fine day, in the very same theatrical tradition as sets the footlights ablaze when an actor walks on carrying a little candle. Here it was different, here spring was a slow invasion emerging from the depths of the soil and the moisture of the fields. It was like a haze lifting.[74]

Marcuse does not quote this passage, but I do so here because it demonstrates the layered nature of the writing in a way which, incidentally, supports Marcuse's reading of the novel: first, the reference to spring is factual and metaphorical, denoting an imminent shift in the plot which reveals a truth about feelings (the lifting of a haze); second, it cites memories of better times (childhood in Provence) coloured by present springtime (as the *promesse du bonheur* in reality); third, the image of the footlights draws attention to the artificial character of the romance.

Bérénice gazes at the flowers – 'blue flowers everywhere ... She lent against the iron gate and fell into reverie.'[75] Two pages later, 'He had called her again. It was not a dream. Aurélien was there in Claude Monet's garden, and he was looking at her, and he had tears in his eyes.'[76] Marcuse reads this meeting as the artistic culmination of the novel, exhibiting 'an almost unbearable tenderness, sorrow and desperation'.[77] It is the revolutionary promise of love, a realm of joy outside the established order:

> All the others live within and without their love.... In contrast, Aurélien's and Bérénice's relationship binds itself to a 'promesse du bonheur' which transcends the happiness of the others as much as a free order of life transcends all liberties within the established order of life. And because it does, it must end at once, automatically, when it is adjusted to the normal state of affairs.[78]

The novel's main story was set in 1922. The final part of the novel, an Epilogue, is set in 1940. Aurélien is a captain in the defeated French army. He is married and has children – has become an ordinary person in other words. Marcuse reads this as 'the only chapter in which politics enter in a decisive role'.[79] Aurélien arrives at the town in which Bérénice now lives with her husband, but in a separate life, and is now active with the Left. The lovers meet again. Marcuse summarises:

> Alone with Aurélien, politics stand between them. They don't speak the same language anymore, or, the language of politics silences the language of their dead love which they still try to speak. She is a new, a strange Bérénice – not the ghost of the beloved one. Then follows the weird drive into the night, into the dark country.[80]

They drive to a remote farmhouse where they eat and drink. In the car, the two lovers are pressed close together. On the return drive they are surprised by the Germans: 'Aurélien is pressed against Bérénice on the front seat. For the first time, he holds her tight in his arms – but he does not feel her: she is a strange and cold person. From the dark, the Germans strafe the road ... only after a while does he notice that he is embracing a dead Bérénice.'[81] The passage from Aragon reads, 'And the light fell on the dangling hand, that embrace of the supposed lovers, the bleeding arm that held Bérénice, and how the blood had run down her dress, and her drooping head.'[82]

For Marcuse, the language of politics is alien to that of love: 'Their love, which has been destroyed before, dies in politics.'[83] Bérénice's call for action is 'the negation of the "Invitation au voyage"'. But, Marcuse continues, 'the negation reveals ... the true relation between the two realities: their final identity ... in Bérénice'.[84] But the lesson is that political action is the death of love, even when the aim of political action is liberation, even love's liberation from terror. Marcuse adds: 'This goal is the same world which was meant from the beginning of their fate ... in which the "promesse du bonheur" finds its fulfilment.'[85]

The story is sad to the end. Today, the plot would be criticised as misogynist, and Bérénice seen as a victim of men's war games; it could certainly have been different, so that the final roles are reversed and Aurélien is shot. But I think Marcuse's interest is in its rehearsal of an imaginary of bliss in which Bérénice is the personification of feeling, against the grain of political machinations and bourgeois decadence. It is not to be read as a literal depiction but as a literary device. The novel supports this reading, and not least in its use of a layered if at times ambivalent past beginning with Aurélien's memory, after he first meets Bérénice, of a line by Racine: '*Je demeurai longtemps errant dans Césarée*' (I tarried a long time wandering in Caesarea).[86] After dancing with her in a café he tries to remember a song: 'For the first time he became aware of her absence and began to feel her absence from his arms.'[87] Marcuse concludes, in the final section of his 1945 essay:

> The effect is an awakening of memory, remembrance of things lost, consciousness of what was and what could have been. Sadness as well as happiness, terror as well as hope are thrown upon the reality in which all this occurred, the dream is arrested and returns to the past, and the future of freedom appears only as a disappearing light.[88]

But art reconciles and that is its curse. All is reduced to aesthetic contemplation. Even the representation of terror takes the form of art; suffering becomes beautiful. 'Art does not and cannot present the fascist reality ... But any human activity which does not contain the terror ... is ... untrue.'[89] Art's grace is that its non-truths engender a realisation of the untruths of what it cannot adequately represent.

A SAFE HOUSE?

Where, then, does this leave culture in a time of emergency, which, Benjamin notes, 'is not the exception but the rule'?[90] Marcuse's essay posits a joy which is latent in ordinary life, and remembered in love poems even under conditions of total oppression. The life of ease can be glimpsed obliquely, or seen in moments of shock, as when the protagonists in *Aurélien* meet at Giverny. And perhaps Leslie's reading of Benjamin's interest in Aragon's work coincidentally echoes Marcuse's reading of that incident as disrupting 'the accepted order of things'.[91] Marcuse writes that 'The artistic form ... stays and brings to rest. ... all content becomes the object of aesthetic contemplation, the source of aesthetic gratification.'[92] Richard Wolin argues that for Benjamin a work's meaning 'bursts forth and its link to the realm of redeemed life is thereby revealed'.[93] Marcuse did not invoke redemption, rather an imagined tragedy which distances the life of ease to a point at which it is glimpsed as radically other than the present. That is when order is perceived as disorder, a denial of what is implicit in the imagination of what could be but, in the prevailing conditions, cannot be. In *Aurélien*, the promise of joy denied is aligned with France, pictured in the face of the dead Bérénice: 'This illusory identification is corrected by the true identification of the fatherland [*patrie*] with the "promesse du bonheur." Only rarely has art dared to dissociate the idea of the fatherland from all patriotic context and to make it the symbol of ultimate human fulfilment.'[94] The fatherland is not a national territory but all 'the liberated earth'.[95] Marcuse reads this as political, returning to the contradiction of art which conjures the promise of a future joy but does so only in remembrance.

Finally, I want to make a tenuous link to Julia Kristeva's remark that, in Paris in the 1960s, an intellectual could turn 'to "the exquisite crisis" of which Mallarmé spoke, which led one to the borders of madness without causing one to topple into it'.[96] The journey to a near loss of self might be juxtaposed to the journey to self-knowing of the German artist-novel; if art becomes an investigation of the artificial, so the need for liberation is instantiated in art as a form of unreality. In Baudelaire's 'Invitation au voyage', from the 1850s, the reader is drawn towards an isle of luxury and ease, beauty and voluptuousness, as a refusal of alienation. Exotic lands are as far as possible from grey streets. The paintings of Paul Gauguin exemplify this, and are read as escapist in consequence (unjustifiably in my view because they are pervaded by sensuousness). In terms of Marcuse's 1945 essay such paintings might be interpreted, not as exotic, but as affirming sensuality in opposition to the repressed sexuality of bourgeois culture. I do not have scope to extend this idea here, but would suggest that both the states of psyche which were art's content for Mallarmé, and the sensuality depicted by Gauguin in the same period, are realms where oppression is negated. Obviously – in keeping with modern art's claim to autonomy as successor to the bohemian disregard of social and moral conventions – this is regardless of Gauguin's real sex life in Tahiti. Marcuse does not identify the status of the love poetry he cites with the political commitment of its authors but with a vision of a world other than that of actuality.

Art is a safe house in an occupied land. In the 1960s, Marcuse takes a leap into optimism when he encounters the emergent counter-culture as a real enactment of human sensuality, or the actualised glimpse of the life envisioned in the latent image of the *promesse du bonheur*. In the 1970s, after the failed revolt of 1968, he reflects on a dire political realm in which art again stands as the medium of a remembered freedom, and a future glimpse of joy, as it turns away from engagement in an un-free and increasingly totalitarian world. The germ of that optimism, and equally of that pessimism, appear, I think, in the 1945 essay, which can be read as a turning point in Marcuse's aesthetic theories generally. I take up the story of optimism in the next chapter, of the problem of its realisation in Chapter 6, and of artistic withdrawal in Chapter 7.

5
Society as a Work of Art

The war in Europe ended in the summer of 1945. It was followed by several years of austerity, the Cold War, and the economic boom of the 1960s in the West. Marcuse remained in government service until 1951 before becoming a philosophy professor. By then Ernst Bloch had taken up a professorship at Leipzig (in the East), and Adorno had returned to Frankfurt (in the West). Marcuse remained a relatively obscure figure until his moment came in 1967 – the year of the Summer of Love in San Francisco, the counter-culture, the student movement, and protest against the war in Vietnam. These distinct but overlapping social, political and cultural currents had in common a refusal of the received values of what had become the affluent society.

Aged 69,[1] in July and August 1967, Marcuse lectured at the Free University, Berlin, and the Dialectics of Liberation Congress in London,[2] then went to Salzburg to take part in the 3rd Conversation on Humanism.[3] At the Roundhouse, surrounded by the flower children, it seemed as if a new society had come into being – a society as a work of art. But the moment of 1967 did not arise from nothing.

The student movement had been mobilised since the early 1960s, and the Summer of Love followed the Freedom Summer of the Civil Rights campaign in Mississippi in 1964. Street theatre was established in San Francisco by 1965 and the Diggers began free food distribution there in October 1966. The moment was also more politicised than its media coverage revealed, but this was politicisation in the realm of personal life, when ways of living were refusals of the dominant society. And, from the mid-1960s, as David Farber notes, 'white middle-class youths restocked the medicine chest' with marijuana and LSD.[4] This, along with new music and communal living, was a purposeful denial of mainstream society. At the same time, paradoxically, it marked the beginning of a commercialised youth culture. For Jim McGuigan, the 'hippies ... were usually weekenders' pursuing pleasure as a lifestyle choice.[5] By the end of 1968 it had become clear that the counter-culture could not change the world, and that well-organised occupations of factories and universities in Paris could not bring down the government. Yet the moment of the late 1960s was more than a distraction. It may have been ephemeral, and for some of those who were there it was a-historical, but there was a legacy in that social, cultural and political horizons were extended in a personal sense of liberation – a hope that the world could be as it was imagined.

In this chapter, I reconsider Marcuse's response to that moment, looking in particular at his idea of a society as a work of art – which he describes as 'the oldest dream of radical theory and practice' and 'the most utopian ... possibility of liberation today.'[6]

I find a degree of continuity between Marcuse's 1945 essay on French literature and his perception of an incipient society coloured by a promise of joy (*promesse du bonheur*) in 1967. In the next chapter I ask how such a society might be realised, drawing on Marcuse's Berlin lecture, 'The End of Utopia'[7] and *An Essay on Liberation*.[8] Here, I outline the context for his 1967 papers in relation to the New Left and the counter-culture. I then reconsider two short papers, 'Liberation from the Affluent Society' and 'Society as a Work of Art', both from 1967.

THE NEW LEFT(S)

By 1967, Marcuse had become a key figure for the student movement and the New Left – two overlapping constituencies. He spoke in Europe and North America, and his books, *Eros and Civilization*[9] and *One Dimensional Man*,[10] were both republished in paperback editions in 1966, the former with a new 'Political Preface'. He had become a widely publicised contributor to radical thought and student unrest, integrating politics and philosophy in a way seldom encountered in the conservative university system in the US. Angela Davies recalls Marcuse's presence when she was a student at Brandeis University in the early 1960s: 'there was something imposing about him that evoked total silence and attention when he appeared'.[11] Other ex-students have noted his references to topical events such as the Cuban missile crisis in 1963. When he taught a course on the Warfare State, however, Brandeis let his contract lapse. So, in 1964, Marcuse moved to the University of California at San Diego, keeping a lower profile for a while.[12] Andrew Feenberg, a colleague of Marcuse's there, recalls that 'He took his intellectual mission seriously but he also demonstrated with us for our causes which were his as well.'[13] Feenberg adds that Marcuse defended

Angela Davies when she was attacked politically despite the danger to himself – a real danger, since it provoked death threats and led in the end to termination of his contract. But in 1967, in a moment of social transformation, Barry Katz observes, 'Marcuse's ... name began to acquire the mystical aura of familiarity that the media have the power to create.'[14]

Marcuse saw his new status as evidence that 'everything can be co-opted, everything can be digested' by the media.[15] Radical politics had no need for auras, and the New Left had no formal leaders. The New Left was a regrouping of intellectuals and radical students mobilised by the war in Vietnam and a general dominance of the Right in North America (and Western Europe). The old Left was doctrinaire, and tainted with complicity in authoritarian regimes after the suppression by Warsaw Pact forces of the Hungarian uprising in 1956. The New Left was a free-thinking, neo-Marxist departure from traditional (scientific Marxist) agendas such as class struggle. Douglas Kellner reads the New Left as pluralist, and engaged with 'emergent cultural forms and social movements', while concerned with issues of 'gender, race, sexuality, the environment, [and] peace'.[16] Vincent Geoghegan emphasises the urgency of the New Left's appeal as a responsive current rather than another institution. He quotes Marcuse, speaking in December 1968: 'we cannot wait and we shall not wait. I certainly cannot wait. And not only because of my age. I don't think we have to wait.... Because I literally couldn't stand it any longer if nothing would change. Even I am suffocating.'[17]

Even in December 1968, when hope began to fade, Marcuse remained committed to socialism: 'We must be able to show, even in a very small way, the models of what may one day be a human being. ... I still believe the alternative is *socialism* ... that *libertarian* socialism which has always been an integral concept of socialism, but is only too easily repressed and suppressed.'[18] Libertarian socialism does not seek to seize power, he explained, but to diffuse it in an open, transparent formation. This seems prescient of single-issue campaigning in the 1990s, for example in anti-roads protest – described by George McKay in 1996 as 'diffused, concentrated in small groups and around local activities, small groups which are highly flexible and autonomous'.[19] Perhaps such formations epitomise revolutionary practice throughout modern history, from the Levellers and the Diggers during the English Revolution of the 1640s to the eco-village communities of the 1990s (some of which began as intentional communities in the late 1960s, leaving cities for experimental ways of living beyond the media gaze). But new formations emerged in a specific way in the 1960s, from plural roots in higher education, culture, social activism and radical religion.

In 1959, the Student League for Industrial Democracy (established in 1905) was re-constituted as Students for a Democratic Society (SDS). It was inspired by and drew its tactics from the civil rights campaigns, using techniques such as the sit-in and sit-down developed by the Student Nonviolent Coordinating Committee (SNCC). Local, non-violent interruptions of routine repression gained public attention and showed campaigners to be willing to risk their safety by undertaking civil disobedience. From the beginning, SDS rejected institutional structures for experiential tactics. New ideas arose collectively among participants in localised cultural situations. James Farrell cites historian Sara Evans noting that the student activism of the 1960s arose amid 'the folk music and philosophical conversations of campus coffeehouses'.[20] The old Left played a role in a North American return to folk music from the 1930s,[21] as it had in Britain where the Communist Party was instrumental in the folk revival,[22] but with an emphasis on traditional music. The emerging folk scene of the 1960s renewed that legacy in hybrid forms, and a new vernacularism in the form of protest.

There were also links to radical Catholicism, Quakerism, and the work of theologian Thomas Merton. In Merton's prolific writing, divine love was personal and social. He wrote, too, on Existentialism, and Ghandian non-violent resistance.[23] Farrell observes that like Merton, 'the students posed empathy and activism against apathy'.[24] Apathy was aligned with institutions, the de-humanising aspect of which was shown by the trial of the Nazi Adolph Eichmann in Jerusalem in 1963. Hannah Arendt, an observer at the trial, saw Eichmann as a functionary in an authoritarian system, who claimed to be unaware of the consequences of his actions, complaining that his abilities were never adequately recognised by promotion to the highest rank.[25] Hannah Pitkin sees Arendt as struck by his ordinariness: a 'desk murderer' speaking 'in stock phrases'.[26] The trial took place in the same year as the Cuban missile crisis, and the triple ghosts of Auschwitz, Hiroshima and the anti-communist witch-hunts of the 1950s hovered over the students and professors who opposed a society which relied on institutions – not least the university with its campus rules, gender segregation and dress codes – to maintain the power base of military and industrial interests.

Against a total institutionalisation, then, personal experience and imagination were inherently oppositional (as a love poem was in face of total oppression). Farrell cites the Quaker concepts of inner light and redemptive community as sources of student radicalism, informing the rise of conscientious objection to military conscription (the draft).[27] A conference at Port Huron in June 1962 brought together speakers from secular and religious backgrounds, philosophy, social science and politics, to agree on shared values. The event produced a 'human independence' that was not an 'egotistic individualism', but which embraced personal connectivity against estrangement and atomism. Farrell emphasises the model of a participatory democracy using consensus decision-making in decentralised situations.[28] Citing the then well-known sociologist C. Wright Mills' 'Letter to the New Left', Farrell describes how a new radicalism grounded in new conditions was initiated:

> Unlike the Old Left, which had organized around the economic issues of the Depression and anti-fascism ... the New Left would confront 'newer discontents like powerlessness, moral disaffection, the purposelessness of middle-class life' – the issues of an affluent society.... the New Left looked for other agents to challenge the alienation, bureaucracy, and cultural hegemony of Cold War America.[29]

Similarly, historian Doug Rossinow sees liberation as the idea which united the New Left: 'when young political radicals said "The revolution is about our lives," they fused their desire for individual empowerment with the dissident cultural politics'.[30] Rossinow adds that the New Left within the student movement developed its own counter-culture parallel to that of the hippies in San Francisco, as a means to attract participants and as a model of culture which had political agency.[31] He, like Sara Evans, notes the place of folk music in the New Left counter-culture, but the New Left looked equally to the Beat poets (such as Jack Kerouac) and singer-poets such as Bob Dylan, while also requiring an 'authentic masculinity' epitomised by 'male heroes like C. Wright Mills and Fidel Castro'.[32] Leonie Sandercock has written recently that awareness of gender was not integral to radical politics at the time (or since).[33] The radical texts of the period use a normative masculine which went unchallenged before the rise of feminism in the 1970s; even among the associates of the Frankfurt Institute only Bloch made a case for the historical role of women in revolutions, citing, for instance,

Louise Otto, a 'red democrat', and founder in 1865 of the General Association of German Women.[34] Marcuse also emphasises the importance of Mills' work in the Introduction to *One-Dimensional Man*. Differentiating critically between the tendency to personalism and the appropriation of ordinary life by consumerism, he argues that 'The political needs of society become individual needs and aspirations' but that 'their satisfaction promotes business and the commonweal'.[35] The coercion to produce precludes free human development along the path to happiness; alienating work produces a need for leisure which is subsumed in the round of alienation, and peace is maintained by the threat of war: the affluent society enacts utter irrationality in the guise of (instrumental) Reason.

Yet within those conditions are forces which 'break this containment and explode the society'.[36] In the next decade this occurred with the women's movement. In the 1960s, the great refusal was a rejection of consumerism and the warfare state. Meanwhile an expansion in higher education in the post-war years meant that campus life became a site of contested values within a broader class spectrum,[37] and, with the escalation of US bombing in Vietnam, claims for personal freedom were fused with demands for an end to war (to all wars):

> The first teach-in took place March 24, 1965, at the University of Michigan. The suffix suggested a connection with the sit-ins of the civil rights movement and of the 1930s labor movement, and defined learning as a political experience. In both cases, people occupied and transformed the spaces of their own lives, bringing social protest into established American institutions.[38]

Teach-ins had the effect of deconstructing the barriers between academic disciplines as well as defining the questions posed to the holders of power. If the political was personal, it was philosophical, social, cultural and psychological as well. It spawned an inter-disciplinarity, and gave rise to Free Universities, first at San Francisco State University in 1965, then at Berkeley in 1966, and in 150 sites by 1971.[39] Some of the Free Universities had offshoots such as the free school in which I took part in Bristol in the summer of 1968.

Marcuse spoke often to student groups throughout 1967 and 1968, and it was a student group in Germany, German Socialist Students (*Sozialistischer Deutscher Studentenbund*, also SDS), who organised his lectures in Berlin. But the New Left was not an exclusively student movement as such, and included intellectuals or members of what in Europe was called an intelligentsia. It was interested in questions of national liberation and in civil rights campaigns in the US, and Marcuse, a migrant from a European intelligentsia, shared these concerns, taking the emergence of diverse oppositional social movements as evidence of a possibility that radical change could emerge within the affluent society, 'returning him to the utopian and emancipatory themes' of *Eros and Civilization*.[40]

From the outset, the New Left was pluralist, linking student with anti-war protest, resistant tactics from the civil rights campaigns with campus occupations, and anti-consumerism with refusal of the draft. In late summer 1968, Marcuse was interviewed for the French magazine *Express*. Noting an anarchist strand in the student movement, he said: 'This means that the students have perceived the rigidity of the traditional political organizations' outside of which 'revolt spontaneously occurs'.[41] He added, however, that it is not enough to be spontaneous – organisation is required (but not leaders): 'In the actual movement there are no leaders as there were in the Bolshevik Revolution.'[42] For others at the time, even the New Left was too orthodox. Ken Kesey, from the activist group The Merry Pranksters, addressed an anti-war meeting in Berkeley in 1965: 'turn your backs and say ... Fuck it' – politics is 'what *they* do'.[43] Rossinow cites Todd Gitlin, ex-SDS President, in 1967 saying that its old-guard had never sampled LSD and were suspicious of marijuana.[44]

1967

The media coverage of the Summer of Love depicted a scene in which mainly affluent young people in bright and motley garments wore flowers in their hair, listened to new music, smoked marijuana, and made free love. The writer Joan Didion moved into the Haight-Ashbury district of San Francisco (the District) in 1967 to see what lay behind this bland picture. Her account, 'Slouching Towards Bethlehem', depicts a sometimes dysfunctional but politicised scene, in reaction to an atomised society: dropping out as community. She begins apocalyptically, reporting bankruptcy notices, casual killings, abandoned homes, and vandals unable to spell the four-letter words they graffitied on walls. This was the affluent society, not what was then called the Third World:

> It was not a country in open revolution. It was not a country under enemy siege. It was the United States of America in the

cold late spring of 1967, and the market was steady ... It might have been a spring of brave hopes and national promise, but was not.... All that seemed clear was that at some point we had aborted ourselves and butchered the job ... San Francisco was where the social hemorrhaging was showing up. San Francisco was where the missing children were gathering and calling themselves 'hippies'.[45]

Reviewing the context for 1960s poetry with a comparable bleakness, Eric Homberger cites a notebook of Robert Lowell's from 1967–68 listing a series of crises and conflicts: 'a terrible accumulation of war, riots, deaths, demonstrations, politics and revolution, bracketed by Vietnam.... a nightmarish actuality'.[46] Still, within that actuality new forms of culture were produced. Often, they merged art, literature and performance, as in the art-happening.[47] New, intermediate art forms departed from tradition, just as the successive movements of modernism had since the 1880s. This was (as in the 1880s) a departure from the market, as poets and bands gave free public performances, and artists refused to make objects for dealers to sell. It worked for a while, before the photographic record of a happening or an artist's walk became a commodity and dealers traded reputations instead of goods.

Street theatre was a politicised emerging cultural form, however, which did not lend itself to assimilation. It arose in parallel to informal actions in public space, from the beat poet Allen Ginsberg's gesture of standing outside a women's prison in New York in the winter of 1964 to protest against the criminalisation of marijuana,[48] to the Merry Pranksters' public acid parties in San Francisco in 1966. Jerry Garcia (from the band The Grateful Dead) saw 'thousands of people all helplessly stoned ... in a roomful of people none of whom any of them were afraid of. It was magic, far out, beautiful magic.'[49] Farber writes that the Pranksters' Acid Tests involved the use of electronic feedback devices, fluorescent paint, film loops and strobe lights, all 'geared toward maximizing psychic, sensual input, loading up the mind and pushing tripsters toward a vast collective experience'.[50] This contrasted with the controlled experiments with consciousness-changing substances conducted by Timothy Leary, who drew on the terminology of biology to describe society as an expansion and contraction of impulses, from which LSD offered release. Leary describes social processes as follows:

The free, expansive vision is moulded into the institutional. Hardly has the institutional mortar set before there is a new cortical upheaval, an explosive, often ecstatic or prophetic revelation. The prophet is promptly jailed. A hundred years later his [sic] followers are jailing the next visionary.[51]

If universities train 'consciousness contractors',[52] newly available substances 'expand your awareness, open your mind',[53] and an open cortex produces ecstasy: 'The nervous system operating free of learned abstractions is a completely adequate, completely efficient, ecstatic organ.'[54] For the Merry Pranksters, acid visions were an alternative to anomie, 'a belief in the possibility of a communal youth consciousness'.[55] Use of LSD was criminalised in 1966. Drug raids probably politicised those affected.[56]

For more radical groups, though, there had never been a line separating the use of alternative substances and the adoption of alternative political tactics. The Diggers used LSD and undertook provocative street actions; Farber quotes founder-member Peter Coyote that their aim was to encourage people to '"de-school" yourself, to continually transcend limits when you discover them'.[57] Their distribution of free food to young runaways in the District (Didion's 'missing children') was part of this de-institutionalising process.

The Diggers arose within but separated from the San Francisco Mime Troupers, a street theatre group that had been working in San Francisco since 1959. Michael Doyle calls the Mime Troupe's work 'guerilla theatre', an avant-garde practice within the emerging counter-culture.[58] He situates the Mime Troupe in 'the van of New Left activism', citing their 1966 production *A Minstrel Show, or: Civil Rights in a Cracker Barrel*. Trading on the minstrel show in which white singers blacked-up as negroes, they politicised the form and introduced provocation of the audience. As Doyle recounts: 'Audiences found it perplexingly difficult to discern the true racial identity of the six masqued performers, a predicament that rendered the actors' raucous banter all the more unsettling.'[59] No subject was taboo. The show toured, with a performance at the New York Town Hall.[60]

Didion may have seen an off-shoot of the minstrel show in Golden Gate Park in 1967, of which she recalls Troupers made up with black faces, 'tapping people on the head with dime-store plastic night-sticks ... wearing signs on their backs'.[61] They pick on a black man and ask if he is getting annoyed, exacerbating tension between the white youths for whom dropping out is a luxury and the local black people; they ask him if his music has been stolen by white performers, getting a hostile reaction from both white and black on-lookers. Approaching a member of the Troupe, Didion asks what is going on; the member turns out to be new and replies hesitatingly, 'you see the capitalists are taking over the District, and that's what Peter – well, ask Peter'.[62] Peter was Peter Berg. But Didion did not ask him because he hated journalists. She notes that some members moved to the Troupe from the Artists' Liberation Front, a group 'for "those who seek to combine their creative urge with socio-political involvement"'.[63] Didion remarks that the activists knew that media coverage of the counter-culture missed the point, which was radical social change, but she also characterises it as 'the desperate attempt of a handful of pathetically unequipped children to create a community in a social vacuum'.[64] Perhaps it was inept; perhaps it was also liberating for at least some of those who there. (I was not, so I cannot say.)

Looking back across more than 40 years, it is clear that many strands converged in the counter-culture, which overlapped with the New Left, which itself linked closely to the student movement. The Mime Troup, for instance, provided the SDS with an office at their base at Howard Street, San Francisco in 1965; the Diggers saw the use of consciousness-changing drugs as opening a path to communal life, while music, drugs and communal living were personally experienced political action. The Diggers seem not to have researched the English group of that name who dug up St George's Hill in Woking on 1 April 1649, in order to grow food for free distribution using the most advanced seed and agricultural techniques.[65] But they shared 'a vision of the total transformation of social and economic relations, a dedication to bringing about the New Jerusalem by peaceable means, a reliance on pamphlets and direct appeals [... and] a belief that exemplary actions were the key to realizing their ambitious goals'.[66]

The personalisation of activism was linked to a refusal of technological (instrumental) rationality, informed by Eastern and Western religions. Technological rationality saw nature as a resource; but, as Farrell writes, 'counterculturalists began to look for ... personal, relationships with nature'.[67] This led to an interest in shamanism and forms of Western primitivism appropriated from non-Western cultures, but also drew on a Western myth of Eden to validate drugs as offering an escape from objectivism into an Edenic state of nature 'before the snake of socialization'.[68] For his part,

Marcuse saw the counter-culture as less important than movements for national liberation in Latin America, Africa and South-East Asia, the civil rights campaign, and the student movement – which latter challenged US foreign policy and upset the system by which a managerial and professional elite of lawyers, managers, and teachers was trained.[69] As he wrote:

> I have never said that the student opposition today is by itself a revolutionary force, nor have I seen the hippies as the 'heir of the proletariat'! Only the national liberation fronts of the developing nations are today in a revolutionary struggle. But even they do not by themselves constitute an effective revolutionary threat to the system of advanced capitalism. All forces of opposition today are working at preparation and only at preparation – but toward necessary preparation for a possible crisis of the system. And precisely the national liberation fronts and the ghetto rebellion contribute to this crisis, not only as military but also as political and moral opponents – the living, human negation of the system.[70]

Meanwhile the Diggers were the 'worker-priests' of the counter-culture, believing in free housing, free health care and an economy of sharing; co-opting private property as public property and producing a free news service.[71] It is not difficult to understand how the counter-culture might have been seen as replacing the working class in evolving (rather than calling for) a new society, when the conditions for revolt in North America and Europe were not impoverishment but affluence. That was the position adopted by the New Left: a revolutionary force in a coalition of students, intellectuals and radicals who no longer demanded better working conditions but the transformation of work as play.

LIBERATION FROM THE AFFLUENT SOCIETY

Marcuse undertook a programme of intense activity from 1966 to 1968. He took part in a teach-in at the University of California at Los Angeles in March 1966, and spoke at a conference on Vietnam organised by German Socialist Students in May of that year. The German SDS organised his lectures in Berlin in July 1967. Few students read Marcuse in Paris in 1968,[72] but, in the same year, the German student leader Rudi Dutschke took Marcuse's ideas as legitimating the tactics of revolt.[73] Marcuse arrived in London for the Dialectics of Liberation congress directly from Berlin, and spoke in a session which included the black power activist Stokely Carmichael. In the spirit of 1967, it began with a Living Theatre performance and a reading of mantras by Allen Ginsberg. The congress was organised by a group of four anti-psychiatrists, including R.D. Laing. Opposing the abjection of 'people who are called mad', Laing pointed to the tendency to scapegoat individuals within a family as 'someone who will consent ... to take on the disturbance of each of the others'.[74] Co-organiser (and editor of the papers) David Cooper writes that in the Congress they sought to balance theory and practice, inviting Marcuse, Gregory Bateson and Lucien Goldmann for theory, and Carmichael to represent practice. They sought a bridge, too, between analyses of the individual's destructive tendencies and those of society. Cooper comments:

> It seems to me that a cardinal feature of all revolutions has been the dissociation of liberation on the mass social level ... and liberation on the level of the individual and the concrete groups in which he [*sic*] is directly engaged. If we are to talk of revolution today our talk will be meaningless unless we effect some union between the macro-social and micro-social, and between inner reality and outer reality.[75]

Marcuse was not, as it happens, persuaded by Laing's alternative psychiatry. Looking back to a conversation in 1971 he says, 'Well I met Laing, but we seem to be unable to find common ground.'[76]

Marcuse geared his contribution to the audience of hippies, intellectuals and political activists, many of whom camped out in the festive ambience of the Roundhouse. For Kellner, 'Marcuse's contribution vividly synchronized New Left political perspectives with affirmations of the counterculture.'[77] Marcuse acknowledged the hippies: 'I am very happy to see so many flowers here and that is why I want to remind you that flowers, by themselves, have no power whatsoever, other than the power of men and women who protect them and take care of them against aggression and destruction.'[78]

He continued that his topic was the liberation of intellect and body, and that liberation emerged from within a system as a product of the falseness of the system's values. As he said: 'That is a decisive point.... liberation by virtue of the contradiction generated by the system.'[79] Asserting that liberation is 'a biological, sociological and political necessity',[80] he insisted that freedom is attained within the conditions of technological advance:

If today these integral features, these truly radical features which make a socialist society a definite negation of the existing societies, if this qualitative difference today appears as Utopian ... this is precisely the form in which these radical features must appear if they are really to be a definite negation of the established society: if socialism is indeed a rupture of history, the radical break, the leap into the realm of freedom – a total rupture.[81]

These conditions are a historical exception. While the affluent society shows no signs of disintegration, and the working class is captured by the quasi-satisfaction of needs, opposition arises when awareness of the contradictions of capitalism are sufficiently widespread. A need to resist arises and produces ruptures. Marcuse gives an example of such a rupture which may seem incidental, even quaint, but repays reconsideration:

Walter Benjamin quotes reports that during the Paris Commune, in all corners of the city ... there were people shooting at the clocks on the towers of churches, palaces ... consciously or half-consciously expressing the need that somehow time has to be arrested; ... the established continuum has to be arrested, and that a new time has to begin – a very strong emphasis on the qualitative difference and on the total rupture between the new society and the old.[82]

I say this is worth reconsideration because the quantitative time in question is that of the established regime not only in its ubiquitous presentation on public clocks but also of the regulation of labour and the working day, with its prescribed times of start and finish. Lewis Mumford cites the regulation of the hours of monastic life as the source of this time, which migrates from prayer to secular society where 'The clock, not the steam engine, is the key-machine of the modern industrial age ... consummation of this technics in every department of industrial activity.'[83] The idea of re-starting time is inherent in major revolutions. For Marcuse at the Roundhouse, a clean slate began with the total negation of the existing society, overcome by a free and happy life in which work gives way to play.[84] Work is not play under the regime of the clock, and aesthetic reality is not bound by such constraints, retaining – Marcuse writes in *Eros and Civilization* – 'its freedom from the reality principle'.[85]

Marcuse's definition of the aesthetic is both philosophical and psychological, a revision of Freud's psychodynamic model of an unrestrained desire for pleasure (Eros) and its denial in favour of deferment on which Western civilisation is built. That deferment is the reality principle, like a voice over the shoulder saying wait until tomorrow. In 1967, the message was that we want the world and want it now! But if the total, immediate gratification of desire is chaotic – even if it was the aim of the Merry Pranksters – in modern, industrial society the deferment of pleasure has reached new heights. Repression is political and psychological, and the repression of libidinal, life-affirming consciousness continues to increase despite the liberalisation of sex (its commodification in fact). To fracture this repression is the aim of aesthetic reality:

> This task involves the demonstration of the inner connection between pleasure, sensuousness, beauty, truth, art, and freedom – a connection revealed in the philosophical history of the term *aesthetic*. There this realm aims at a realm which preserves the truth of the senses and reconciles, in the reality of freedom, the 'lower' and the 'higher' faculties of man [*sic*], sensuousness and intellect, pleasure and reason.[86]

Put this way, Marcuse's vision is not incompatible with Marx's early writing, where the sensuous is emphasised. For instance, in his fifth Thesis on Feuerbach, Marx says: 'Feuerbach, not satisfied with *abstract thinking*, appeals to *sensuous contemplation*; but he does not conceive sensuousness as *practical*, human sensuous activity.'[87] For Richard King, Marcuse integrates a Marxist notion of alienated labour with Freud's idea of non-libidinal work.[88] Although Marcuse's analysis of repression was damning of Western society, Geoghegan reads his prognosis as optimistic: 'it maintained that contemporary civilization can blossom and achieve a thoroughly liberated existence under the rule of a new reality principle'.[89] The old reality principle, transposed to a performance principle in industrial society can, then, be set aside and replaced by a new, re-libidinised, non-repressive principle, and a new social equilibrium.

This utopian vision may have seemed luxurious compared to Carmichael's depiction of the aims of black power: 'that black people see themselves as part of a new force ... we see our struggle as closely related to liberation struggles around the world'.[90] But perhaps there was common ground in Marcuse's statement that a dialectics of liberation meant 'the construction of a free society ... the vital need for abolishing the established systems of servitude; and ... the qualitatively different values of a free human existence'.[91] The idea of a *qualitatively* new society – as opposed to the *quantitative* advances of consumerism – runs throughout Marcuse's papers in the late 1960s, and is most fully examined in *An Essay on Liberation* (see Chapter 6 below). The new, libidinal reality links the objective conditions of an affluent society (which include a suppressed potential to end toil) with the subjective condition of a growth of a new sensibility. The demand for quantitative change in terms of better living conditions is prevalent in the Third World (the global South), while qualitative change is now viable in the rich world but, Marcuse asserts, is still 'perverted by the capitalist organization of society'.[92] He continues:

> I think we are faced with a situation in which this advanced capitalist society has reached a point where quantitative change can technically be turned into qualitative change, into authentic liberation. And it is precisely against this truly fatal possibility that the affluent society, advanced capitalism, is mobilized and organized on all fronts, at home as well as abroad.[93]

Abroad was the war in Vietnam. At home was the total mobilisation in the form of consumerism and the mass media. A war in all but name was waged against citizens in order to advance the interests of the military-industrial complex which governed their lives. I use terms not used by Marcuse himself here, but his argument is that the affluent society represses its potential to be free through 'this comfortable servitude' in a society 'spreading terror and enslavement' worldwide.[94] Hence, 'the capitalist Welfare State is a Warfare State. It must have an Enemy', while the perpetuation of servitude intensifies a primary aggressiveness to a degree hitherto unknown.[95]

Marcuse remains committed to socialism, but sees the qualitative transformation of society as defining socialism in its most utopian way: 'the abolition of labour, the termination of the struggle for existence – that is to say, life as an end in itself and no longer a means to an end – and the liberation of human sensibility and sensitivity.'[96] This means the unity of work and play, necessity and freedom. At this point Marcuse puts forward the idea of a society as a work of art:

> This means one of the oldest dreams of all radical theory and practice. It means that the creative imagination, and not only the rationality of the performance principle, would be a productive force applied to the transformation of the social and natural

universe. It would mean the emergence of a form of reality which is the work and the medium of the developing sensibility and sensitivity of man [*sic*].

   And now I throw in the terrible concept: it would mean an aesthetic reality – society as a work of art. This is the most Utopian, the most radical possibility of liberation today.[97]

It is terrible only in its shock value – convulsive like beauty, almost Surreal. Although Marcuse disagreed with Norman O. Brown on the interpretation of Freud, there is an element of common ground between Marcuse's idea of a terrible concept of aesthetic reality and some of Brown's quasi-mystical assertions in *Love's Body*, such as 'Love is all fire; and so heaven and hell are the same place', or 'Fire is freedom. Spontaneous combustion. Spontaneity is ardor.'[98] Brown's theme in *Life Against Death* of a reclamation of the body and the power of all the senses as inherently oppositional may also be relevant. Brown writes: 'The resurrection of the body is a social project', which will become a practical possibility when those who govern 'are called upon to deliver happiness instead of power'.[99] I look further at the idea of a new sensibility in Chapter 6, but need to emphasise here that an aesthetic society *is* a society in which a new and free sensibility has been produced. As King summaries: 'the goal of the new sensibility would be an aesthetic ethos in which society would essentially become "a work of Art"'.[100]

SOCIETY AS A WORK OF ART

At the Roundhouse, Marcuse attempted to say what a society as a work of art would be 'in concrete terms'.[101] He speculates that play and imagination will reconfigure the cities and the countryside, restoring nature after its exploitation in capitalism. But this also involves provision of space for privacy and tranquillity, and 'the elimination of noise, captive audiences, of enforced togetherness, of pollution, ugliness'.[102] At first, this appears a negation of North American society with its mass media and spectacles of false social unity. But Marcuse repeats that this is a socialist vision – 'I believe that the idea of such a universe guided also Marx's concept of socialism'[103] – which entails the emergence of new biological needs to re-instantiate a desire for happiness which is inherent in resistance under capitalism. I leave discussion of how the new biological needs arise to the next chapter. Here, I simply observe that the idea of a society in which work is play is not Marcuse's invention but an established concept in utopian thought since at least the early nineteenth century, where it figures prominently in the writing of Charles Fourier.

Fourier envisaged a libidinal society in which work relations, as social relations, are of their nature erotic (in a broad sense). They imply a form of sociation in which people of complementary passions enjoy collaborating, which Fourier articulates at length in an idiosyncratic and complicated way. Growing pears, for example, involves different types of pear and different stages of cultivation, from which a sympathy is charted with certain personality types who would, as if naturally, carry out the tasks required together. The whole of France is to be reorganised in a new social group, the Phalanstery, in which the numbers of each personality type are calculated to ensure libidinal efficiency. He also advocates a sexual minimum (a minimum availability of sex, like a minimum wage).[104] Marcuse does not do that. Yet the idea of an aesthetic society can be situated in this libidinal utopianism, just as it inherits a tradition of millenarianism envisaging an immanent revolution: the abolition of work and office, the Land of Cockaigne in the here and now.[105] At the Roundhouse in July, 1967 it might have seemed that this revolution was being re-enacted in flower-power against the false Cockaigne of affluent consumerism. But what was (is) a society as a work of art?

In Salzburg in August 1967, Marcuse argued that the creative imagination can be the agent of a qualitatively different society because a possible transformation of labour is viable through technological advance. In a post-scarcity economy, the requirement for work diminishes and opportunity for creative ease increases. This is repressed by the mechanisms of capitalism while, in implicit opposition, affluence produces the idea of real liberation and thereby demonstrates the contradictions of a false liberation from want. A few years later, the designer Victor Papanek argued in *Design for the Real World* for a revision of the wants produced by consumerism as if they are genuine needs of human life.[106] In relation to the green thought of the period, Marcuse's psycho-political analysis sat well beside ecological critiques in a refusal of consumer culture.

Marcuse attaches particular importance to art in the exposure of contradictions in the dominant society, and as a vehicle for radical imagination. Citing the concept of false consciousness in Marxism, he states: 'The power of knowing, seeing, hearing, which is limited, repressed and falsified in reality, becomes in art the power of truth and liberation.'[107] He begins his Salzburg paper, however, by saying that the function of art is to bring peace. This might suggest the affirmative culture of bourgeois society (see Chapter 3), but relates to the promise of happiness. Citing the Expressionist painter Franz Marc, Marcuse reads the 'crisis' of art in the 1910s as 'a rebellion against the entire traditional function of art' in which the object of depiction is dissolved.[108] The old art offered a 'beautiful semblance' but the new art is – and here Marcuse cites the Berlin Dadaist Raoul Hausmann – a '"*critique of cognition*"'.[109] Hence art should now 'no longer be powerless with respect to life, but should instead help give it shape – and none the less remain art'.[110] Going on to cite Surrealist poetry as the evocation of a new world in a new language, Marcuse writes: 'art is rescued in its dual, antagonistic function. As a product of the imagination it is semblance, but the possible truth and reality to come appear in this semblance and art is able to shatter the false reality of the status quo'.[111] There is then a productive tension between art's semblance and its authentic expression. But a difficulty appears: if art is to dissolve reality as art, it remains a non-material entity, a semblance in the form of a negated reality. Marcuse's tactic is to align art as the articulation of the beautiful with the sensibility (the mind-set of sensuousness) which is a prerequisite for radical social change, and is produced in radical personal transformation. Society, he claims, must create the conditions for 'the truth of art to be incorporated in the social process itself and for the form of art to be materialized'.[112] I think this means that the new society produces the context in which the new sensibility renders all as art.

Rationally, 'The beautiful belongs to the sphere of non-repressive sublimation, as the free formation of the raw material of the senses and thus the sensuous embodiment of the mere idea.'[113] Reconfiguring the problem of affirmative culture, and avoiding mysticism, Marcuse argues that 'Every work of art is consummate in this sense, self-sufficient, meaningful and as such it disturbs you, consoles you, and reconciles you with life.'[114] This applies to abstract as well as figurative art. And since there are very few cases of authentic literature (in contrast to the romantic literature of consumerism) with a happy ending, negativity is 'sublated' in the language of form, while art removes what is unjust or remains un-reconciled.[115] This is complex, and combines modern art's claim to autonomy – the independence of its language of form and colour from perception – with a cathartic function. Art is far from affirmative: 'In the consciousness of the avant-garde artist, art becomes ... a more or less beautiful, pleasant *decorative background in a world of terror*.

This luxury function of art must be destroyed. The protest of the artist becomes passionate, socially critical analysis.'[116] He cites the work of Samuel Beckett as a recent case of such work. Beckett is also cited by Adorno in his *Aesthetic Theory*, published posthumously in 1970.[117]

Marcuse argues that although technology and art are traditionally separated (as the beautiful and the useful, as he sets out at the beginning of his essay on affirmative culture), the distinction can be collapsed, and the divide between work and play dissolved. This is 'the idea of a possible artistic formation of the life world'.[118] Form is the form of freedom, the form of the practice of life, 'which free people in a free society are able to provide for themselves'.[119] This is not far removed, coincidentally, from Joseph Beuys' idea that everyone is an artist – or has a creative imagination in which to envisage new social forms (see Chapter 8). Marcuse concludes:

> For art itself can never become political without destroying itself ... The contents and forms of art are never those of direct action, they are always only the language, images, and sounds of a world not yet in existence. Art can preserve the hope for and the memory of such a world ... the uncompromising *rejection of illusion*, the repudiation of the pact with the status quo, the liberation of consciousness, imagination, perception, and language from its mutilation in the prevailing order.[120]

But it is hard to match this to the art produced in the late 1960s, ranging from pop art with its appropriations of advertising images to colour-field painting and formalism (or colour-field painting). Most of Marcuse's references are literary, from an earlier time. Nonetheless, his writing at this time was a response to a historical moment of immense optimism. That moment is now encapsulated in history and the question of how a new sensibility arises is not resolved in these papers. In a lecture given in Berlin, 'The Problem of Violence and the Radical Opposition', Marcuse spoke of the forms of resistance used in the student movement – the sit-in, the be-in and the love-in – as constituting an existential community which fused a political rebellion with a 'sexual-moral rebellion'.[121] I think that was one element in a wider personalisation of social, political and cultural directions which marks out the time. Julia Kristeva remembers 1968 as 'a worldwide movement that contributed to an unprecedented reordering of private life'.[122] Perhaps that is its legacy. But if optimism gave a wondrous glimpse of how a society might evolve, according to a new need for freedom and through a new, libidinal form of social relations, optimism alone was not enough to change the world. Perhaps, though, changing the world was not the point; a perpetual topic of discussion at the time was whether the world could be changed without first changing the mind-sets of those who would spontaneously become the citizens of a new world.

6
The End of Utopia

In Chapter 5 I discussed Marcuse's idea of a society as a work of art in the context of the counter-culture, the New Left and the optimism of the 1960s. But I ended by saying that optimism would not change the world. In 1968, spontaneous but well organised campus and factory occupations in Paris failed to bring down the French government. After 1968, new insights into the processes of social change appeared to be necessary. Marcuse had begun to address this in papers delivered during 1967, and he goes further in *An Essay on Liberation* (written in 1967, revised in 1968 and published in 1969),[1] writing of new biological needs arising from the contradictions of the affluent society. That a new society remains unrealised is attributed to its repression by the mechanisms of the existing society. But how do the conditions for its realisation arise?

My aim in this chapter is to examine the problems of a new sensibility and new needs as discussed by Marcuse in the late 1960s. While I begin by doubting the biological status which Marcuse ascribes to the need for freedom, I draw on more recent work in the field of consumption to suggest that needs do, indeed, change, and on a reading of Darwinism to suggest that biology, too, is produced, not given, which means that it can in theory be socially produced. The difficulty, which subsequent insights on the sociology of sub-cultures demonstrate, is that new needs articulated at street level can be assimilated into the dominant market-led society – just as transgressive practices such as graffiti have been appropriated by the art market. This leads to a further issue as to whether the realisation of radical social change requires a critical class, such as the working class or the intelligentsia, to drive it forward – or not.

Looking at these issues, I compare Marcuse's work with that of André Gorz – who draws on Marcuse's ideas in his own *Farewell to the Working Class*[2] – and to Rudolf Bahro's critique of socialism from within the East bloc.[3] I begin with Marcuse's lecture 'The End of Utopia' given in Berlin in July 1967,[4] focusing briefly on his reference to the concept of a historical break. I then outline the lecture's argument that utopia is viable through technological advance, and re-state a question posed by a member of the audience as to how a new consciousness can arise within the conditions of the existing society. Marcuse recognised a dilemma from which he had no exit; I end the chapter by suggesting that the ground of the problem can be moved from time to space, or co-presence, as a revolution within the existing society – an idea derived from Henri Lefebvre's theory of moments.

ENDLESS POSSIBILITY: THE BREAK

Marcuse's lecture 'The End of Utopia' was one of a series of five organised by the German Socialist Students organisation, which went on to offer its own alternative courses for the 1967–68 academic year.[5] Three of the lectures examined revisions of psychoanalysis, and one offered provisional legitimacy for revolutionary violence. The latter was a contentious subject: struggles for national liberation in ex-colonial states were armed, while the Weathermen in the US (and later the Red Army Faction in Germany) adopted tactics including sabotage in what they took to be parallel struggles for liberation in North America and Europe.[6] Marcuse condoned violence only as a right of resistance and a last resort. In a radio interview in April 1979 he confirmed his position, looking back on the New Left:

> Advocacy of violence ... should be taboo. Violence may be considered justified only as counter-violence ... a natural right of resistance for suppressed minorities after all legal means have been exhausted.... I also added that if then these minorities rebel, that might break the chain of violence which we had throughout history.[7]

In 1979 he adds that he is less optimistic about the ending of violence: 'breaking the chain of violence is probably only thinkable in a long historical process'.[8]

His main concern in 'The End of Utopia' is the transition from a world of alienating toil to a world of ease enabled by technological advance: the ending of scarcity as the basis for a new life, a Land of Cockaigne.[9] He argues that the life of ease is no longer utopian in the sense of fantasy, and asserts:

> Today any form of the concrete world, of human life, any transformation of the technical and natural environment is a possibility ... we have the capacity to turn the world into hell, and

are well on the way to doing so. We also have the capacity to turn it into the opposite of hell. This would mean the end of utopia.[10]

In contrast to the historical concept of utopia as an unrealisable dream, utopia is now possible – 'the material and intellectual forces for the transformation are technically at hand' – but is suppressed by the 'total mobilization' of the affluent society 'against its own potential for liberation'.[11] This echoes ideas Marcuse proposed in *One-Dimensional Man*,[12] but the Berlin lecture is more optimistic – perhaps in response to the audiences he was then addressing. Gerd-Rainer Horn notes that between 1967 and 1969 Marcuse spoke at 'public meetings in overcrowded and smoke-filled auditoria' and to students' groups in New York, London, Berlin, Amsterdam, Paris, Oslo and Rome.[13] As suggested in Chapter 5, these audiences were an incipient new society. Suddenly, in a manifestly irrational society,[14] the end of utopia was at hand.

The end of utopia, then, is the end of daydreaming which relegates transformation to a realm which I read as being distanced from actuality in the same way as freedom is distanced in the affirmative culture of bourgeois society (see Chapter 3). Hence the end of utopia is the end of utopian mystique, the danger of which (though Marcuse does not reference this) is that it leads to the false millenarianism of fascism.[15] But, also, utopia as really possible liberation is the end of social *evolution* (quantitative improvements combined with continued alienation), replaced by *revolution* as a 'break' in history.[16]

The idea of the break poses difficulties, however. Ernesto Laclau argues (in 1996) that the way emancipation is envisaged is either as a chasm – the future disconnected from the past (a New Jerusalem descending from the sky) – or a reformism in which change is scripted within, and hence on the terms of, the old society.[17] This can be applied to the ending of the chain of violence, too: either a new consciousness supersedes the need for violent resistance, or violence reproduces an aspect of the society within which its perpetrators seek revolution. This exemplifies the problem of how a new society emerges, beginning within the existing society yet seeking to be radically other than, or counter to, that society, while its tactics are drawn from the existing society because its vocabulary of possibilities is that which is currently available. For many student radicals and probably most of the counter-culture's incipient social groups, however, non-violence was more than a refusal of violence (as the motif of the existing society) and became a way of life informed by, for instance, Buddhism and Ghandian philosophy.

Marcuse was more pragmatic, seeing a need for violent struggle in certain conditions. But he is clear (in 1979, cited above) that he sees violent resistance as legitimate only as a last resort in struggles for liberation. In 1967, in his Berlin lecture 'The Problem of Violence and the Radical Opposition', he cites resistance in Vietnam as keeping in check the suppression of liberation by 'the most efficient system of destruction of all times'.[18] Speaking of the opposition within the affluent society – in teach-ins, sit-ins, be-ins and love-ins – he sees an 'existential community' which, like non-violent demonstrations, is necessarily opposed to (and by) the dominant society, and which breaks from institutions which limit protest to an ineffective ritual.[19] So, opposition is rendered as violence by the inherent violence of the system it opposes; this inevitably makes real protest into civil disobedience, which may break the pattern of violence offered by the authorities through tactics such as sitting down in the street. Marcuse gives an example from his experience of an anti-war demonstration: when demonstrators met a heavily armed line of police, instead of seeking to break through it they sat in the road, played guitars, and began 'necking' and 'petting'.[20] Marcuse reads this as a spontaneous unity and anarchy, likely to persuade even the police. It is, too, a literal interpretation of the slogan Make Love Not War, in keeping with the personalisation of politics, and a spontaneous, un-planned break with violence. I read this as of more than passing interest in that it suggests a revolutionary tactic which is not a reaction to, or on the terms of, the existing society (whether or not it persuaded the police in that case or others like it).

The idea of a break is found in Marxist-Leninism. Esther Leslie finds the word 'Leap' written four times in the margin in Lenin's annotations to Hegel's *Logic*.[21] She adds that 'leap equals spontaneous activity equals self-movement',[22] which sounds like the situation at the demonstration described above. Walter Benjamin employs the concept of the break, too, in his 'Theses on the Philosophy of History': 'The same leap in the open air of history is the dialectical one, which is how Marx understood revolution.'[23] But Marcuse also sees a cultural break in Surrealism's rupture of the codes of perception of the dominant society. In his paper 'Society as a Work of Art' (see Chapter 5), he cites the Surrealist poet Benjamin Péret: 'The poet can no longer be recognized as such today, unless he [*sic*] opposes the world in which he lives with *total nonconformity*. The poet stands opposed to everything, including those movements that act only in the political arena and thus isolate art from the totality of cultural development.'[24] He quotes the same passage in French in *An Essay on Liberation*,[25] arguing there that the poetic imagination is fundamentally other to instrumental rationality.

Surrealism thus constitutes a break, and has neither plan nor programme except to interrupt. Like Dada, it attacks bourgeois society's institutions and via them the normative values they enshrine. In contrast to reformism, when the outcomes of specific interventions are predicted, and when licensed dissent maintains power, then art can fracture the codes and categories used to maintain and to normalise power. In 1967, the counter-culture enacted a similar refusal of normalisation. In *An Essay on Liberation*, Marcuse writes of the language of sub-cultures as a 'rupture with the linguistic universe' which reclaims the words of ordinary language to denote acts and attitudes categorised as taboo: 'This is the Hippie subculture: "trip", "grass", "pot", "acid", and so on.'[26] In an article in *Partisan Review* in 1972, he writes that black music speaks 'pain, sorrow, and indictment'[27] and that the language of black militants constitutes a linguistic rebellion. But does linguistic rebellion end capitalism?

Returning to 'The End of Utopia', Marcuse argues that technology can now erase the economic problem of scarcity, but that the affluent society deploys surplus repression to prevent it – that is, repression beyond that of the deferment in which gratification of desire is delayed for an envisaged greater good, and individual desires subsumed in a collective need – as the normative process of civilisation defined by Freud. In face of surplus repression, Marcuse sees new needs emerging which 'signify the liberation of a dimension of human existence'[28] beyond basic needs (such as food, shelter, and so forth). The new needs invoke a revolutionary consciousness, but a question arises as to whether this requires an equally new environment in which to break from history and become a new social formation. Marcuse argues that the task of critical theory is to go beyond the call for social improvement to practices of freedom: 'Today we must try to discuss and define … the qualitative difference between socialist society as a free society and the existing society.'[29] He distinguishes this qualitative difference (an aesthetic-erotic society, in which work is play) from the quantitative reform evident in, for instance, increased productivity, which is the norm of the existing society. But how does the new society arise? A member of the audience observes: 'The centre of your paper today was the thesis that a transformation of society must be preceded by a transformation of needs.... this implies that changed needs can only arise if we first abolish the mechanisms that have let the needs come into being as they are.'[30] Marcuse replies:

> You have defined what is unfortunately the greatest difficulty in the matter. Your objection is that, for new, revolutionary needs to develop, the mechanisms that reproduce the old needs must be abolished. In order for the mechanisms to be abolished, there must first be a need to abolish them. That is the circle in which we are placed, and I do not know how to get out of it.[31]

I think this arises also in relation to Marcuse's Salzburg and London papers (see Chapter 5). If the conditions of an affluent society produce a possibility of liberation but deny it in surplus repression, how is the leap made to the ending of surplus repression? Do new needs produce new conditions, or are new needs a means to social transformation only when conditions enable them to be consciously articulated and expressed? Taken at face value this is a chicken-and-egg dilemma, beyond resolution. But what is the nature of the needs? Are they cultural (the product of nurture) or are they biological (an intervention within nature)? And what would be the implications of lending them a biological status for the agency of social groups in realising the society such needs imply?

NEEDS AND ALIENATION

In *An Essay on Liberation*, consolidating ideas from various earlier papers, Marcuse writes of the new needs as having a biological status: 'The development of qualitatively new human needs appears as a biological necessity: they are needs in a very biological sense.'[32] New needs, then, are produced by the repressive mentality of bourgeois society and instrumental rationality, while a class-based society restricts the need for freedom by constricting the imagination to a 'controlled play'[33] affirming the status quo. In contrast, in certain moments, imagination enters 'into the projects of a new social morality'[34] which states the perennial need to be free in an 'aesthetic-erotic dimension'.[35] Marcuse relies on the biological status of a need to be free, then, rather as (coincidentally) Ernst Bloch relies on the status of hope as being equivalent to that of a drive (in Freudian terms) in *The Principle of Hope*. The biological status of new needs allows Marcuse to read their emergence as the result of a spontaneous eruption of a new sensibility or awareness. This might in turn suggest that the concept of agency ceases to be useful, if the new needs become pervasive of their own accord. I return to this below, but the status of the envisaged new needs must first be clarified.

When Marcuse writes that 'the new sensibility has become a political factor',[36] I take this to mean that, as an underlying principle of social organisation, the new sensibility which expresses the perennial need to be free replaces that of instrumental rationality. Marcuse consequently revises Marx's position that work does not become play but is only reduced in quantity through technological progress, writing instead of a society in which people 'speak a different language, have different gestures, follow different impulses' and develop 'an instinctual barrier' against brutality.[37] Asking rhetorically if this is utopian, he answers that it *is* 'the May rebellion in France'[38] in which, as was cited in Chapter 2:

> the piano with the jazz player stood well between the barricades; the red flag well fitted the statue of the author of *Les Misérables* [Victor Hugo]; and striking students in Toulouse demanded the revival of the language of the Troubadours, the Albigensians. The new sensibility ... crosses the frontier between the capitalist and the communist orbit; it is contagious because the atmosphere, the climate of the established societies, carries the virus.[39]

This reads as a positive equivalent of the ghetto cry of pain. In answer to the dilemma posed by the questioner in Berlin, it appeals to a spontaneous new consciousness articulated in new cultural forms and new ways of living – the student occupations of May 1968, a revolution in private life and an occupation of space. And if to revive the songs of the troubadours (who sang mainly of unrequitable love in the langue d'Oc)[40] seems less revolutionary, the history of modern art exhibits repeated appropriations of forms from outside the European mainstream – such as the use of African masks in Cubism – to catalyse a break from the dominant language of form. Similarly, in the 1992 occupation of Twyford Down in the south of England by anti-roads protestors calling themselves the Donga tribe, a sub-culture spontaneously denoted a resistant, qualitatively different society.[41] I am left, however, with a nagging doubt as to the biological nature of these needs, and the possibility of lasting change on a social scale if they are most often manifest in marginalised groups (and may be a means to become self-marginalised).

Introducing the fifth volume of Marcuse's Collected Papers, Douglas Kellner, Clayton Pierce and Tyson Lewis cite the Lacanian analyst Adrian Johnston claiming that a radical break with the present is possible only through '"a break with needs altogether"'.[42] This may be an even more utopian possibility than that envisaged by Marcuse in 1967. C. Fred Alford writes, however, that despite the idea of new biological needs being Marcuse's 'most problematic concept' he is drawn to its 'instinctual basis for socialism in the demands of Eros'.[43] Alford helpfully summarises Marcuse's arguments:

> What Marcuse wants to say is that society reaches so deeply into the human being that it can manipulate and exploit humanity's deepest instinctual needs. Society has always done this, of course, but never with the effectiveness of advanced industrial society ... Yet if Eros is merely a creature of history, then it loses its great revolutionary virtue: its utter demandingness (for Eros, too much satisfaction is never enough), as well as its desire for real and genuine fulfilment now and forever. It is these virtues that render Eros immune to the intrusions of history ... and that make Eros such a potent and permanent revolutionary force, even in exile, so to speak, deep within the alienated body and one-dimensional mind.[44]

Alford concludes that Marcuse never solved the dilemma of making Eros historical. I tend to agree, and in retrospect would ask whether newly produced needs, even if they are biological, are yet subsumed in market economics, and thereby turned to reverse effect. I come to that later. Here, I want to dwell a little longer on the status of the new needs.

I have raised doubts about the use of biological metaphors in the dominant planning theory of the inter-war years as a naturalisation of a historical process (seeing history as the process of human intervention in the conditions in which human acts are shaped).[45] To see the transitional zones of cities growing through inward migration as the inevitable sites of conflict, as the urbanists of the Chicago School did, is a crude Darwinism trading on a notion of survival of the fittest. But a more careful look at Charles Darwin's theories of evolution leads to a reconsideration of human needs: Darwin does not explain the origins of species but he does explain that no entity in the natural world is simply as it is (as if given by god); all life is *produced*, as it is *made* and as it *becomes*, as a product of evolving conditions. Writing on Darwin's theories of natural selection, Elizabeth Grosz argues that he saw the natural world as devoid of plan, and produced by processes of proliferation, mutation and adaptation which are endless.[46] Evolution is also random, as is mutation. It leads to some forms which thrive and some which die. The human consciousness is also produced in a process which involves contingency and adaptation, though one in which – if Marx is correct (and Marcuse remains a Marxist) – intervention inflects the direction of mutations. Perhaps, tentatively, I could say that Marcuse moves towards a dialectical Darwinism, arguing that needs are biologically produced, while retaining a Marxist vision of a society which is produced in human intervention and can therefore not just change but change for the better. I realise this is rather speculative.

I could leave it there, as a non-specialist, but the dialectical model has another side: if needs are produced, perhaps the market has as much ability to intervene as does the revolutionary class (if there is one). The owners of the means of production, that is, are able to manufacture consumer wants, which are then felt as human needs, in order to expand their markets. I do not venture here a critique of the sociology of consumption,[47] but part of the literature on the subject holds that consumers are not simply dupes of the market but can use it knowingly for the purpose of identity-consumption. That argument relies on another which it supersedes, that consumers were once persuaded to consume what the market offers through its manufacture of false needs. Conrad Lodziak argues that consumers' needs are, contrary to this, not produced by manipulation in advertising but in a more pervasive, underpinning way.[48] Citing Gorz, Lodziak argues that it is alienating work which produces the need to consume in the first place, as a form of compensation, regardless of the distinctions between specific products or the advertising campaigns used to sell them. For Gorz, it is not fashion which creates a desire for new goods but the 'relationships of production' characteristic of a society in which producers are alienated from the products of their toil.[49] Writing with Jeremy Tatman, Lodziak summarises Gorz's argument that it is necessary to consider

> First, how the capitalist system distances people from their experienced needs, offering 'compensations' for this 'loss' in the form of consumer goods and services. Second, how capitalism's need for consumers translates into socialisation for consumerism, and third, how effective socialisation for consumerism leads to a

dependency on commercial products and services, which by their very nature do not match experienced need.[50]

From this, needs produced in alienating work are met by goods which do not satisfy. I would add that they fail to satisfy not because they are designed that way, for example through built-in obsolescence (though they are), but because the need they address is not one which can be met by consumption at all, only by removing alienation. In the bind of toil-and-consumption, or work-and-leisure, then, consumption leads to further desire and the need to work more to pay for more leisure or lifestyle goods, and so on, and on, and on. Taking this into account, Marcuse's model of new needs arising in a realisation of the dominant society's contradictions can be read as a reclamation of the production of needs not unlike that of language in sub-cultures. Verbal language, too, was Darwin's model for evolution.[51] Marcuse describes a not dissimilar process to that of biology when he writes that

> The new sensibility, which expresses the ascent of the life instincts ... would foster, on a social scale, the vital need for the abolition of injustice and misery and would shape the further evolution of the 'standard of living.' ... Emergence of a new Reality Principle: under which a new sensibility and a desublimated scientific intelligence would combine in the creation of an *aesthetic ethos*.[52]

The aesthetic ethos in question is that of work made play, the utopian-erotic life. All this consolidates arguments that Marcuse first made in *Eros and Civilization*[53] and which in the 1960s appeared as evidence of a new social and cultural formation outside the society ruled by the military-industrial complex, an outcome of instrumental rationality and the perpetrator of the war in Vietnam.

BUT...

But new needs are not immune to co-option by the dominant society, as subsequent experience shows, and they may be neutralised as cultural artefact or appropriated by the market. Sociologist Sharon Zukin writes of New York street culture in the 1980s:

> Styles that develop on the street are cycled through mass media ... divorced from their social context, they become images of cool.... The cacophony of demands for justice is translated into

a coherent demand for jeans. Claims for public space ... inspire the counterpolitics of display in late 20th century urban riots.[54]

Jim McGuigan also argues that 'cool', as a term for the street-level culture which he sees as beginning in the permissive ambience of the 1960s, is a means to neutralise opposition. The market can adopt any critique and 'turn it around to the advantage of capitalism itself'.[55] Citing Judith Williamson's *Decoding Advertisements*, in which a popular impression of advertising as lies is assumed to be a social norm, McGuigan argues that even that norm is used as persuasion in mass culture:

> advertising can incorporate its mythic status (as a lie) into itself with very little trouble. Advertisements will always recuperate by using criticisms of themselves as frames of reference which will finally *enhance*, rather than destroy, their real status. It is like the use of the liberated woman ... even she will go crazy about aftershave.[56]

McGuigan and Williamson differ from Lodziak in taking advertising's claims to persuade at face value. But I leave that aside, to suggest only that capitalism retains power through the mechanisms of both production and exchange. What is to be done? And by whom? These are naive but necessary questions, and I move now to the question of class, and the possibility that a new revolutionary class emerged in 1967 and 1968 through the counter-culture, the student movement, the New Left, and what Marcuse calls a young intelligentsia – all overlapping publics. Of course, the same argument can be applied to class as Johnston applies to needs (above): that the new society will break from the category of class entirely (and for Bloch, utopia is a classless society). I take it as a paradox, though – rather than an insoluble dualism – that while new needs arise spontaneously, yet a necessity remains for intervention by a group within the existing society in ways conducive to a realisation of the awareness implicit in those needs on a social scale (the outcome of which is a new society). This does not, however, erase the difficulty that intervention tends to emanate from marginalised groups – inevitably because, as Marcuse argues, any group venturing to intervene will be marginalised as a threat to the status quo, and suppressed as far as the Establishment is able.

THE END OF CLASS?

Marcuse argues that opposition to advanced capitalism is isolated 'from the masses and from the majority of organized labour' who become an 'integrated majority' so that refusal is taken up instead by minorities, such as young middle-class professionals and technocrats – the new intelligentsia – and by ghetto populations.[57] In the late 1960s black power was an active force, and the young intelligentsia had not become the 'boho' generation of young professionals who became the drivers of gentrification in the 1980s (and remain that in the de-industrialised cities of the globalised economy).[58] As Elizabeth Wilson remarks, 'Bohemia first emerged as a counter-space in opposition to the repressive authority of bourgeois society.'[59] But bohemians become conformists adopting the edge or rawness of marginal zones as inverted chic in another case of appropriation of dissent by market forces. Wilson remains optimistic that 'This does not mean that the desire to change society has disappeared.'[60] But is there a working class in opposition to the power of capital today?

Marcuse accepts that 'It is of course nonsense to say that middle-class opposition is replacing the proletariat as the revolutionary class.'[61] This is because the militant intelligentsia has separated from white-collar workers. Marcuse also accepts that his position on class, and his emphasis on biological needs, is 'an intolerable deviation ... regression to bourgeois, or even worse, aristocratic ideologies'.[62] Undaunted, he reasserts the role of an emergent subject (self) and the onset of a period of education 'which turns into praxis: demonstration, confrontation, rebellion'.[63] He compares this to the role of the party in preparing the ground for mass revolt in Marxist-Leninism. In 1968, however, the French Communist Party was ambivalent towards the student occupations,[64] while Marcuse identified the students and young technocrats as a new intelligentsia and an oppositional community.

It appeared to Marcuse that advanced capitalism neutralised the conditions for revolt which were seen by Marx as the necessary objective factor for change by bringing the working class within the affluent society; the subjective forces – consciousness – were similarly absorbed into consumerism. In this situation, black power and the New Left are resistant. Looking to Europe, Marcuse sees a range of relations between student movements and other groups: in fascist countries – Spain and Portugal then – students were supported by agricultural workers, but in Germany they met violent opposition from organised labour.[65] The situation is nuanced, and no united oppositional agency seems to be present. But rather than replace the prediction that the working class will overthrow capitalism by another claiming that the student movement and young intelligentsia will do so, Marcuse states:

> The search for specific historical agents of revolutionary change in the advanced capitalist countries is indeed meaningless. Revolutionary forces emerge in the process of change itself; the translation of the potential into the actual is the work of political practice. And just as little as critical theory can political practice orient itself on a concept of revolution which belongs to the nineteenth and early twentieth century.[66]

This suggests a revision not only of the identification of the force which produces change, but of the concept of agency as well. Marcuse sees two possible developments out of this: first, struggles for national liberation in ex-colonial countries will threaten the economy of advanced capitalism; second, the absurdities of advanced capitalism will provoke resistance within the West in a 'collapse of work discipline, slowdown, spread of disobedience to rules and regulations, wildcat strikes, boycotts, sabotage, gratuitous acts of non-compliance'.[67] For those who refuse the system's irrationality, there is solidarity:

> expressive of a true harmony between social and individual needs and goals, between recognized necessity and free development – the exact opposite of the administered and enforced harmony organized in the advanced capitalist (and socialist?) countries. It is the image of this solidarity as elemental, instinctual, creative force which the young radicals see in Cuba.[68]

The term solidarity has since taken on a loaded meaning after its adoption by a group of shipyard workers in Poland in the 1980s, and the way Cuba is perceived may have undergone a shift as well, since Fidel Castro's handing over of power to a pragmatic regime. Likewise, the student movement and young intelligentsia who comprised the young radicals have since been supplanted by anti-globalisation protestors,[69] squatter avant-gardeners,[70] and participants in the network society.[71] Outside the global North, as the affluent society has become, a new opposition to globalisation and its colonisation via development[72] has arisen, and has become networked.[73] After a proliferation of new social movements and new social technologies[74] since the 1980s and 1990s, the young intelligentsia of 1968 might now seem a force which never quite coalesced or cohered in revolutionary terms. But in an interview in 1971 Marcuse differentiated himself from Horkheimer and Adorno in supporting the student movement and the young intelligentsia as a vital socio-political force.[75] If the issue of agency has shifted in its specifics, perhaps the need for small groups operating within but departing from the dominant society remains, at least in making opposition visible. But if this is the case, who are these groups? Are they now diverse and worldwide, or does the working class still hold some currency within post-industrial societies as a potential agent of change?

In *An Essay on Liberation*, Marcuse discusses the agency of specific social groups for transformation, extending his critique to art as a potentially productive force for the material and cultural transformation of (Western) society.[76] This means 'reversing the development of socialism from scientific to utopian' unless groups within advanced industrial societies can be identified to support such a notion.[77] Hence, remembering that the old utopia is daydreaming, the project of radical social change regresses to utopian dreaming unless there is a material process towards the envisaged leap.

Marcuse rehearses the shift in advanced capitalist society from a model of labour as alienating toil to one in which consumption is enforced by toil, and luxuries are seen as needs.[78] In face of instrumental rationality, when a freedom to consume is presented as a social benefit, the vital leap is into a rationality of joy. Historian Richard King observes that in his earlier writing Marcuse used a model of 'reason, freedom, and happiness' in which a joyless, un-free reason produces technical rationalisation, and happiness separated from reason and freedom is mindless hedonism.[79] Marcuse saw this tripartite equilibrium in the outlook of the students whose protests reached 'a dimension which, as aesthetic dimension, has been essentially apolitical'.[80] He adds that 'organic elements' emerge as a new sensibility of rebellion.[81] But they emerge among specific groups even if Marcuse does not have in mind here the hedonism of the counter-culture. What he does have in mind is the role of intellectuals in a reoccupation of public life, arguing that intellectuals have a responsibility to demonstrate (literally) the possibility of a new society. In 'The Problem of Violence and the Radical Opposition', he states:

> Now the liberation of consciousness ... means ... demonstrations, in the literal sense. The whole person must demonstrate his [sic] participation and his will to live.... The established order is mobilized against this real possibility. And, if it harms us to have illusions, it is just as harmful ... to preach defeatism and quietism, which can only play into the hands of those that run the system.[82]

The reference to quietism may reflect his memories of the withdrawal of intellectuals from public life in the Weimar Republic; or an ambivalence towards groups who left the cities in 1968 to found intentional communities in rural places.[83] But the point is that Marcuse consistently envisages new revolutionary agencies enacting a new sensibility in personal and political life, outside a traditional concern with production:

> Even on the left the notion of socialism has been taken too much within the framework of the development of productive forces, of increasing the productivity of labor, something which was not only justified but necessary at the level of productivity at which the idea of scientific socialism was developed but which today is at least subject to discussion.[84]

He notes that a fusion of technology and art parallels the convergence of work and play advocated by Charles Fourier in the early nineteenth century, so that 'socially necessary labor can be organized in harmony with the liberated, genuine needs of men [sic]'.[85] He concludes that, 'because the so-called utopian possibilities are not at all utopian but rather the determinate socio-historical negation of what exists, a very real and very pragmatic opposition is required'.[86] Kellner, Pierce and Lewis comment:

> Marcuse exhorts philosophers to engage in socio-political action.... he concedes the importance of the concerns of the existing individual, the needs of human subjectivity and the drive towards authenticity. But he argues that a real change of inauthentic existence pre-supposes a transformed society.... every individual is a social individual, living in and conditioned by a social-historical situation.[87]

Yet the relation between individual consciousness and new social formations remains vague. It seems, too, that the young intelligentsia does not replace the working class, but that the model of a leading force is abandoned in favour of a diffusion of agency. If this is the case, then it no longer matters whether the working class is mobilised against (or has been entirely subsumed within) capitalism, or whether there is a self-identified working class; what matters is how localised campaigns undermine and subvert the system in ways it cannot as yet suppress, or at least not without exposing its own violence and irrationality. But I run ahead, outlining my own position on the issue. To return to the texts, I look briefly now to Gorz.

In *Farewell to the Working Class*, Gorz argues that trades unions and employers both affirm quantitative improvement, and that this is compromised in so far as higher earnings are accompanied by a denial of the shorter working week (which Gorz sees as allowing greater time for free activities replacing leisure-consumption). Lodziak and Tatman quote Gorz: 'A political strategy centred on the reduction of working hours may be the main lever with which we can shift the balance within society, and put an end to the domination of the political sphere by the economic. And this would mean the extinction of capitalism.'[88] Marcuse similarly argues that 'a theory which has not caught up with the practice of capitalism cannot possibly guide the practice aiming at the abolition of capitalism'.[89] Gorz looks to 'the extinction of political economy' in 'freely determined possibilities for happiness rather than quantities of exchange value',[90] and cites Bahro as reviving Marxist thought.[91] Bahro himself writes of 'a path of increasing self-management from below in all society's institutions'.[92] Gorz quotes Bahro to the effect that an advanced industrial society can meet its material needs (as Marcuse said); hence the need for qualitative change and what Bahro calls a cultural-revolutionary economic policy. Within the quotation is this passage, which might be put beside Marcuse's texts from the 1960s:

Historical examples show, moreover, that the same or similar results of human development and human happiness are compatible with fairly great differences in the quantity of available products. In no case can the conditions for freedom be measured in dollars or roubles per head. What people in the developed countries need is not the extension of their present needs, but rather the opportunity for self-enjoyment in doing, enjoyment in personal relations, concrete life in the broadest sense.[93]

Bahro, a member of the managerial class in the German Democratic Republic who remained a communist despite being attacked and for a short time imprisoned by the regime, similarly seeks an updating of theory to reflect new practices in capitalism.

Gorz cites Marcuse in *Farewell to the Working Class*, paraphrasing his argument for a cultural shift which replaces competitiveness with reciprocity, tenderness and a love of life.[94] Gorz argues that the working class in a post-industrial society has no vision of a new society while 'The non-class engendered by the decomposition of present-day society can only conceive of the non-society of which it is the prefiguration.'[95] He looks to feminism as a qualitative revolution; and to autonomous cooperation and the free availability of 'convivial tools'.[96] The term convivial is also used by Ivan Illich:

> The crisis [of advanced capitalism and social breakdown] can be solved only if we learn to invert the present deep structure of tools; if we give people tools that guarantee their right to work with high, independent efficiency, thus simultaneously eliminating the need for either slaves or masters and enhancing each person's range of freedom.[97]

For Gorz, Bahro and Illich, then, the working class is no longer the obvious force for revolution, and is now integrated in the mechanisms of the dominant society. I think Marcuse adopts this position, too, although at times with a note of caution. In a radio conversation with Bill Moyers in 1974, for instance, he says: 'I never said the students, as a group, would replace the working class as the vehicle of change', adding that he saw the students as preparing the way for the development of a new consciousness.[98] Like Gorz and Bahro, too, Marcuse remains committed to the ideals of communism; but a communism that must be re-visioned in new conditions which – I think – do not include any significant agency on the part specifically of a working class. Not everyone will agree but I leave it there.

MOMENTS BEFORE, MOMENTS AFTER...

King summarises Marcuse's position in *An Essay on Liberation* as ascribing to the intelligentsia the task of theory, and to minorities and students that of exemplifying a new lifestyle. He adds that this position relied on 'the belief that biological needs were socially and culturally formed and that to change them was the goal ... of radical political action'.[99] Marcuse argues in a lecture at Berkeley in 1972 that the situation demands the interface of two political and social forces,[100] and admits that student militancy has declined while 'you cannot have an avant-garde where there is no mass movement behind'.[101] What is left, in which radical students (such as 'my young friend Rudi Dutschke'[102]) play a vital role, is a long march through the institutions as the site in which new needs translate into new formations of knowledge and sociation. Culture and education, then, are the site of revolution by other means.

This leads me to Henri Lefebvre's theory of moments (an earlier version of his theory of space).[103] Though there are few links between their works, Marcuse met Lefebvre in 1968. Marcuse was in Paris for a UNESCO conference on Marxism. He was acclaimed in the press as a leading figure in the student movement, though few French students had read his work at the time.[104] Marcuse was surrounded by journalists on entering the hall, and rescued by a reporter with a car.[105] He asked to meet the North Vietnamese delegation – in Paris for peace talks – and was taken to their hotel where an unplanned meeting duly took place. Walking back to his own hotel he was invited by students from the École des Beaux Arts, which they had just occupied, to join them. He gave a version of his conference paper there, but it disappointed the section of the audience expecting him to urge 'a Chinese-style "worker-peasant alliance" against capitalism'.[106] When they met later, Lefebvre, too, was disappointed with Marcuse's views. He recalls:

I met Marcuse several times. We had some points of agreement on the critique of bourgeois society and one-dimensional man ... but I didn't agree with him on the fact that one could change society by aesthetics ... According to Marcuse, industrial society, by its mode of social control, provokes a reductionism of possibilities for individuals and an integration (or disintegration) of the working class. The attack on the system can only come from an encounter between critical theory and a marginal substratum of outcasts and outsiders. But in May 1968 this attack took the form of a formidable working class general strike.[107]

Marcuse's reliance on the student movement as a young intelligentsia contrasts with Lefebvre's belief that the working class retained a vital role in revolution. Marcuse said in 1968 that 'the students showed the workers what could be done', and that 'the workers followed the slogan and the example of the students'.[108] This may have reflected the situation in North America – but not in France. Lefebvre knew that more than a million French workers had taken part in a general strike in 1968, reviving the tactic of occupation previously used in 1936. Kristin Ross writes:

> Occupation was generally viewed as a mark of the strength and seriousness of the strike, since it meant a clear departure from tired, artificial forms like meetings and petitions, or the partial 'symbolic' strikes that bore the trappings of the trade-union movement and no longer mobilized workers.[109]

Marcuse may have been unaware of the significance of this, seeing the student occupations of French universities as equivalent to teach-ins in the United States. Lefebvre taught at Nanterre, where the occupations began, and understood the meaning of occupation as qualitatively different from the normalised, quantitative demands of unions.

Lefebvre was critical, too, of Marcuse's view of total repression. As Andy Merrifield writes, 'Lefebvre could never comprehend modern capitalism as seamless; his mind revelled in openness not closure.'[110] For Lefebvre, the system always leaked. And that was evident in sudden moments of clarity within the dulling routines of everyday life under capitalism. Lefebvre articulates his theory of moments in 1959,[111] defining the moment – which is a moment of sudden clarity available to anyone, but unannounced – as an attempt to intuitively realise the possibility of life amid its dulling actualities. Merrifield reads this as analogous to the French Symbolist poet Stéphane Mallarmé's metaphor of a space between words, a secret door allowing the reader to enter: 'Once inside the reader can subvert each verse, rearrange its rhythm, reappropriate the poem as a covert author.'[112] Merrifield adds that the moment is 'an opportunity to be seized and invented. It is both metaphorical and practical, palpable and impalpable, something intense and absolute, yet fleeting and relative.'[113] He adds that it is like the sense of festival – which might be compared with Marcuse's image of the jazz player at the barricades. Earlier, in *Critique of Everyday Life*, Lefebvre argued that capitalism manipulates leisure as distraction. When the 'constitutive elements of leisure' are found in media such as film,[114] work remains unchanged and the otherness of leisure is a non-radical alternative in a continuum of work-play (quite distinct from what Marcuse means by work becoming play). Sexuality is conscripted to the project in a 'wearying, mechanical' eroticism.[115]

And so, Lefebvre writes, 'we work to earn our leisure, and leisure has only one meaning: to get away from work. A vicious circle.'[116] This resembles Lodziak's position that alienation drives the leisure industry, and is compatible with Marcuse's critique of consumer culture. But I return to the problem of how a new society emerges, where I think there is another difference between Lefebvre and Marcuse (which neither asserts at the time).

Marcuse sets the problem in *time*. Regulated time was the target of the Communards who shot at public clocks as if they were enemy soldiers. Time also dictates that a new society *succeeds* an old society according to a linear trajectory. But suppose that old and new can be co-present in a metaphorical *space*. That is, on the old model, change is the actualisation of a tomorrow the outline of which was scripted yesterday. This is the social philosophy of the bourgeoisie, and reminds me of a sign outside a public house in Exeter: 'Free beer tomorrow for those who missed it yesterday'. (The sign is no longer there, but I doubt as a result of the cost of dispensing free beer.) This is partially ruptured in the model of revolution in which time starts again as Year One. Leslie comments on re-enactments of the Bolshevik Revolution in Leningrad in 1920: 'the past was preserved and cancelled at the same time'.[117] But is there another possibility? Rather than re-enactment is there a pre-enactment, as, I would say, in the experimental living of eco-villages and intentional communities co-present with the dominant society? Is the long revolution the gradual shift from one to the other?

Is the long march the revolution which is co-present within the existing society which gradually transforms it radically but from within? For those who took part in the emergent social and cultural formations of the late 1960s, being there was probably transformative. To recognise this shifts the ground of Marcuse's dilemma in Berlin from time to space, if only metaphorically. And, indeed, if a new consciousness arises spontaneously, as he says, then it is today, not tomorrow, that is the location for a new society defined, in rather 1960s terms, as living in the moment. I am not sure if this matters, but it might.

7
The Aesthetic Dimension

In this chapter I move on to Marcuse's last book, *The Aesthetic Dimension*,[1] published in 1978. *The Aesthetic Dimension* echoes aspects of Theodor Adorno's *Aesthetic Theory* (published posthumously from an unresolved manuscript in 1969),[2] in considering art after Auschwitz. Yet if art speaks obliquely in face of terror, in a political impasse art retains its criticality through its autonomy, its radical otherness and apartness from a world which it still regards from a memory of hope. Art has a capacity to render the contradictions of the dominant society visible, and paradoxically, while being of the world, it looks on the world as if externally, and can indict it. In these conditions – which are the layered conditions of post-1968, post-Auschwitz, and post-the failure of the German revolution in 1919 – *The Aesthetic Dimension* elaborates a contingent possibility for resistance. Marcuse states towards the end of the book that 'Art remains marked by unfreedom; in contradicting it, art achieves its autonomy'.[3] The paradox of unfreedom and autonomy runs in various forms through Marcuse's aesthetics but perhaps reaches its most succinct form in *The Aesthetic Dimension*. Hence the book gives no solution to unfreedom, and a limited answer to the question of art's role and its responsibility in an increasingly darkening world. Part of its argument was rehearsed earlier in *Counter-revolution and Revolt*,[4] published in 1972, which is a more direct response to the failure of revolt in Paris in 1968. I begin, then, with that book, particularly with a re-reading of the section on art and revolution. I then reconsider *The Aesthetic Dimension*, and end by comparing responses to Marcuse's aesthetics from art historian Carol Becker and art critic Peter Fuller.

THE 1970s AND COUNTER-REVOLUTION

In 1967 Marcuse saw the world as facing hell or its opposite. By the 1970s it seemed that the choice had been made, but unfortunately not for hell's opposite. So, in the opening pages of *Counter-revolution and Revolt*, Marcuse argues that capital will go to more or less any length to ensure its dominance:

> The Western world has reached a new stage of development: now, the defense of the capitalist system requires the organization of counterrevolution at home and abroad. In its extreme manifestations, it practices the horrors of the Nazi regime.... Torture has become a normal instrument of interrogation around the world.... a constant flow of arms from the rich countries to the poor helps to perpetuate the oppression of national and social liberation.[5]

For Marcuse to cite the horrors of the Nazi regime is not a trope but a reference to the history which led to him flee Germany in 1932. In the 1970s he saw a return of dark times, not as history repeating itself but in the form of a new totalitarianism of consumption supported by an unscrupulous exploitation of labour, of the ex-colonial world, and of the earth's natural resources.[6] He says at the beginning of *The Aesthetic Dimension*:

> In a situation where the miserable reality can be changed through radical political praxis, the concern with aesthetics demands justification. It would be senseless to deny the element of despair inherent in this concern: retreat into a world of fiction where existing conditions are changed and overcome only in the realm of the imagination.[7]

That miserable reality became evident to Marcuse, again personally, in 1969 when he was accused of supporting violence in student demonstrations, attacked by the Right, and threatened with compulsory retirement from the University of California. When he received death threats and was forced to leave his house temporarily it was guarded by students. In 1970 he agreed to retire but retained an office in the university and was allowed to teach informally. Marcuse also came under attack from the Marxist Left, accused of being a CIA stooge on account of his wartime intelligence work.[8] Douglas Kellner writes that Marcuse's gloom about the demise of radical opposition was set aside in 1967;[9] but by December 1968, at an event organised by the British newspaper *The Guardian*, Marcuse stated that a free society had become more remote than it had seemed to be. He now saw the New Left as an umbrella movement for diverse interest groups who made up a political and cultural opposition, and whose tactics constituted a new form of politics. The new New Left, as it were, would consist of 'small groups, concentrated on the level of local activities', and would foreshadow – in a reference to a more conventional form of revolution – a new form of libertarian socialism, 'namely councils of manual and intellectual workers, soviets ... organized spontaneity'.[10]

Organised spontaneity precludes leadership, and Marcuse began his talk in December 1968 by disowning media claims that he had ever been a leader of the New Left or the student movement, saying: 'And there is one thing the Left does not need, and that's another father image, another daddy.'[11] To the Federal Bureau of Investigation in the United States, however, Marcuse was a leader, and a sufficient threat to social order that it bought copies of all his books and wrote reports on them.[12] Capitalism works in strange ways, at times not so different from those once used on the other side of the Iron Curtain.

Although a new realism was necessary after the failure of revolt in 1968, and in face of the extraordinary lengths to which those in power were prepared to go to suppress freedom (well beyond buying books), many arguments begun in 1967 surface again in Marcuse's post-1968 work. In *Counter-revolution and Revolt*, for example, he resumes his discussion of needs, identifying an inherent instability which arises spontaneously when 'capitalism cannot satisfy the needs which it creates'.[13] As in the discussion of needs in *An Essay on Liberation*, Marcuse sees a possibility for a transformation of needs in 'the *qualitative* leap' by which capitalism is transcended.[14] He continues that such a transformation appears in 'the fight against the fragmentation of work, the necessity and productivity of stupid performances and stupid merchandise ... against pollution as a way of life'.[15] (This reference to environmentalism, a theme Marcuse takes up in the 1970s, lies outside my scope here.[16]) Marcuse adds that the New Left engages not only in ecological issues but in 'a new sexual morality' as well, in the context of the women's liberation movement and, in parallel, a liberation of aesthetic needs.[17]

The basic argument is that to undermine capitalism requires a counter-value structure entailing non-competitive work and a refusal of productivity. As in his writing from the 1960s, Marcuse echoes a libidinal utopianism found in the writing of Charles Fourier; he calls for a 'rejection of the anti-erotic puritan cult of plastic beauty and cleanliness' as a means to 'articulate the deep malaise prevalent among the people at large'.[18] The difficulty, he accepts, is that such counter-values tend to separate the New Left which embraces them from the wider public who lack the sensibility which results from – or produces – a free society in place of the freedom of choice of consumer culture, as in the de-politicisation of 'the hippie sector'.[19] Marcuse argues that the conditions facing the New Left after 1968 differ from those of the period of civil rights campaigning and the anti-war demonstrations of the early 1960s. If, he adds, the dominant society was unprepared for revolt in the mid 1960s, it had made up the deficit after 1968 'to such an extent that the very survival of the radical movement as a political force is in question'.[20] Marcuse cites the German student activist Rudi Dutschke (whom he met in 1968) as advocating 'the *long march through the institutions*: working against the established institutions while working in them ... by using the resources and modes of knowledge available for counter-purposes'.[21]

I noted this in Chapter 6, and add here only that it can be compared to the concept of a long revolution through education and culture proposed by Raymond Williams.[22] But there is a difference: while Williams saw adult education as an entry route for working-class people into the learning associated with work in universities, Marcuse argues in a more radical mode for counter-institutions, like the 1960s teach-in. Williams rejected Marcuse's attempt to link Marxism and psychoanalysis, but put on record his respect for Marcuse 'as a man' acting and speaking 'with an exemplary and quite uncommon dignity' under pressure.[23] For Marcuse, though, the counter-institution was the means to build a new society within the old, a revolution by other means or, so to speak, a revolution before the revolution.

ART-REVOLUTION

The third chapter of *Counter-revolution and Revolt* deals with art and revolution. Here, Marcuse begins to examine some of the questions which were to preoccupy him later in *The Aesthetic Dimension*. Among them – and counter to an orthodox Marxist reading of art as reflecting the conditions of its production and its class character – is how works of art retain a capacity to evoke meaning after the time of their making:

> The work of art first transforms a particular, individual content into the universal social order of which it partakes – but does the transformation *terminate* in this order? Is the truth, the validity, of the work of art *confined* to the Greek city state, bourgeois

society, and so on? Evidently not. Aesthetic theory is confronted with the age-old question: what are the qualities which make the Greek tragedy, the medieval epic still true today – not only understandable but enjoyable today?[24]

The answer is that art 'reveals the human condition' through aesthetic transformation of its subject matter. Form in art instantiates intellectual qualities which are constant, like beauty and tenderness, and which have their own order distinct from that of the prevailing social order. In its radical otherness, then, 'art opens the established reality to another dimension: that of possible liberation'.[25] Art evokes an unreal world as the counter-institution by which art's affirmative character in its bourgeois institutions is refused. But here, instead of a promise of happiness, Marcuse invokes a promise of secular redemption by which art transcends its class content 'without eliminating it'.[26]

Art retains that content and goes beyond it. It represents historically and culturally specific realities but in doing so it appeals to a humanity beyond those realities. It would be too easy, I think, to call that content universal, though Marcuse does derive part of his theory from the Kantian concept of disinterested judgement – that is, beauty is accessed without vested interests, as a constant quality the representations of which in ordinary perception are partial and ephemeral. But rather than universalise concepts which, in keeping with critical theory, I see as historically produced, I suggest that the image specific to individual experience is transposed through its depiction in art to a socially accessible scale. Marcuse does not put it that way, but he does argue that even in bourgeois art there is a truth content which has meaning beyond the circumstances of its class character or its affirmation of the prevailing order. It is always nuanced. Art's truth permeates its appearances, as 'an illusion in which another reality shows forth'.[27] Or, I might say that the content or meaning of a painting is constructed by the viewer regardless of its subject matter (a vase of flowers or a crucifixion). Marcuse seems metaphorically to equate the quality of beauty with the quality of freedom, in the sense of a qualitatively new society. As he argues in *An Essay on Liberation*, that qualitative revolt requires a new sensibility, an aesthetic of negation speaking of the new society within the old. Negation is art's radical contract:

The relation between art and revolution is a unity of opposites, an antagonistic unity. Art obeys a necessity, and has a freedom which is its own – not those of the revolution. Art and revolution are united in changing the world – liberation. But in its practice, art does not abandon its own exigencies and does not quit its own dimension: it remains non-operational. In art, the political goal appears only in the transfiguration which is the aesthetic form.[28]

Marcuse then cites the Surrealist writer André Breton's comparison of two different revolutionaries, the painter Gustave Courbet – a functionary of the Paris Commune in 1871 – and the poet Arthur Rimbaud – a bohemian who sympathised with but was not an operator, so to speak, of the Commune. For Breton, Courbet depicts his protest and his insight into sensuality in the still-life paintings he produced after the Commune, while Rimbaud, though he wrote a constitution for a communist society, writes in the same way both before and after the Commune: 'The revolution was in his poetry from the beginning and to the end: a preoccupation of a technical order, namely, to transfigure the world into a new language.'[29] To me this is less helpful as an analysis of Courbet's work (which was revolutionary in the 1840s and 1850s in including non-privileged subjects in monumental scenes), but more so in relation to Rimbaud, in the context of Marcuse's 1945 essay on French literature (see Chapter 4).

Again prefiguring the text of *The Aesthetic Dimension*, Marcuse concludes that art and revolt are held in an insoluble tension. Art does not change reality, but is another reality, and as such is always inherently revolutionary. He paraphrases Adorno's view that, in the conditions of advanced capitalism's counter-revolution, 'art responds to the total character of alienation and administration with total alienation'.[30] The music of John Cage, Pierre Boulez and Karl-Heinz Stockhausen are cited as examples along with Samuel Beckett's plays, which offer a world devoid of hope yet which refuse all accommodation with actuality: 'to make end with things as they are'.[31] Similarly, Adorno says of Beckett's *Waiting for Godot*:

> At ground zero ... a second world of images springs forth, both sad and rich, the concentrate of historical experiences that otherwise, in their immediacy, fail to articulate the essential: the evisceration of subject and reality. This shabby, damaged world of images is the negative imprint of the administered world.[32]

Earlier in the same passage, Adorno writes of the artfulness of anti-art taken to a point at which it becomes the annihilation of reality (in art). Adorno refers later in *Aesthetic Theory* to Beckett's work as evoking a 'crepuscular grey as after sunset and the end of the world', presented with no suspension of disbelief – the audience know it is on stage – yet unable to completely renounce the circus garb.[33] He adds, citing Beckett's *Endgame* and *Godot*: 'Art emigrates to a standpoint that is no longer a standpoint at all because there are no longer standpoints from which the catastrophe could be named or formed, a world that seems ridiculous in this context.'[34]

After Auschwitz comes the threat of nuclear war as total catastrophe again (a reality brought home to millions by media coverage of the Cuban missile crisis in 1963). But there is a continuum: standpoints – places from which to make detached observations – no longer exist in the second half of the twentieth century. Despair is the most likely emotion, while mundane cruelty occurs on a daily basis. The late twentieth century is a period of barbarism, and art is ineffective against it: 'Art can do nothing to prevent the ascent of barbarism – it cannot by itself keep open its own domain in and against society. For its own preservation and development, art depends on the struggle for the abolition of the social system which generates barbarism as its own potential stage: potential form of its progress.'[35]

Except, as Marcuse argues in *An Essay on Liberation*, art contributes to, gives form to, a new sensibility. In advanced capitalism this is not a revolutionary consciousness among the working class; revolutionary art has no longer any reason to represent a class now integrated into consumerism. Only 'the *rupture*, the *leap*' prevents illusion.[36]

AN AESTHETIC DIMENSION

The idea of art as rupture suggests either anti-art, as in Dada, or the rupture of visual codes as in Surrealism. But in *The Aesthetic Dimension* Marcuse draws closer to the argument advanced in 1945 in his essay on French literature in the 1940s.[37] There, he argued that a literature of intimacy was the last refuge of a consciousness of freedom in those specific conditions. Now he argues that a political sense is integral to aesthetic form: 'I see the political potential of art in art itself, in the aesthetic form as such.'[38] In the Preface, he contends that art's aesthetic form is autonomous, standing apart from the conditions of its production (such as social relations) as negation, able to subvert the prevailing consciousness of the dominant society. He also reasserts the exemption of art from the representation of class consciousness. Yet the theory which Marcuse puts forward here remains Marxist, even if it involves a major revision of Marxism's previous tenets – first, that art's authentic hope lies in its reflection of the consciousness of an 'ascending class' (the proletariat) whose aspirations writers will articulate; and, second, that a declining class (the bourgeoisie) produces only decadence.[39] These ideas are no longer credible because they rely on a separation of an economic base from a cultural superstructure. Instead, revolution requires a new consciousness as a subjective condition throughout a society. Again echoing his 1945 essay, but also the importance of the leap (see Chapter 6), he argues that 'Subjectivity strove to break out of its inwardness into the material and intellectual culture. And today ... it has become a political value as a counterforce against aggressive and exploitative socialization.'[40] This echoes his remarks in the Preface, that 'there may be more subversive potential in the poetry of Baudelaire and Rimbaud than in the didactic plays of Brecht'.[41] He goes on to outline his thesis as follows:

> The radical qualities of art ... its indictment of the established reality and its invocation of the beautiful image (*schöner Schein*) of liberation are grounded precisely in the dimensions where art *transcends* its social determination and emancipates itself from the given universe of discourse and behaviour while preserving its overwhelming presence. Thereby art creates the realm in which the subversion of experience proper to art becomes possible: the world formed by art is recognized as a reality which is suppressed and distorted in the given reality.[42]

There is, then, both a drawing together of strands from his previous writing and a newly heightened paradoxical aspect which should not, I think, be reduced to ambivalence. This is clear, for example, when Marcuse says that aesthetic sublimation both has an affirmative character (making suffering acceptable) *and* is simultaneously 'a vehicle for the critical, negating function of art'.[43] Art stands as reconciling other *and* rebellious subjectivity, at the same time.

This leads to a definition of authenticity – responding to the difficulty of illusion – as the transposition of content into form, and the transposition of the sedimented traces of conditions of unfreedom into aesthetic form. Form is not pure but arrived at through experience, in a view of cultural production not unlike that implied by the life-journey of the artist or writer in the German artist-novel on which Marcuse wrote his doctoral thesis (see Chapter 2). For him, 'Aesthetic form, autonomy, and truth are inter-related. Each is a socio-historical phenomenon, and each *transcends* the socio-historical arena.... The truth of art lies in its power to break the monopoly of established reality ... to *define* what is *real*. In this rupture ... the fictitious world of art appears as true reality.'[44]

To loosely paraphrase Marcuse's argument: imagining the world as it could be, rather than accepting the monopoly of the given, involves the incipient realisation of that world in the process of its articulation as a counter-reality. Reading Marcuse today I am reminded that art offers a viable arena for the articulation of imaginative worlds, as a safe house within the terrain occupied by advanced capitalism, as a zone of experiment, a process of improvisation rather a manufacture of solutions, which *is* the revolution.

The imaginative reconstruction of society, then, takes place in the subjective element of revolution while having the capacity to contribute through imagination to conditions conducive to its realisation. Hence, 'Art breaks open a dimension inaccessible to other experience', in which the tyranny of the reality principle (conformity) is broken.[45] But how? In the five sections of *The Aesthetic Dimension*, Marcuse sets out arguments on the need to revise the tie of conventional Marxist aesthetics to a proletarian culture, on autonomy, and on art's rendering of suffering as beauty – among other issues. Here I want to look briefly at autonomy and the representation of suffering.

AUTONOMY

Art's power of negation lies in its otherness from the society and values it negates. But if it is so set apart, how and what does it communicate to the members of that society? This is reminiscent of the problem of a new sensibility in Marcuse's Berlin lecture 'The End of Utopia' (see Chapter 6), when a new sensibility requires, yet is a product of, the new conditions envisaged in it. Or, as Marcuse puts it, art is 'inevitably part of that which is and only as part of that which is does it speak against that which is'.[46] But within the seemingly contradictory relation of being in (or being formed by) and of denying a specific reality is the possibility of the leap, the historical break. In an imagined world, that is, which Marcuse calls 'fictitious',[47] reason, imagination and a memory of joy are freed from their adaptation to conformity within the dominant society to become autonomous agents of a new mental universe which is the first instantiation of a new reality. '[T]he aesthetic sublimation thus liberates and validates childhood and adult dreams of happiness and sorrow.'[48] Even realist novels transform the conditions of the actual world to make their subject matter compelling in the particularities of language. In this way, language is 'tightened or loosened, forced to yield insights otherwise obscured'.[49]

Marcuse cites two contrasting examples of language in this respect: 'the immediacy of the need for change' in Brecht, and Becket's 'schizophrenically diagnostic language' which does not speak of change.[50] For Marcuse as for Adorno, Beckett conveys the absurdity of the world in the absurdity of text. Perhaps (though Marcuse does not) it is worth citing a short passage from one of Beckett's texts. This is from *The Unnamable*, a text of 132 pages in English, with no paragraph breaks after page 20:

> Air, the air, is there anything to be squeezed from that old chestnut? Close to me it is grey, dimly transparent, and beyond that charmed circle deepens and spreads its fine impenetrable veils. Is it I who cast the faint light that enables me to see what goes on under my nose? There is nothing to be gained, for the moment, by supposing so. There is no night so deep, so I have heard tell, that it may not be pierced in the end, with the help of no other light than that of the blackened sky, or of the earth itself. Nothing nocturnal here. This grey, first murky, then frankly opaque, is luminous none the less. But may not this screen which my eyes probe in vain, and see as denser air, in reality be the enclosure wall, as compact as lead?[51]

There is little hope, or some hope, then the wall like lead. But that is not the point. In a biography, Deirdre Bair notes that Beckett admitted optimism was not his way; and that what comforted him was acceptance of depression, and making it work for him.[52] He wrote at night. When he had written as much as possible he walked the streets of Paris, went to a bar to drink spirits, and slept through the day. Beckett lived in Paris throughout the German occupation. Although an Irish citizen, hence a neutral, he joined the Resistance. Bair notes how 'a spontaneous desire to organise and overthrow sprang up all over France – especially in Paris, where so many highly educated and articulate people congregated'.[53] This is a generalisation, but it echoes Marcuse's idea that a need for liberation can arise spontaneously. There were links among that literary resistant milieu after the war, too: Max-Pol Fouchet, who published Paul Éluard's poem *Liberté* (see Chapter 4), remained editor of the magazine *La Fontaine*, and accepted a text by Beckett, *L'Expulsé* (*The Expelled*).

Adorno notes Beckett's dry humour,[54] and his 'indifference' to the conventions of development in literature (the progression of a plot): 'Consciousness recognizes the limitedness of limitless self-sufficient progress as an illusion of the absolute subject.'[55] Marcuse was more direct, writing to Beckett in 1978 to thank him for a poem he had written for Marcuse's eightieth birthday, apologizing in case his letter 'would just be another fan letter but I can't help it'.[56] He goes on to say that he always sensed 'that in the hopeless suffering of your men and women, the point of no return has been reached. The world has been recognized for what it is.... Hope is beyond our power to express it.'[57]

I make this detour into Beckett's work and its links to critical aesthetic theory first because his texts draw out neatly that paradoxical quality which is embedded in Marcuse's late writing; and, second, because they likewise carry the burden of the catastrophe of the twentieth century. Elsewhere, Marcuse cites Beckett as achieving a communicable 'estrangement' in his prose, in the context of the question as to whether it is possible to write poetry after Auschwitz,[58] and he comments on Beckett in an interview: 'I think it is precisely the total absence of all false hopes that brings out the depth of the necessary change.'[59]

The paradox is that while art's social and aesthetic dimensions are radically separated, they are not mutually disabling. It may be that 'the artist's desperate effort to make art a direct expression of life cannot overcome the separation of art from life'.[60] Still, the separation enables a distancing without which art would be uncritical. 'The work of art can attain political relevance only as autonomous work. The aesthetic form is essential to its social function.'[61] This brings me back to autonomy and to the scope for art to indict society, especially, through beauty and its evocation of sensuality. This happens, for instance, in Charles Baudelaire's collection of poems *Les Fleurs du mal* (written in the 1850s): 'the indictment does not exhaust itself in the recognition of evil; art is also the promise of liberation'.[62] Art offers glimpses of another reality which intersects the existing, miserable reality, consistent with Marcuse's essay on French literature, in which he concludes:

> The incompatibility of the artistic form with the real form of life may be used as a lever for throwing upon the reality the light

which the latter cannot absorb, the light which may eventually dissolve this reality (although such dissolution is no longer the function of art). The untruth of art may become the precondition for the artistic contradiction and negation.[63]

Or, in *The Aesthetic Dimension*: 'Art's unique truth breaks with both everyday and holiday reality.... Art is transcendence into this dimension where its autonomy constitutes itself as autonomy in contradiction.'[64]

From this, Marcuse argues against anti-art because it seems to be a rejection of art's responsibility to show 'the cosmos of hope'.[65] In the 1970s, the mainstream fine art practices in North America were colour field painting and minimalist sculpture. Marcuse's points of reference are to earlier movements such as Surrealism, however, though these continued and had North American as well as European formations. Marcuse made contact, for instance, with a Chicago Surrealist group in 1971,[66] sending them an essay on the contradiction between art and politics in which he asserts that the ending of that contradiction would also be the end of art. The contradiction must, then, remain unresolved as the ground of seeing through one reality to another of a radical otherness. Influenced by Adorno,[67] Marcuse sees closure of the argument as the worst option. Perhaps this reflects his disillusionment with Soviet Marxism,[68] following his work on the Soviet system for the US government in the late 1940s, but it is more a realisation that even in a progression to socialism there will be cause for critique. This is not pessimism but Marcuse's equivalent of Realism as the appropriate mode of cultural production in the conditions after the failure of revolt in 1968. It is not a rejection of the optimism of 1967 but it does amount to a retreat from the claim that an aesthetic society was taking place. Asked by Kellner whether he had changed his position from the 1960s to the 1970s, Marcuse said that he had not, but that counter-cultural art in the 1960s – such as Bob Dylan's songs – was simply better than that of the 1970s.[69]

SUFFERING'S BEAUTIFUL IMAGES

The second problem I want to investigate via Marcuse's writing is the beautification of suffering. This is a question of representation and authenticity and it becomes more pressing after Auschwitz – does any art make the depiction of suffering acceptable, so that the real suffering depicted is no longer unacceptable? This can also be read, however, as part of the wider paradox in which, for instance, 'art is permeated with pessimism' while also offering a liberating laughter.[70] Marcuse uses this idea to differentiate art from mere propaganda, citing Georg Büchner's play *The Death of Danton* as a case of pessimism which permeates even literature which celebrates revolution. Büchner's writing offers a good example of paradox, as John Reddick argues in the introduction to a paperback edition of his work: 'his disjunctive mode with its relentless insistence on fragments and particles is always the expression of a radiant vision of *wholeness*'.[71] This affirms Marcuse's argument that the form of art and literature itself carries meaning – quite apart from its subject matter. If art follows autonomous laws of harmony or beauty, it follows that this harmony or beauty will be communicated to the spectator regardless of whether the work's subject matter is a vase of flowers or the execution of a martyr.

Marcuse begins section IV of *The Aesthetic Dimension* by asserting that the realm of art never deals only with 'the given world of everyday reality' but that neither is it only 'fantasy' or 'illusion', because all it contains relates to reality. Yet at the same time it transposes those elements of reality which it represents, taking them into an aesthetic unreality which is qualitatively other than the given.[72] 'As fictitious world, as illusion (*Schein*), it contains more truth than does everyday reality.'[73] The world is thus turned upside down, the mundane becomes illusory. This is important because, in capitalism – and this remains a Marxist analysis – ordinary life is the domain of false consciousness, not least in the manufactured wants of consumerism. The purpose of art under such conditions is to reveal the contradiction between a claim to happiness (the underlying, dormant or latent, utopian desire) and ways of producing happiness which prolong unhappiness, and to offer a glimpse of another, made-up world in which happiness is real. At this point Marcuse cites Hegel to the effect that reality is deception, and that true reality lies beyond.[74] This is an Idealist position, and Marcuse follows the quotation from Hegel with a reminder that dialectical logic (Marx's dialectical materialism) may justify art's claim to represent happiness, but that 'in the confrontation between art and reality they become mockery'. But Marcuse also insists that, after Auschwitz and the gratuitous killing of Vietnamese civilians by US soldiers at Mai Lai (widely reported in the press at the time), reality can be all too real. This leads to an impasse: 'Art draws away from this reality, because it cannot represent this suffering without subjecting it to aesthetic form, and thereby to the mitigating catharsis, to enjoyment. Art is inexorably infested with this guilt.'[75] And there is no way out of that.

The difficulty of representation which mitigates reality does not, however, release art (or artists and writers) from the responsibility to recall 'again and again' what survives in reality and might lessen the possibility of its repeat performance. Hence 'Authentic art preserves this memory in spite of and against Auschwitz.'[76] This means that art is possible after the Holocaust, after all. But Marcuse's argument, although it is stated in other terms, remains compatible with Adorno's own contention that:

> Even the most extreme consciousness of doom threatens to degenerate into idle chatter. Cultural criticism finds itself faced with the final stage of the dialectic of culture and barbarism. To write poetry after Auschwitz is barbaric. And this corrodes even the knowledge of why it has become impossible to write poetry today.[77]

This does not mean that it is impossible to write poetry after Auschwitz: the poetry of Paul Celan expresses the destruction of meaning occasioned by the Holocaust while retaining a distinct poetic form. Celan writes under an assumed name, however, and his poetry lies at the limit of what can be said, its form itself degenerating almost into chaos. This shows, too, that form (aesthetic reality) accommodates a history of reduction to nothing (or almost so). For Adorno, the difficulty that 'it becomes ever harder for artworks to cohere as a nexus of meaning' leads to a response that 'the very concept of meaning' is rejected, while 'even prior to Auschwitz it was an affirmative lie ... to ascribe any positive meaning to existence'.[78] This becomes miserable, and almost void. In the circumstances, to seek escape is inappropriate. Marcuse writes in an unpublished essay that the negation of form remains literature even as the slaughter goes on.[79] The indictment uttered by annihilated victims is silent, but the preservation of memory is 'the legitimation of literature after Auschwitz'.[80]

But Marcuse strikes out in a direction against Adorno when he says that, facing the totalitarianism of exchange relations in consumer society, the production of 'non-works' by the avant-garde has a playful quality: 'they are exactly what they want to oppose: abstract'.[81] It is instead the ordering of words and style (crafting) of literature which speaks. Style can be negation. Since the reality of Auschwitz is a point of no return:

Literature can remind us of it only through breaks and evasions: in the representation of people and conditions that led to Auschwitz and the desperate struggle against them. Representation remains obligated to the transformational mimesis: the brutal facts are subjugated to form-giving; reportage and documentary become raw material for formation through creative love (the principle of hope) and creative hate (the principle of resistance). The two principles of formation constitute an (agonistic) unity, which is the political potential of art.[82]

I am unsure how much any of this means to readers today for whom the history of the Holocaust (for which the term Auschwitz stands already in a degree of mythicisation) belongs to their grandparents' generation. Efforts to reclaim fragments of that history exist,[83] but from increasing remoteness. A question arises as to why the topic captivates attention. I am reminded, simply, that, as Marcuse writes, 'The revolution is for the sake of life, not death.'[84] And, 'The final outcry is that of rebellion; it affirms in all that horror the powerless power of love.'[85]

Finally, in *The Aesthetic Dimension*, Marcuse notes his departure from the Marxism of class consciousness. Conventional Marxist aesthetics has little use for beauty (which is seen as linked to bourgeois elitism), yet Marcuse reads beauty as inherently revolutionary. Beauty is convulsive. Beauty interrupts, if not suffering itself, then the lies by which capitalism renders suffering on a social scale mundane. Beauty stands in direct relation to Eros, and hence stands against the reality principle which suppresses desire's gratification. The moment of beauty, though ephemeral, is transformative and political: 'The return of the repressed, achieved and preserved in the work of art, may intensify this rebellion.'[86]

Everything remains paradoxical, stretched between opposites; but even the scenes of madness in Büchner's story *Lenz* contain for Marcuse a certain kind of beauty. I end this section of the chapter with an extract from *Lenz* followed by an extract from *The Aesthetic Dimension*, and would ask the reader to compare the former with the passage from Beckett's *The Unnamable* cited above.

Lenz, a writer, has arrived in the village of Wadersbach (Waldbach in the text), where he is given lodging by the pastor Oberlin. After an attack of madness, and a period of calmness, he goes walking:

He wandered through the mountains hither and thither, broad slopes funnelled down into the valleys, few trees, nothing but mighty sweeping lines and, further beyond, the distant smoking plain, in the air a mighty rushing, nowhere any trace of man save here and there an empty hut ... perched forlornly on the mountainside. He grew quiet, perhaps almost in a dream, for him everything melted into a single line, like a wave of water rising and falling between heaven and earth, it was as though he were lying by the edge of an infinite, gently undulating sea. Sometimes he sat down, then he carried on walking, but slowly and in a dream. He sought no path. It was profoundly dark when he came to an inhabited hut.[87]

As in *The Unnamable*, description crosses freely between fiction and reality, through spaces which are credible as landscape but which function simultaneously as depictions of a mental state. Beauty walks beside depression, too. Maurice Benn writes of Büchner that he sees in aesthetics a need for a new art recognising the oppression perpetrated by the social order, and in philosophy the 'untenability of the prevailing religious and idealistic attitudes' of life.[88] He thinks Büchner goes to excess on both sides, but that his pessimism, which is mainly prevalent, is yet only one part of his expression. Benn notes that Büchner withdrew from political activism, but did so because he was no longer by then in a revolutionary situation (which might be compared to the situation of the 1970s). Benn summarises Büchner's position as recognizing the 'profound and eternal tragedy of the world' while suggesting that this could be answered by the idea – which Benn draws from Ludwig Feuerbach – that 'human beings nevertheless have an innate drive towards happiness'.[89] I would see that idea as being glimpsed in some of Büchner's descriptions of landscape, though they tend to be liable to disintegration as well.

Marcuse emphasises art's integrity with sensuousness, and the autonomy of the realm of beauty; he adds:

The medium of sensibility also constitutes the paradoxical relation of art to time – paradoxical because what is experienced through the medium of sensibility is present, while art cannot show the present without showing it as past. What has become form in the work of art has happened: it is recalled, re-presented. The mimesis translates reality into memory. In this remembrance, art has recognized what is and what could be, within and beyond social conditions.[90]

Marx wrote of 'human-sensuous activity' in his fifth 'Thesis on Feuerbach'.[91] If the point of art is to change the world, in a world in which death is reproduced mundanely in the pursuit of profit, revolution is a re-engagement with life; that is, in the imagined society which enacts its content in its antagonistic negotiation of polarities. It may be that that seems fanciful, but for Marcuse, 'art represents the ultimate goal of all revolutions: the freedom and happiness of the individual.'[92]

CODA: TWO RESPONSES

Carol Becker was a graduate student at the University of California at San Diego who worked with Marcuse after his official retirement. She remembers taking long walks with him during which they debated the women's movement, the role of intellectuals in pre-revolutionary conditions, and the role of art in social change.[93] She recalls Marcuse saying that 'It was within the imagination that the desire to envision the idealized state of utopia and push the world to its realization resided',[94] and that images of liberation arise from repression, just as a critical rupture emerges within bourgeois culture to become potentially revolutionary. Becker admits she doubted this, and saw Marcuse as 'trapped in modernism'[95] and unaware of how far the popular imagination was controlled by the mass media. Becker maintains that view, but now accepts that Marcuse's view of liberation is also viable – that making art can be a resistant act, and that images can be subverted when art-work becomes non-alienating labour.

Becker notes Marcuse's justification for aesthetics in *The Aesthetic Dimension*, and points to the indirect ways in which Marcuse sees art as representing social relations. She links his refusal of Freud's reality principle there to his earlier discussion of it in *Eros and Civilization*, to arrive at a definition of art as a location 'where freedom is experienced'.[96] For Becker this is a 'psychic location'[97] intersecting the physical space of the art object. She emphasises the liberating character of art in 'the possibility of fulfilment, which only a transformed society could offer'.[98] The experience of art, in this liberating sense, is not easy; the vision is utopian and, as she says, 'Marcuse is not ingenious about how this transcendence will occur.'[99] Art has a paradoxical relation to reality. It cannot abandon its estrangement. It interrupts, or as Becker puts it, 'It must dislocate the viewer ... by its refusal and inability to become part of the reality principle.... Art should not help people become assimilated in the existent society.'[100]

How was that received in the 1980s and 1990s, after Marcuse's death? Becker notes the vogue for pastiche, and a return to political art (though in a largely uninformed way). She argues that Marcuse's argument for an indirect relation between aesthetics and politics is hard to understand, because the relation between subjective feeling and collective politics is unexplored. Nor, she complains, does the Left appreciate that the message of revolutionary art may be not in its subject matter but in its language. She returns to Marcuse's view of anti-art as reproducing what it fails effectively to critique – offering no glimpse of the utopian whole in place of social fragmentation. Becker draws out two 'necessary conditions' for art from Marcuse's analysis: 'that the artist has a responsibility to help society deal with its hidden conflicts and contradictions', and that 'the work must embody hope in whatever way possible'.[101] I worry that this suggests a return to the instrumentalism which Marcuse refused, or to an avant-garde position of leading society to a new dawn. But I agree with Becker, reading Marcuse, that 'hope lies in the particularly human ability to envision what does not exist'.[102] I agree also with her concluding remark, when she justifies the re-reading of Marcuse today: 'Postmodernism may have changed the discourse and terms of the debate, with the introduction of issues of postcolonialism and the notion of the divided, decentred subject. But it has not helped artists understand how to position themselves.'[103]

For the British art critic Peter Fuller the need was to dismiss what he regarded as the dross of 1970s art, particularly the monochrome canvas. Becker saw the 1970s as the beginning of postmodernism, but Fuller saw its art as a last gasp of modernism under the influence of New York modernist critic Clement Greenberg. In his autobiography, Fuller recalls seeing an exhibition including 'a coloured slab, leant against the wall' which told him that 'art was already set on walking the plank to this blankness'.[104] Looking for art which had not walked the plank, Fuller turned to figuration, especially to images of the mother-and-child as depicting a universal human content. But around 1980, having begun as a Marxist critic, Fuller sought an answer as to why art retained its resonance outside and long after the end of the conditions in which it was produced.

For Fuller, art had to be more than a record of class consciousness. He writes, in an essay on 1970s art, that 'There is nothing mysterious about the individuality to which authentic art bears witness.'[105] Fuller argues that as well as a social setting for art there is a biological one, mediated by environmental (educational) conditions but nonetheless the underlying condition of human beings.[106] The one-dimensionality of the art of the 1970s denies this for Fuller. He cites Marcuse's claim that art evokes a universal humanity which is set apart from class origins. Reading *The Aesthetic Dimension* soon after its publication in English was a transformative experience for Fuller, making good, as it were, the deficit he found in Marxist aesthetics.[107] Fuller writes in 'The Journey: A Personal Memoir' that he could still remember the excitement with which he read Marcuse's book.[108] I can see why. Fuller's argument for a biological basis for aesthetics is not the same as Marcuse's argument for new biological needs, but it is not so far away. Fuller seeks deep meaning in art – a critique of the human condition but also a reaffirmation of a kind of wholeness – which roughly equates with Marcuse's concern for sensuousness and a unity transcending a fragmented reality (though for Marcuse the latter is also there). Clearly, this is a modernist position reliant on art's autonomy, which is in turn reliant on an independent language of form which rejects the reproduction of ordinary visual perception, asserted in Western art from the 1880s onwards. This position may also subsume a privileging of the artist and writer as members of an intelligentsia, in practice seeking a social contract after the decline of court and church patronage from the late eighteenth century onwards. The storm and anxiety which Büchner articulates is a response to an introjected natural reality (using bleak landscapes and vile weather, or vast chasms, as invoking states of psyche), but it is a reaction also to the trials of having to make a precarious living by writing. Precarity has become a new frame of reference today – as the revolution through the institutions continues – and will remain 'the concern of generations, while "the final crisis of capitalism" may take all but a century'.[109]

8
Legacies and Practices

Marcuse lectured in Frankfurt in May 1979. Setting out '25 Theses on Technology and Society', he re-stated the idea that freedom from consumerism requires a radical transformation of the consciousness and depth-psychology of individuals.[1] Such a transformation would entail, too, the emergence of a new sensibility in protest at the total repression of Eros. This would be a protest 'from all classes of society' arising from 'a deep, visceral, and intellectual inability to comply' with a 'socially organized death-instinct'.[2] This echoes ideas from both *An Essay on Liberation*[3] and *Eros and Civilization*,[4] revising Marxism towards a realisation that the working class were no longer the motivating force for revolution, and that the process would in any case be long, educational and cultural, not a sudden mass uprising on the nineteenth-century model. Art becomes an element in that long revolution in a way it could not credibly have been in the model of mass revolt.

Near the end of *The Aesthetic Dimension*, Marcuse writes that art preserves memories of failed goals but that it also preserves the hope for joy: 'art represents the ultimate goal of all revolutions: the freedom and happiness of the individual'.[5] He died on 29 July 1979 in Starnberg, Germany, where he had been a guest of Jürgen Habermas, then the Director of the Max Planck Institute. While in Starnberg, Marcuse met the French philosopher Jean Marabini, to whom he confided that he would like to go to Italy but was worried he might die in Venice like the character in Thomas Mann's novel.[6] He never made the visit, but had hoped to investigate the work of Italian radicals such as Antonio Negri, and the violent activism of the red brigades. In the summer of 1979 he was also involved in a campaign in East Germany to free Rudolf Bahro, who had been imprisoned as a result of his critique of really existing socialism (the campaign was successful – Bahro was released a few days after Marcuse's death).[7] Bahro occupies an equivalent position to Marcuse, both Marxist revisionists, except that Bahro worked within a socialist state.[8] Ten years later, in November 1989, East Germans took down the Wall, and crossed in large numbers at the checkpoints to be welcomed with 100 marks to spend in the affluent society.[9] In 1990, the Polish-Canadian artist Krzysztof Wodiczko projected an image of an Eastern-bloc shopper in a striped shirt, his shopping trolley loaded with electrical goods (a common sight, briefly), onto Nikolai Tomsky's *Lenin Monument* (a colossal statue in red granite). Shortly after, the monument was demolished; some of its stones were subsequently placed on the grave of Rosa Luxemburg.[10] As Marcuse said, art preserves the memory of failed goals. The impact of the projection, however, may have been to emphasise the triumph of false consciousness in 1989, a mass revolt in the opposite direction to that predicted in the revolutionary trajectory of scientific Marxism. As to the longer-term consequences of those events, it is too soon to judge.

SINCE

Looking back on Marcuse's aesthetic theory, the question as to what role art plays in the social transformation which is yet to come, apart from its preservation of a latent hope, remains unanswered. It was not Marcuse's style to prescribe. In any case, within his theory is the idea that a new sensibility will arise spontaneously, which is itself the outcome of hope's preservation, inflamed by the contradictions of the existing society.

In the 1970s, Marcuse saw art as the radical other to, or negation of, the terrible reality of a totally administered world. Art refuses compliance, negating the existing society. Art intervenes in the categories by which the world is understood, undermining the credibility of the notion, peddled by those in power, that there is no alternative to the way things are (just as public monuments in stone and bronze previously lent the weight of history to insecure regimes). Art interrupts and is potentially convulsive. This is a Romantic idea, but also millenarian, echoing 'the libertarian sects of the Middle Ages' and the ideas of Charles Fourier as well as early Marx.[11] But is it still relevant today? Perhaps the realities of climate change, mass migration and wars over water in the mid to late twenty-first century will provoke a millenarian upheaval. By then, art may be a redundant category; indeed it has already changed since the negating culture on which Marcuse and Adorno wrote in the 1960s and 1970s. Examples of that last phase of modernism might be Samuel Beckett's near-nihilist drama, or the empty, sometimes grey and sometimes black, paintings of the 1970s. A more engaged art is represented by Adrian Mitchell's poems. Now, the borders between art, architecture, fashion, performance, text, media and publicity are no longer policed, while critical frameworks in feminism and post-colonialism have replaced critical theory in much academic work (but not all, as the turn to a 'post-Marxism' testifies). New social movements, too, have changed the way revolt is conceptualised, using de-centralised tactics, fusing local, pluralist knowledges and the worldwide web.

In my view, however, Marcuse's critique of totalitarianism in technology and consumerism, along with Adorno's of the culture industry, nonetheless remain pertinent.[12] Nina Power gestures towards Marcuse with the title of her recent book *One-Dimensional Woman*, writing that 'What looks like emancipation is nothing but a tightening of the shackles',[13] while 'feminism offers you the latest deals in lifestyle improvement', in sex and in business.[14] All this highlights the difficulty that arises when departures from consumer culture are regularly subsumed within the mainstream. Art is no exception. In 1995, New York artist Martha Rosler complained that

> The anti-institutional revolt was unsuccessful, and the art world has now completed something of a paradigm shift. The mass culture machine and its engines have long redefined the other structures of cultural meaning, so that patterns of behaviour and estimations of worth in the art world are more and more similar to those in the entertainment industry.[15]

Yet power leaks. Some independent curators do manage to subvert art's institutions from within, though this may not address the gap between audiences and museums.[16] But if much contemporary art is subsumed by the market, some does at least grapple with its state of confinement in an emerging cultural dissidence in the West. This is an issue I take up below via the work of Freee Art Collective, as one of four cases I will examine as an after-text to my reconsideration of Marcuse's aesthetics, ranging from the 1930s through the 1960s to the 1990s and today. The four cases are Pablo Picasso's mural-scale painting *Guernica*; Joseph Beuys's efforts to create an open studio as a model of direct democracy; the *Monument Against Fascism* by Jochen Gerz and Esther Shalev Gerz, in Hamburg; and *Protest Drives History*, a photographic-performative work by Freee Art Collective (Andy Hewitt, Mel Jordan and Dave Beech). I begin by reviewing certain strands in Marcuse's aesthetics from the preceding seven chapters, as a context for my critique of these four cases.

ART-NEGATION

Vincent Geoghegan describes Marcuse's theory as involving 'a conception of the individual as a free creative subject'.[17] Geoghegan is refering to Marcuse's social theory, but I would argue that it is an appropriate summary of his aesthetic theory, too. The difficulty, as Peter Bürger puts it, is that bourgeois art 'projects the image of a better order and ... protests against the bad order that prevails' but ensures that the protest is contained in 'an ideal sphere'.[18] While that describes the affirmative culture of bourgeois society which Marcuse examines in his 1937 essay, it could also denote the assimilated radicalism of cool culture more recently. In the late 1960s the student movement and the counter-culture seemed to break with such histories, fusing cultural and political action in new ways of living with others. It was at this point that Marcuse introduced the idea of a society as a work of art – of an aesthetic, ludic and libidinal society. But for this to emerge at a social rather than individual scale requires a new sensibility, which Marcuse argues is grounded in new biological needs produced in the contradictory conditions of advanced capitalism. After 1968, Marcuse reaffirms art's autonomy: the freedom of the laws of form is the space of art's criticality in a longer revolution. Obliquely, that criticality interrupts the social order, as a reminder that alternatives are always possible. Informing his later theory, the idea that a literature of intimacy may be a site of freedom in the conditions of totalitarianism (in his 1945 essay on French literature) appears to me to retain interest, especially in light of that personalisation of politics and politicisation of personal life which is a lasting legacy of the 1960s. The *promesse du bonheur* looks towards a life of ease, which is glimpsed in the counter-culture. Beauty as non-repressive order is a protest against the prevailing social order; to put it simply, beauty is itself a protest.

But there is a tension between a spontaneity implied in a glimpse of bliss and art as the everyday profession of those who work in its institutions. There may be no exit from this other than to see art as a paradoxical field. Art is institutionally validated as art, while it seeks to smash institutional structures which include those which validate art. But paradox is a recurrent theme in Marcuse's work. In the artist novel, the artist's life-journey is governed by the opposing forces of an inner freedom which separates the artist from the bourgeoisie, and a conformity requiring negotiation of a place in (or linked to) bourgeois society. Michael Löwy and Robert Sayre read the artist-hero of such literature as protesting against the 'mechanization of economic and cultural life' and the alienation of the spiritual in modern society.[19] The German word *geistig* has a range of meanings, however, from ghostly to intellectual. The term may denote the artist's state of psyche, or membership of an intelligentsia, rather than a yearning for religiosity. These appear to be the polarities between which a modern artist operates, making work which is radical in content while seeking recognition from art's critical apparatus (which tends to conservatism in various ways).

Marcuse ascribes to art the function of interruption. He sees this in Surrealism, and I read it in art practices today, inside and outside the gallery. Surrealism had no political programme, and the French Surrealists had an ambivalent attitude to the Communist Party. Indeed, if art has an interruptive force it is this which the inherited agencies for change, such as the Party, cannot understand because it threatens their position as well as that of the elite in power. The effect of art's interruptions is rhizomatic, or virus-like, defying organisation – it is contagious.[20] Nevertheless, despite widespread media coverage, art is limited in the publics to whom it speaks, maintaining a divide between audiences and producers which ensures the privileged voice of the artist or writer (on the model of an avant-garde). Still, the awkward edge between activist art and political activism is interesting,[21] especially if everyone might be an artist – as Beuys proposes – directly re-visioning the world. Marcuse argues that direct action is required if 'the democratic system of corporate capitalism' renders the extant liberal civic ordering 'as a counter-revolutionary force'.[22] Art has a parallel responsibility: 'Reality has to be discovered and projected. The senses must learn not to see things any more in the medium of that law and order which has formed them.'[23] But how does art do that?

GUERNICA

In 1937, German aeroplanes bombed the Basque city of Guernica. Picasso had been invited to exhibit in the Spanish Republic's pavilion at the Paris World Exposition, and completed *Guernica* in a month – a short time for a mural-scale painting (349 x 777 cm).[24] After touring Europe the painting went on long-term loan to the Museum of Modern Art (MoMA) in New York because Picasso refused to let it go to fascist Spain. After the death of General Franco (and Picasso himself), it did return and is now exhibited in the Prado, Madrid, as a national treasure. I recall seeing it shortly after its transfer to Spain, under armed guard in a special pavilion. *Guernica* has become a monument against fascist terror. But in 1945, Marcuse referred to it in these terms: 'All indictments are easily absorbed by the system which they indict ... *Guernica* is a cherished museum piece.'[25] Does this erase its message, or was the message always compromised? Marcuse writes:

> The picture itself seems rather to negate the political content: there is a bull, a slaughtered horse, a dead child, a crying mother – but the interpretation of these objects as symbols of fascism is not in the picture. Darkness, terror and utter destruction are brought to life by grace of the artistic creation and in the artistic form; they are therefore incomparable to the fascist reality. (They appear in the picture as the individualization of universal forces and as such they transcend the fascist reality into a 'supra-historical' order. They have a reality of their own: the artistic reality. That is perhaps the reason why Picasso refuses to call them 'symbols.' They are 'signs,' but signs for a bull, a child, a horse, etc.)[26]

I quote the passage at length because it can be read in several ways. First, the images depict suffering, but are signs within an artistic language; second, they universalise the particular and locate it beyond present reality; third, the painting's status in the canon of modern art follows this distancing.

I leave aside the question of art's depiction of suffering (which the painting obviously raises), because I think that the question has no answer, and look instead at the work's institutional status. This is connected to its location in a museum, and equally to its location in modern art's visual language. *Guernica* is certainly an iconic image of fascist terror, but it is also framed by an idea of modern art which may be recognised first. If so, the painting communicates its generalised situation within a field, and happens to depict one of the recurrent themes for which that field – mid-century modernism – is known. After that, perhaps, it reminds the spectator of the violent deaths of human and non-human occupants of a Basque city in 1937. A documentary film may operate differently, but would not be immune from representing its genre.

Working quickly to get the painting done in time, Picasso used images from previous works, in the style of those works. Although he had begun to move to a neo-classical style in the 1930s, the fragmentation of the figure in *Guernica* echoes Cubism in the 1910s (and several paintings of his lovers in the 1920s and 1930s). Picasso's early Cubist work was limited in colour, too, though as a means to concentrate on form; later collages and paintings introduce strong colour. In *Guernica* there is only grey, a representation of horror without amelioration. The images are re-combined here but not, as they were in Cubism, as the solution to the representation of three (or four) dimensions in two, but as damage. Yet damaged humanity is brought to the gaze of the spectator 'through the grace of the artistic creation', which sets the picture apart from the world as it represents terror. Marcuse wrote of Paul Éluard's poetry: 'In the night of the fascist terror appear the images of tenderness ... the language of love emerges as the instrument of estrangement; its artificial, unnatural ... character is to produce the shock.'[27] Perhaps the problem is that *Guernica* depicts the signs of woman, child, horse and bull, but not the tenderness of humans and animals as what is being defiled. Art historian Paul Wood writes, too, of an ambiguous and 'relatively private symbolism' drawn from Picasso's pictures of bullfights and classical subject matter at the time.[28] The attempt to make a public statement is denoted by the work's scale, and by its site at a world exhibition, but is in tension with a personal narrative which transmuted into a monumental form, presented as a personalised monument.

Such a reading fits with Carol Duncan's reading of another of Picasso's iconic works, *Les Demoiselles d'Avignon*, as depicting women in a 'desecrated icon already slashed and torn to bits',[29] exhibiting the dualism of the female deity and the whore, the decadent and the savage, in 'one horrible painting' which Picasso 'dredged up from his psyche'.[30] Yet Picasso also saw himself as an avant-gardist, reportedly commissioning a pair of trousers with the same green stripes as worn by Gustave Courbet in his large painting *The Studio* (1855). Linda Nochlin writes that Picasso 'symbolically assumes' Courbet's role, literally stepping 'into the pants of an overtly phallic master-painter'.[31] This enhances the case for *Guernica* as the outcome of an interiorised negotiation of meaning: the modern artist's psychic travelogue. Perhaps that is the characteristic of modern art as constructed by curating decisions at MoMA: the artist as the heroic explorer of the dark edges of anxiety (later epitomised in Abstract Expressionism). Such an exploration, despite the analogy to exotic travel, may contain a utopian or a libertarian memory. But the role of the museum is then to license it.

The museum's function in the ordering of society was inherent in the establishment of art museums for public access, such as the Tate Gallery at Millbank, opened in 1897. Making high culture available to the lower classes was a philanthropic gesture, but it was also a means to prevent revolt.[32] By mixing with the educated middle classes, that is, artisans and members of the working class might affect the same manners and conformities as their social superiors. MoMA extends the function in a modernist version; its galleries mimic the rooms in which collectors enjoy private access to art, but they do this for a democratised public while drawing on the design and marketing techniques of retailing.[33] Duncan writes that museum directors are constrained by prevailing cultural constructs, while 'art museums are a species of ritual space'.[34] In such spaces, art is contemplated silently, and canons are constructed to order cultural history in certain ways. *Guernica* was co-opted into the narrative of modern art, and its frequent reproduction as a symbol of this lessens the impact of its content. It functions as a set of signs, and the system of signs within which it functions operates as another form of affirmative culture. This is not, paradoxically, to say that the image has no impact. How it is received depends, after all, on how the spectator reads it.

BEUYS AND DIRECT DEMOCRACY

Art historian Rosalind Krauss writes that Beuys' *Fat Chair* (1964) uses felt, fat, wax and objects 'gathered together as so much detritus' in 'performative rituals'.[35] In the title, Beuys uses a pun (in German, but it works in English too) on the word *Stuhl* (chair) as shit (stool). Krauss cites Beuys saying that the chair 'represents a kind of human anatomy, the area of digestive and excretive warmth processes'.[36] Beuys walks huddled with a felt-wrapped walking stick, wrapped in a felt blanket. There is a coyote in the room. It is the beginning of art as process and concept; it is also haunted by the dehumanising experiences of the war, and a surge towards humanism in post-war art which it refutes and extends. But I speculate (and am no expert on Beuys – I never met him).

Krauss argues that Beuys acts the parts of shaman, wandering Jew, scapegoat, and so forth – these being excluded others. In another work, *Palazzo Regale* of 1985, Beuys laid out the life-goods of a beggar and a king, juxtaposed in glass sarcophagi as if they were memorial goods for the life hereafter. According to Krauss, Beuys acts the bohemian who lives 'where love redeems the lost and dying, and where the only true nobility is that of talent'.[37] She adds that the modern artist was thought of as the 'harbinger of a form of life not territorialized' by the social divisions of industrialization, and that this is 'the incarnation of ... non-alienated labour'. For Krauss,

Beuys, 'eager to promote his own aestheticized version of a post-capitalist Utopia', transposed 'the character of the bohemian into that of the proletarian' about to 'rise from the ashes of capitalism as the controller of his [sic] own labour power, producing his own being as value.'[38] I think the key point here is that Krauss reads Beuys as enacting his dream of a post-capitalist world. From this, she takes Beuys' well-known saying that everyone is an artist to denote a wish to fuse the proletariat and the avant-garde. I am unsure, however, whether she reads Beuys correctly when she says that 'the nurse at her station, the digger in the ditch'[39] epitomise this fusion. But leaving that aside, Krauss rightly draws attention to the shamanistic aspect of Beuys' performances, and to the 'shamanistic figure ... who reveals the form always already locked within the chaos of matter'.[40]

Like Krauss, I have doubts about the appropriation of elements from other cultures, such as shamanism, in Western cultural production. It could be said that Beuys' claim that everyone is an artist is contradicted by his retention of the role of privileged interpreter, or facilitator of spells. But if everyone really is an artist, this means that everyone has a creative imagination, and can hence imagine new social as well as aesthetic formations. That might be really existing socialism. Beuys' idea is not far from Marcuse's own idea of a new sensibility, in which the world is apprehended in a new way. As in a society as a work of art, this means that, if realised, the specialist category of art would become redundant. Beuys also promoted direct democracy as an alternative to the representational democracy of conventional democratic political institutions. There is a link to Marcuse's writing, though coincidental. Marcuse writes, for instance, in *The Aesthetic Dimension*, that 'Direct democracy, the subjection of all delegation of authority to effective control "from below", is an essential demand of Leftist strategy.'[41] But he adds that the demand is necessarily ambivalent, and that effective student participation in running a university 'presupposes that the majority of the student body is more progressive than the faculty and the administration'.[42] There is a risk of the contrary (and might be far more so today). Nonetheless, the idea of a direct, non-representational political system, with its inherent difficulties of scale and the time it takes to make consensus decisions, remains a preoccupation of intentional communities today.

Beuys' use of the gallery as a democratic site remains of interest, too. In 1974, the artist Allan Kaprow cited Beuys' 100-day sit-in at Documenta V in 1972: 'He was available for anyone to discuss with him his current interests in political change and the role the arts might have in this change.'[43] Beuys is, however, the subject of the spectacle; his work remains art in order to be autonomous, implying that he remains *the* not *an* artist. In the period of the Cold War, again, autonomy from the state had a specific meaning. Asked by a visitor to the Office for Direct Democracy at Kassel, in Documenta V, Beuys argued as much against top-down decisions in the Soviet Union as in the West.[44] This seems to be an attempt to step outside ideological history. As Benjamin Buchloch writes:

> The private and public mythology of Joseph Beuys ... could only be developed and maintained on the ahistoricity of aesthetic production and consumption in post-war Europe. The substantially retarded comprehension of European Dada and Russian Constructivism ... determined both European and American art up until the late 1950s and served for both producers and recipients as a basis for mythifying subsequent aesthetic work. Once put into their proper historic context, these works would lose their mystery and seemingly metaphysical origin.[45]

In contrast, the art critic Caroline Tisdall views Beuys' relation to materials as 'a form of corrective' to industrialised society's lack of any 'intense physical and psychological contact with the material world'.[46]

Beuys saw his shamanistic pose as 'transformation through concrete processes of life, nature and history'.[47] Without seeking a return to archaic culture, he saw the shaman's 'nature' as therapeutic.[48] In *The Reenchantment of Art*, Suzi Gablik echoes the critique of modern life as devoid of real connectivity,[49] asserting that shamanistic culture is an antidote to the instrumentalism which produces environmental destruction. This is one reading of modern art. In keeping with Buchloch's remarks (above), it is linked to the artist's social contract as hero of psychic journeys, stand-in for humanity in flirting with psychosis.[50] But the representation of psychosis is already mediated by the codes of art when it reaches a public; it remains art not mental life even if it evokes states of psyche – a zone in which there are no real stand-ins. It is subsumed in a grandiose narrative of modernism by its visual codes and institutional validation, just as political reactions are subsumed in the negotiations of elected representatives. Direct democracy, then, raises the issue of alternatives to representation in art, which leads, yet again, to the redundancy of art as a category.

In fact, modernism had casualties for whom art was not therapeutic: Jackson Pollock, Arshile Gorky and Mark Rothko all committed suicide; Willem de Kooning was one of many modern artists with a drink problem. More importantly, at the conceptual level, therapy as represented by Beuys (not as in psychoanalysis) is bound to the role of the shaman. Such an appeal to magic is an anti-Enlightenment pose, against which critical theory argues that reason delivers us from rule by mysterious Fate. If reason is utilised to control nature and other humans (instrumentalism), it can be revised from within.[51] When Beuys says social sculpture is 'how we mould and shape the world in which we live' in which 'everyone [is] an artist',[52] I think of Marcuse's idea of a society as a work of art. Yet an abiding image of Beuys is as interpreter of the world. Donald Kuspit writes of Beuys' art as a convalescent fantasy in which the disturbed patient 'always threatens to tumble down again, yet always keeps on climbing'.[53]

AGAINST FASCISM

In 'Society as a Work of Art', Marcuse elaborates a post-vangardist position:

> Great art has never had any problem coexisting with the horrors of reality. Just think of contradictions such as ... the Parthenon and a society based on slavery; ... Racine and the mass famines of his time .... In its beautiful form art has also produced its transcendent content. Here in the beautiful form lies the critical element of aesthetic reconciliation, the image of the powers to be liberated and pacified. This ... which is antagonistically opposed to reality, is neutralized and occupied by the repressive society itself.[54]

Or a society which is a work of art is a society whose members live in the moment (in a Lefebvrian sense – see Chapter 6). But the horrors of reality are not always self-evident, being often camouflaged or allowed to fade. Like the statues of forgotten kings and military men which provide a convenient site for birds to sit in public parks, events recede in public memory. A possible function for art, then, is to redress the loss of memory, and with it an ideological deficit. For example, Christoph Schäfer's *Diffusing Red: Anti-Monument for the Red Ruhr Army* (2010) temporarily re-coded a water tower in Essen as a historical-ideological site. Far-right groups were besieged there in 1920, after the Left's opposition to the invasion of the Ruhr by the Freikorps. Surrounded by workers' groups, the Rightists gave up; but some threw hand grenades into the crowd as a last-ditch gesture. In the resulting skirmish 11 occupants of the tower and an unknown number of workers were killed. But a description of the events written 50 years later cited the 'dozens of brave policemen' who were 'bestially slaughtered by the reds'.[55] In March 1934, Hermann Goering took part in a remembrance service for the Freikorps dead. Schäfer's aim was to reassert the real history of the event – the workers' refusal of fascism – by flying red flags from the tower (a large building with a public clock, replacing the original structure). In the 1980s the municipality placed explanatory boards by the tower, classifying it as a memorial. But for Schäfer, the boards do not break the dominance of a right-wing memorial landscape: 'The memory of the victims on the side of the workers is nearly invisible.'[56] Red flags counter the 'organised amnesia'.[57] As Wodiczko says of his projections onto public monuments, once seen, the memory lingers and the monument is not perceived in the same way.

The function of re-making history can be read as an effort to subvert the institutional neutralisation of past events, and perhaps can do this from within by using the form of the public monument – like the water tower in Essen – as a site of contested meaning. In contesting history, the ownership of history (and by implication the present image of society) is brought into question, or interrupted. And the point of departure for any history is contingent, as Paolo Bianchi writes: 'Images of the world can only be pieced together from the fragments of broken mirrors: there is no clear shape.'[58] Bianchi adds that, now, strategies for survival, or for making meaning, are no longer 'defined as the counter-images of a power ... but are based upon one's own ... experiences of the world'.[59] But art is as likely to be appropriated as it is to create an agonistic public sphere: 'Our world is drowning in consumerism, lunacy and art.'[60] Bianchi nonetheless cites the work of Jochen Gerz as evidence that art's illusions can be broken in public authoring of art. In 1969, for instance, Gerz asked 600 workers at the chemical company Hoffman-La-Roche questions such as 'Do you personally know a (a) painter (b) pop-singer (c) actor (d) writer' and so on, exhibiting the completed questionnaires in the Basel Kunsthalle.[61] In 1988, he posed another public question in a photo-text work, *Quod a me expectur?* (what is expected of me [as an artist]?). For Bianchi this asks whether the artist is a super-subject 'who always has an answer to everything'[62] – a statement which can be set beside the discussion of Beuys above. But the point is that there is no universal answer, nor any universal narrative or history; and Gerz was not a spectacular presence in the event.

I want to take this further by looking at a work in which Gerz collaborated with his partner (as she became) Esther Shalev, in Harburg, a suburb of Hamburg, between 1986 and 1993: *Mahnmal gegen Faschismus* (Monument against Fascism). It is a 12-metre-high steel column surfaced in lead, over an underground shaft of 14 metres. The shaft is built into a small brick tower with a platform and railings at the top. The site is in a shopping centre, consisting of mainly small shops, but near a mall. The work was commissioned by the municipality in 1983 after a long process of internal discussion, as a monument against fascism; that is, not as a memorial to the victims of fascism but as a protest against fascism. A design competition was held in 1984. The project was contracted in June 1985. The column was erected, with two steel pens attached which citizens and visitors were invited to use to endorse the monument. As a section was filled, the column was lowered into the shaft beneath to release further space for endorsement. The success of the work would lie in covering its whole surface with signatures, like a petition against fascism. It was completely sunk into the shaft on 10 November 1993, seven years and one month after its dedication. A small photo-text display at the site – at the base of the tower, which has a window onto the shaft, and in identical form on the viewing platform – now shows eight stages of the monument, with texts in German, Turkish, English, French, Hebrew, Russian and Arabic. While in progress, an accompanying text stated:

> Monuments against fascism ... almost always show no daring or energy or artistic meaning; and ... arouse no sense of identification among the broader public.... The inconceivability of the social developments of the twentieth century (National Socialism, and so forth) stands in crass contrast to the memorials that refer to them...

> As opposed to the notion of ... permanence ... the idea of a different function ...: permanence is 'sacrificed'. The 'sacrifice' of permanence is a social and religious act. The population of Harburg ... cause the monument to disappear. The visible becomes invisible, the memorial turns into memory.[63]

The work was described as a buried monument for a buried history, a history that was too painful for the post-war generation who lived through it to recall openly, for two reasons: first, the destruction of cities such as Hamburg and Dresden by bombing, with massive loss of civilian life;[64] and, second, the persistence of that history as an invisible current after 1945. The eco-artist Hermann Prigann told me that, as a child after the war growing up in Gelsenkirchen in the Ruhr (also heavily bombed), he came down from his room one night to see his parents and some of their friends dressed in Nazi uniforms, remembering the (good) old days. He crept back unseen.[65]

Returning to the monument in Harburg, both buried and present-day histories became visible on the column's lead surfaces. The project did not go according to plan. Gerz stated that 'We will one day reach a point where anti-Fascist memorials will no longer be necessary, when vigilance will be kept alive by the invisible pictures of remembrance.'[66] James Young claims that Gerz and Shalev 'hoped for row upon row of neatly inscribed names, a visual echo of the war memorials of another age'.[67] What they got was graffiti, from lovers' hearts and initials to tags and racist hate. Young continues:

> Execution did not follow design ... after a couple of months: an illegible scribble of names scratched over names, all covered in a spaghetti scrawl ... People had come at night to scrape over all the names, even to pry the lead plating off its base. There were hearts ..., Stars of David, and funny faces daubed in paint and marker pen. Inevitably, swastikas began to appear. How better to remember what happened than by the Nazi's own sign?

When I saw the site of the monument in 2010, a star of David and the word Judas (the betrayer, not the German *Juden*) was written in black marker pen on the plaque on the viewing platform (see Figure 1). The local newspaper reported: 'This filth brings us closer to the truth than would any list of well-meaning signatures.'[68] But to what truth does it bring people closer? A continuing prejudice aimed at Turkish guest workers? A resurgent far-Right? Street-level tagging and low-level vandalism? Teenagers asked if it was art when they graffitied the monument, and art is probably not in a position to deny them that when anything an artist does is art. Maybe everyone is an artist, but not in the way intended (itself a contradiction).

The *Mahnmal gegen Faschismus* is an anti-monument in its refusal of the conventions of commemoration and its adoption of a

Figure 1   Esther Shalev Gerz and Jochen Gerz, 'Monument Against Fascism' (1986–1993), Harburg, Hamburg (photo M. Miles)

temporary form. That form, however, proved antagonistic, drawing out love (the lovers' hearts and names) and hate (swastikas). It lent temporary visibility to a reality of Harburg as a seemingly respectable suburb, in a city the centre of which was destroyed in 1943. A shop at the railway station sells postcards of pre-war views of the city, but it is only for the generation born after around 1960 that the city's previous history can be discussed – as said, the trauma of the destruction is beyond communication. The fire storm lasted for three hours. Glass in windows melted. Smoke rose 8,000 feet. As W.G. Sebald notes: 'When day broke, the summer dawn could not penetrate the leaden gloom above the city.'[69] The refugees took to the roads in any direction. The literature on the event is sparse, and Sebald explains this as 'the tacit imposition of a taboo'.[70]

There is no *Guernica* for Hamburg. The site of the monument is quiet, leaf-strewn and outside the destroyed centre. Graffiti continues to appear on the plaque, after the interment of the column, suggesting not so much the communicative public sphere imagined by Jürgen Habermas,[71] as a space of conflicting claims. Awkwardly and inarticulately, this graffiti which continues states social life as it is.

PROTEST DRIVES HISTORY

Finally, I look at a project by Freee Art Collective (Andy Hewitt, Mel Jordan and Dave Beech). *Protest Drives History* is a billboard-scale work. The title is the slogan inscribed on a large bright red banner which the artists hold on view against the dark grey backdrop of Bayston Hill quarry, Shropshire (one of the largest quarries in England, a vast scar on the landscape). In front of them the waters of a hole in the ground take on a slightly artificial blue-green colour (see Figure 2). Holding the banner in this bleak site, the artists are alone in the wind, defiant. But it is posed as a representation of defiance, a posed photograph for public viewing elsewhere, in the art gallery – no public will see it in the quarry. The work is performative in that it begins with this act, a monument refusing the bleakness of history, but then inserted into art's habituial realm, the gallery. But it is not cool culture. If the market triumphs, turning almost everything in sight into profit, the artists refuse complicity when they state that protest – not profit – drives history. I read this speculatively as the free imagining of a world as it could be rather than that to which there is no alternative. The work also obliquely references the sublime in the English landscape tradition: the dark walls of the quarry stand metaphorically for the catastrophe of late modernity.

But I am being Romantic; the artists made the work for an exhibition at the Institute of Contemporary Arts (ICA), London, where it was exhibited in the bar from June 2008 to January

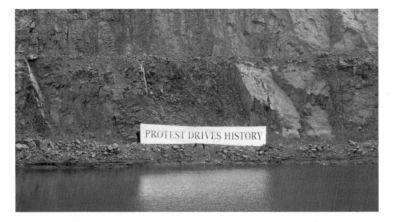

Figure 2   Freee Art Collective, 'Protest Drives History' (2009), Institute of Contemporary Arts, London (photo courtesy Freee Art Collective)

2009. Another billboard was displayed on a commercial billboard site in Hassard Street, off Hackney Road in east London, at the same time. Hackney is a hot-spot for art and regeneration, in its de-industrialised chic – another iconic space of the merging of post-modern art and the sign systems of capital. The artists write:

> We chose to occupy the main wall of the most public part of the building, the bar. Here, unlike in the galleries, we would expect a large number of passers-by ... It functions as background ... in the manner of billboards and advertising rather than painting.... we ask questions about the public for the work and cause friction and division within the existing society.[72]

Causing friction is, again, not the harmonious development of a public sphere. But it accords with Leonie Sandercock's argument that 'An agonistic politics entails broad social participation in the never completed process of making meanings and creating values.'[73] Sandercock adds that there is no mainstream in this political formation, and that a quest for common ground should not erase the right to difference. Nor should it restrict anyone's right to the city – to occupy its spaces and to participate in its affairs.

This is a radically democratic vision, based in the realities of migration and a parallel contingency of values. That contingency now informs art, as the separation of art and life is deconstructed by departures from the gallery and by redefinition of the museum from within. Nikos Papastergiadis writes: 'the most radical gestures in contemporary art are no longer positioned outside the dominant institutions of art or on the moral high ground from which the artist can pour scorn on the foibles of everyday life'.[74] Freee operate in billboard sites and in galleries, exhibiting billboard-scale posters in galleries and art fairs to problematise the definition and meaning of both kinds of space. Their works tend to be provocatively aesthetic – made with the care of choice in colour and form characteristic of art, yet using that to communicate refusal to agree with current requirements of art as a post-modern equivalent of affirmative culture. Asked whether they have worked in culturally led urban regeneration projects, Freee reply: 'They wouldn't want to touch us because our slogans are too critical of their ideology.'[75]

Freee have worked collaboratively, democratising ownership of the project as well as its realisation. For example, in a project called *Futurology* at the New Art Gallery in Walsall, near Birmingham, in 2004, Hewitt and Jordan (before linking with Beech to form

Freee, though already working with him on this project) shared the authorship of the project with several other artists, some of whom in turn shared it with school students. The funding for the project came from a government programme to bring art into schools, in this case in the Black Country, an area of de-industrialisation. Such projects tend to be constrained by the agendas set by funding bodies, but Hewitt and Jordan saw the project as an opportunity to liberate resources to lend some visibility to the inadequacy of the prescribed agenda. They write:

> Like everyone else, artists are part of the economic system of contemporary cultural production. We are interested in understanding these conditions so that as agents in culture, we reflect on how we might act and where we might intervene. Our primary interest in developing the *Futurology* project was to explore the function given to art within what has become known as culture-led regeneration.[76]

Their stance is that they refuse the prevailing agenda's implicit values, and make this known in public billboards and art-spaces. Their constituency, however, seems to me primarily the art world, including inhabitants of the political/aesthetic terrains which determine that world's constitution. Their role within the process of determination is to be irritants. In another poster-scale work, on an attractive mid-blue ground, white text states that the concept of public space, 'beloved of lonely myopic law-abiding right-on gushing morons', assumes the public as 'a mass of bodies'. The concept of the public realm is 'preferred by shifty piss-guzzling half-witted busy-body nerve-wracked self-serving technocrats'. While the concept of a public sphere, in the tradition of critical theory, 'imagines the public producing itself through politicized acts of cultural exchange'.[77] This work was shown at the International Project Space, Bournville in 2007. On another wall the artists were depicted, also billboard-scale, holding a wreath of plastic yellow flowers spelling out the text Protest Is Beautiful.

This work is in two forms – one against a blue-painted interior background, the other outdoors in a green field under a cloudy sky (see Figure 3). The artists do not look joyful, as might be expected, but as though they are at work.

I agree with the sentiment but would put it the other way round: as said above, beauty is a protest. In his 1967 paper 'Society as a

Work of Art' Marcuse argued that beauty is non-repressive order; that is, beauty is, as beauty, a protest against war and fascism. He describes art as other than reality, or negated reality, and thereby imbued with a force of liberation: 'In this way art is rescued in its dual, antagonistic function. As a product of the imagination it is semblance, but the possible truth and reality to come appear in this semblance and art is able to shatter the false reality of the status quo.'[78] The slogan, however minimal, has that scope to interrupt. Freee do not see the use of plastic flowers as ironic, though I wonder if it is a sign of the artificiality of art, or of social relations in consumerism. They stand slightly awkwardly, as they do in the quarry – as ordinary people, not the prophets of a new age or criers of a New Jerusalem.

Figure 3   Freee Art Collective 'Protest is Beautiful' (2007), 1000000 mph Project Space, London (photo courtesy Freee Art Collective)

What I respect is their refusal to let go of the idea that history might be driven by protest, or that to say this is contagious. Within art's world, but contesting its values, Freee offer one example of how contemporary art can interrupt, and in process enact other, more democratic but also personal ideas of what the world might be, against capital's rhetoric that there is no alternative. Money may drive most history now; but to claim that protest drives it is revolutionary art.

AFTERWORD

There is no exit from art's institutions except in the end of art as a category. In 'Some Social Implications of Modern Technology', Marcuse says that utopia 'would not be a state of perennial happiness'.[79] If human relations are nothing but human, 'they will be permeated with the sadness of their singular content'.[80] Human relations are always transitory, and their ephemerality is enhanced when they are freed from the pressures of material existence. By implication, when the problem of abjection – Marcuse says 'social ostracism'[81] – is abated, a residual sadness will remain. But this is not defeat. The protest against death may transmute into present Eros, a life in the present which is ludic, libidinal and free. I do not know if artists can bring this nearer to realisation, or if, as Marcuse's writing in the late 1960s implies, it happens spontaneously. Times are darker now than when he wrote his last papers, and a retreat into aesthetics is both justified and possibly the only path to memories of bliss. But beauty is not confined to comfort; it is convulsive, and each glimpse is transformative.

Notes

INTRODUCTION

1. W. Benjamin, 'The Work of Art in the Age of Mechanical Reproduction' in *Illuminations*, London, Fontana, 1973, pp. 219–54.
2. e.g. V. Geoghegan, *Reason and Eros: The Social Theory of Herbert Marcuse*, London, Pluto, 1981; B. Katz, *Herbert Marcuse and the Art of Liberation*, London, Verso, 1982; D. Kellner, *Herbert Marcuse and the Crisis of Marxism*, Berkeley, University of California Press, 1984.
3. H. Marcuse, *Collected Papers*, ed. D. Kellner, London, Routledge: Volume 1, *Technology, War and Fascism*, 1998; Volume 2, *Towards a Critical Theory of Society*, 2001; Volume 3, *The New Left and the 1960s*, 2005; Volume 4, *Art and Liberation*, 2007; Volume 5, *Philosophy, Psychoanalysis and Emancipation*, 2011; Volume 6, *Marxism, Revolution and Utopia*, forthcoming.
4. e.g. C. Reitz, *Art, Alienation, and the Humanities: A Critical Engagement with Herbert Marcuse*, Albany, State University of New York Press, 2000; J. Abromeit and W.M. Cobb, eds, *Herbert Marcuse: A Critical Reader*, New York, Routledge, 2004.
5. A. Feenberg, 'Remembering Marcuse' in Marcuse, *Philosophy, Psychoanalysis and Emancipation*, p. 241.
6. 'Critical Philosophy: A Personal Perspective with Dr Herbert Marcuse' in *Philosophy, Psychoanalysis and Emancipation*, p. 232 (interview by Helen Hawkins).
7. H. Marcuse, *An Essay on Liberation*, Harmondsworth, Penguin, 1969.
8. H. Marcuse, *The Aesthetic Dimension*, Boston, Beacon Press, 1978.
9. H. Marcuse, *Counter-Revolution and Revolt*, Boston, Beacon Press, 1972, p. 1.
10. W.I. Robinson, 'The Global Capital Leviathan', *Radical Philosophy*, 165, January/February 2011, p. 4.
11. Kellner, 'Introduction' to Marcuse, *Art and Liberation*, p. 1.
12. Reitz, *Art, Alienation, and the Humanities*, p. 181.
13. Kellner, 'Introduction' to Marcuse, *Art and Liberation*, p. 3.
14. A.Y. Davies, 'Marcuse's Legacies' in Abromeit and Cobb, eds, *Herbert Marcuse: A Critical Reader*, p. 46.
15. See M. Miles, *Urban Avant-Gardes: Art, Architecture and Change*, London, Routledge, 2004.
16. H. Marcuse, *Eros and Civilization*, London, Routledge and Kegan Paul, 1956.
17. N.O. Brown, *Life Against Death: The Psychoanalytic Meaning of History*, London, Routledge and Kegan Paul, 1959.
18. N.O. Brown, *Love's Body*, New York, Vintage, 1966.
19. Marcuse, *The Aesthetic Dimension*, p. 73.

1 AESTHETICS AND THE RECONSTRUCTION OF SOCIETY

1. H. Marcuse, *The Aesthetic Dimension*, Boston, Beacon Press, 1978, p. 1 (first published as *Die Permanenz der Kunst Wider eine bestimmte Marxistische Aesthetik*, Munich, Carl Hanser Verlag, 1977).
2. R. Levitas, 'Utopia Matters?' in F. Vieira and M. Freitas, eds, *Utopia Matters: Theory, Politics, Literature and the Arts*, Oporto, University of Oporto, 2005, pp. 41–6.
3. H. Marcuse, *Zeit-Messungen*, Frankfurt-am-Main, Suhrkamp Verlag, 1975; see D. Kellner, 'Introduction' to H. Marcuse, *Art and Liberation*, London, Routledge, 2007, p. 59, n. 71.
4. Cited in Kellner, 'Introduction' to *Art and Liberation*, p. 59.
5. Ibid., p. 67.
6. Ibid., p. 68.
7. H. Marcuse, 'Irvine March 5, 1979' (lecture notes), cited in ibid., p. 69.
8. Kellner, 'Introduction' to *Art and Liberation*, p. 69.
9. Ibid.
10. Ibid., p. 61
11. Marcuse, *The Aesthetic Dimension*, pp. 3–4.
12. Marcuse, *The Aesthetic Dimension*, p. xiii; see Kellner, 'Introduction' to *Art and Liberation*, p. 61, n. 74 on the addition of this sentence in the English edition.
13. W. Benjamin, 'The Author as Producer' in *Understanding Brecht*, London, Verso, 2003, pp. 85–104 (originally a paper for the Institute for the Study of Fascism, Paris, 27 April 1934; first published in German, in *Versuche über Brecht*, Frankfurt-am-Main, Suhrkamp, 1966).
14. H. Marcuse, *Soviet Marxism: A Critical Analysis*, Harmondsworth, Penguin, 1971, p. 108 (first published, London, Routledge and Kegan Paul, 1958).
15. Ibid.
16. Ibid., p. 111.
17. Ibid.
18. F. Engels, 'Introduction: *The Dialectics of Nature*' in *Marx and Engels: Selected Works in One Volume*, London, Lawrence and Wishart, 1968, p. 343.
19. Benjamin, 'The Author as Producer'.
20. Ibid., p. 88.
21. F. Engels, Letter to W. Borgius, London, 25 January 1894, in *Marx and Engels: Selected Works in One Volume*, p. 704.
22. Marcuse, *Soviet Marxism*, p. 109.
23. Ibid., p. 110.
24. H. Marcuse, 'Philosophy and Critical Theory' in *Negations*, Harmondsworth, Penguin, 1968, pp. 134–58 (first published *Zeitschrift für Sozialforschung*, VI, 1937); M. Horkheimer, 'The Present Situation of Social Theory and the Tasks of an Institute of Social Research' in *Between Philosophy and Social Science: Selected Early Writings*, Cambridge MA, MIT, 1993, pp. 1–14.
25. C. Becker, 'Herbert Marcuse and the Subversive Potential of Art' in C. Becker, ed., *The Subversive Imagination: Artists, Society, and Social Responsibility*, New York, Routledge, 1994, p. 114.
26. Ibid.

27. E. Bloch, 'Discussing Expressionism' in T.W. Adorno, W. Benjamin, E. Bloch, B. Brecht and G. Lukács, *Aesthetics and Politics*, London, Verso, 1980, pp. 16–27; G. Lukács, 'Realism in the Balance' in ibid., pp. 28–59.
28. E. Bloch, *The Principle of Hope*, Cambridge MA, MIT, 1986, 3 volumes (first published as *Das Prinzip Hoffning*, Frankfurt-am-Main, Suhrkamp Verlag, 1959).
29. Marcuse, *Soviet Marxism*, p. 109.
30. V. Geoghegan, *Reason and Eros: The Social Theory of Herbert Marcuse*, London, Pluto, 1981, p. 28.
31. C. Greenberg, 'Avant-Garde and Kitsch' in *The Collected Essays and Criticism: Perceptions and Judgements 1939–1944*, Chicago, University of Chicago Press, 1986, pp. 5–22 (first published in *Partisan Review*, Fall 1939).
32. Ibid., p. 9.
33. Marcuse, 'Philosophy and Critical Theory', pp. 134–58; Geoghegan cites p. 154.
34. Geoghegan, *Reason and Eros*, p. 28.
35. Marcuse, *Soviet Marxism*, p. 110.
36. J. Berger, *Art and Revolution*, London, Writers and Readers Publishing Cooperative, 1969.
37. B. Taylor, 'On AKhRR' in B. Taylor and M.C. Brown, eds, *Art of the Soviets: Painting, sculpture and architecture in a one-party state, 1917–1992*, Manchester, Manchester University Press, 1993, pp. 51–72.
38. C. Cooke, 'Socialist Realist Architecture: Theory and Practice' in ibid., pp. 86–105.
39. Marcuse, *Soviet Marxism*, p. 140.
40. M.C. Brown, 'Aleksandr Gerasimov' in Taylor and Brown, eds, *Art of the Soviets*, p. 138.
41. S. Sim, ed., *Post-Marxism: A Reader*, Edinburgh, Edinburgh University Press, 1998, p. 5.
42. K. Marx and F. Engels, *The Communist Manifesto*, in *Marx and Engels: Selected Works*, p. 38.
43. M. Rose, *Marx's Lost Aesthetic: Karl Marx and the Visual Arts*, Cambridge, Cambridge University Press, 1984, p. 11.
44. Ibid., p. 44.
45. Ibid., pp. 59–60; see B. Bauer, *Hegels Lehr von der religion und Kunst*, Leipzig, 1842.
46. C. H. de Saint-Simon, from the Fourth Fragment, 'On Social Organization' in G. Ionescu, ed., *The Political Thought of Saint-Simon*, Oxford, Oxford University Press, 1976, p. 233, cited in Rose, *Marx's Lost Aesthetic*, p. 13.
47. Rose, *Marx's Lost Aesthetic*, p. 77.
48. Ibid., p. 85.
49. Ibid., p. 95.
50. K. Marx, *Grundrisse*, Harmondsworth, Penguin, 1979, p. 110, cited in ibid., p. 83.
51. Rose, *Marx's Lost Aesthetic*, p. 85.
52. P. Fuller, *Art and Psychoanalysis*, London, Hogarth Press, 1988, p. 13 (first published, London, Readers and Writers Publishing Cooperative, 1980).
53. From K. Marx and F. Engels, *The German Ideology*, ed. C.J. Arthur, New York, 1970, pp. 108–9, cited in Rose, *Marx's Lost Aesthetic*, p. 81.

54. K. Marx, 'Theses on Feuerbach' in F. Engels, *Ludwig Feuerbach and the Outcome of Classical German Philosophy*, London, Martin Lawrence, 1888, p. 74 (first publication, from a notebook dated 1845; see also Marx and Engels, *Selected Works in One Volume*, pp. 28–30; *The German Ideology*, ed. Pascal, R. New York, International Publishers, 1947, pp. 197–9).

55. M. Miles, *Urban Utopias: The Built and Social Architectures of Alternative Settlements*, London, Routledge, 2008, Ch. 3.

56. Conversations with the author, West Surrey College of Art and Design, Farnham, and in London, 1979–1981 (from memory).

57. Marx, 'Theses on Feuerbach', p. 74.

58. Engels, *Ludwig Feuerbach* , p. 10.

59. Ibid., p. 28.

60. Ibid.

61. Ibid.

62. Ibid., p. 74.

63. E. Fischer, *Marx in his Own Words*, Harmondsworth, Penguin, 1973, p. 153 (first published in German as *Was Marx Wirklich*, Vienna, Fritz Molden, 1968).

64. Ibid., p. 154.

65. D. Kellner, 'Introduction' in H. Marcuse, *Towards a Critical Theory of Society*, London, Routledge, 2001, p. 12.

66. Marcuse, 'Philosophy and Critical Theory', p. 143.

67. Ibid., p. 150.

68. Ibid., p. 151.

69. Ibid.

70. Ibid., p. 154.

2   THE ARTIST AND SOCIAL THEORY

1. D. Kellner, 'Introduction' to H. Marcuse, *Art and Liberation*, London, Routledge, 2007, p. 3.

2. M. Weber, 'Politik als Beruf', cited in B. Katz, *Herbert Marcuse and the Art of Liberation*, London, Verso, 1982, p. 32.

3. Katz, *Herbert Marcuse and the Art of Liberation*, p. 32.

4. Kellner, 'Introduction' to *Art and Liberation*, p. 5.

5. F. Engels, 'Preface' to *The Communist Manifesto*, German edition, 1890, in K. Marx and F. Engels, *Selected Works in One Volume*, London, Lawrence and Wishart, 1968, p. 34.

6. O. Figges, *A People's Tragedy: The Russian Revolution 1891–1924*, London, Pimlico, 1996, p. 180.

7. Ibid., p. 123.

8. Resolution of the meeting of the iron-rolling shop of the Putilov works, August 1917, cited in S.A. Smith, *The Russian Revolution: A Very Short Introduction*, Oxford, Oxford University Press, 2002, p. 29.

9. Katz, *Herbert Marcuse and the Art of Liberation*, p. 24.

10. Ibid., p. 27.

11. J. Willett, *The New Sobriety: Art and Politics in the Weimar Period, 1917–33*, London, Thames and Hudson, 1982, p. 44 (first published 1978).

12. Katz, *Herbert Marcuse and the Art of Liberation*, p. 28.

13. C. Reitz, *Art, Alienation, and the Humanities: A Critical Engagement with Herbert Marcuse*, Albany, State University of New York Press, 2000, p. 88.

14. Willett, *The New Sobriety*, p. 45.

15. Katz, *Herbert Marcuse and the Art of Liberation*, p. 25.

16. H. Marcuse, 'Lebenslau' (biographical note attached to doctoral thesis), cited in Kellner, 'Introduction' to *Art and Liberation*, p. 5 (also cited in D. Kellner, *Herbert Marcuse and the Crisis of Marxism*, Berkeley, University of California Press, 1984, p. 13).

17. Katz, *Herbert Marcuse and the Art of Liberation*, p. 25.

18. Ibid., p. 22.

19. Cited in Katz, *Herbert Marcuse and the Art of Liberation*, p. 31 (source not given).

20. Willett, *The New Sobriety*, p. 45.

21. Ibid., p. 47.

22. Katz, *Herbert Marcuse and the Art of Liberation*, p. 31.

23. Willett, *The New Sobriety*, p. 49.

24. Katz, *Herbert Marcuse and the Art of Liberation*, p. 41; see also Kellner, 'Introduction' to *Art and Liberation*, p. 11, n. 28.

25. Kellner, 'Introduction' to *Art and Liberation*, p. 7

26. H. Marcuse, 'The German Artist Novel: Introduction' in *Art and Liberation*, p. 79.

27. Ibid., p. 71.

28. Ibid.

29. Ibid., p. 72.

30. Ibid., citing G.W.F. Hegel, *Aesthetik* III, Berlin, 1835, p. 395.

31. P. Fuller, 'Jackson Pollock' in *Beyond the Crisis in Art*, London, Readers' and Writers' Publishing Cooperative, 1980, pp. 98–103 (first published in *New Society*, 26 April 1979).

32. Katz, *Herbert Marcuse and the Art of Liberation*, p. 43.

33. Marcuse, 'The German Artist Novel', p. 72.

34. Ibid., p. 74.

35. Kellner, 'Introduction' to *Art and Liberation*, p. 9.

36. H. Marcuse, 'The German Artist Novel', from *Schriften* I, Frankfurt-am-Main, Suhrkamp, 1978–79, p. 75, cited in Kellner, 'Introduction' to *Art and Liberation*, p. 9.

37. H. Marcuse, *An Essay on Liberation*, Harmondsworth, Penguin, 1969, p. 30.

38. Marcuse, 'The German Artist Novel', p. 75.

39. Ibid., p. 76.

40. Ibid.

41. Ibid., p. 76, citing H. J. C. von Grimmelshausen, Abenteurlicher Simplizius, *Simplizissimus*, Minden, n.d. (Grimmelhausen lived from 1621 to 1676).

42. Marcuse, 'The German Artist Novel', p. 77.

43. W. Kandinsky, *Über das geistige in der Kunst, Insbesondere in der Malerei*, Munich, Piper Verlag, 1911 (dated 1912); published in English as *The Art of Spiritual Harmony*, London, Constable, 1914; and *Concerning the Spiritual in Art, and Painting in Particular*, New York, Wittenborn Schultz, 1947.

44. Marcuse, 'The German Artist Novel', p. 78.

45. Ibid., p. 79.

46. Kellner, 'Introduction' to *Art and Liberation*, p. 9.

47. Marcuse, *Schriften* I, p. 69, cited in Kellner, 'Introduction' to *Art and Liberation*, p. 11.
48. Katz, *Herbert Marcuse and the Art of Liberation*, p. 50.
49. Ibid., p. 50 (citing Marcuse's doctoral thesis, p. 333).
50. Ibid, p. 51 (citing Marcuse's doctoral thesis, p. 326).
51. Willett, *The New Sobriety*, p. 50.
52. Ibid., p. 53.
53. Ibid.
54. Kellner, 'Introduction' to *Art and Liberation*, p. 16, referencing Marcuse, *Schriften* I, pp. 3, 26ff.
55. Kellner, 'Introduction' to *Art and Liberation*, p. 17, citing Marcuse, *Schriften* I, pp. 328–9.
56. G. Lukács, *The Theory of the Novel*, London, Merlin Press, 1978, pp. 38–9.
57. T.W. Adorno, *Aesthetic Theory*, London, Athlone, 1997, pp. 30–1.
58. G. Lukács, 'Realism in the Balance' in T.W. Adorno, W. Benjamin, E. Bloch, B. Brecht and G. Lukács, *Aesthetics and Politics*, London, Verso, 1980, p. 29.
59. Ibid., p. 31.
60. Ibid., p. 32.
61. E. Bloch, 'Discussing Expressionism' in Adorno et al., *Aesthetics and Politics*, pp. 16–27.
62. Katz, *Herbert Marcuse and the Art of Liberation*, p. 48.
63. H. Marcuse, 'Ecology and Revolution' in *The New Left and the 1960s*, London, Routledge, 2005, p. 175.
64. Katz, *Herbert Marcuse and the Art of Liberation*, p. 55.
65. H. Marcuse, 'Beiträger zu einer Phänomenologie des historischen Materialismus' (1928), in *Schriften* I , cited in Katz, *Herbert Marcuse and the Art of Liberation*, p. 61.
66. H. Marcuse, *Hegel's Ontology and the Theory of Historicity*, Cambridge MA, MIT, 1987.
67. J. Abromeit, 'Herbert Marcuse's Critical Encounter with Martin Heidegger 1927–33' in J. Abromeit and M.W. Cobb, eds, *Herbert Marcuse: A Critical Reader*, New York, Routledge, 2004, p. 139.
68. Ibid., citing Marx in R. Tucker, ed. *Marx-Engels Reader*, New York, Norton, 1978, p. 109.
69. H. Marcuse, 'Theory and Politics: A Discussion', *Telos*, 38, Winter 1978, p. 125, cited in Abromeit, 'Herbert Marcuse's Critical Encounter with Martin Heidegger 1927–33', p. 141.
70. D. Kellner, 'Introduction' to H. Marcuse, *Towards a Critical Theory of Society*, London, Routledge, 2001, p. 3.
71. Reitz, *Art, Alienation, and the Humanities*, p. 51.
72. Kellner, 'Introduction' to *Art and Liberation*, p. 22.
73. Reitz, *Art, Alienation, and the Humanities*, p. 52.
74. Ibid., p. 59.
75. Katz, *Herbert Marcuse and the Art of Liberation*, p. 84.
76. Marcuse, 'Theory and Politics: A Discussion', p. 126, cited in Kellner, 'Introduction' to *Towards a Critical Theory of Society*, p. 3.
77. Katz, *Herbert Marcuse and the Art of Liberation*, pp. 84–5.
78. Kellner, 'Introduction' to *Towards a Critical Theory of Society*, p. 1; see also M. Jay, *The Dialectical Imagination*, Boston, Little, Brown and Company, 1973.

79. P.M. Stirk, *Critical Theory, Politics and Society: An Introduction*, London, Cassell, 2000, pp. 14–30.
80. W. Schirmacher, 'Introduction', *The Frankfurt School*, New York, Continuum, 2000, p. xiii.
81. W. Benjamin, 'Theses on the Philosophy of History' VIII, in *Illuminations*, ed. H. Arendt, London, Fontana, 1973, p. 259.
82. A.Y. Davies, 'Preface' to H. Marcuse, *The New Left and the 1960s*, London, Routledge, 2005, p. xi.
83. H. Marcuse, 'Philosophy and Critical Theory' in *Negations*, Harmondsworth, Penguin, 1968, pp. 134–58.
84. Katz, *Herbert Marcuse and the Art of Liberation*, pp. 130–2.
85. W. Benjamin, 'The Work of Art in the Age of Mechanical Reproduction' in *Illuminations*; see also E. Leslie, *Walter Benjamin: Overpowering Conformism*, London, Pluto, 2000, pp. 130–3.
86. Kellner, 'Introduction' to *Towards a Critical Theory of Society*, p. 6.
87. Ibid., p. 7.
88. Ibid., p. 10.
89. Ibid., p. 18, citing Institute for Social Research, 'Ten Years on Morningside Heights: A Report on the Institute's History 1934–44', p. 11 (Herbert Marcuse archives).
90. Kellner, 'Introduction' to *Towards a Critical Theory of Society*, p. 18.

3 AFFIRMATIONS

1. H. Marcuse, 'The Affirmative Character of Culture' in *Negations*, Harmondsworth, Penguin, 1968, p. 133 (first published in *Zeitschrift für Sozialforschung*, vol. 6, 1, Paris, 1937, pp. 54–94).
2. Ibid., p. 128.
3. B. Katz, *Herbert Marcuse and the Art of Liberation*, London, Verso, 1982, pp. 58–86.
4. D. Kellner, 'Introduction' to H. Marcuse, *Art and Liberation*, London, Routledge, 2007, p. 22.
5. Katz, *Herbert Marcuse and the Art of Liberation*, p. 64; see H. Marcuse, 'Contributions to a Phenomenology of Historical Materialism' in *Heideggerian Marxism*, eds, R. Wolin and J. Abromeit, Lincoln NE, University of Nebraska Press, 2005, pp. 1–33 (first published as 'Beiträge zu einer Phänomenologie des historischen Materialismus', *Philosophische Hefte*, pp. 45–68, 1928; and reprinted in German in H. Marcuse, *Schriften* I, Frankfurt-am-Main, Suhrkamp, 1978, pp. 347–89; first published in English in *Telos*, 4, pp. 3–34, 1969).
6. Katz, *Herbert Marcuse and the Art of Liberation*, p. 64.
7. Ibid., p. 66.
8. Kellner, 'Introduction' to *Art and Liberation*, p. 23.
9. Ibid.
10. Ibid. p 18 (citing Marcuse, *Schriften* I, p. 333).
11. Ibid., p. 23.
12. Marcuse, 'On the Aesthetic Dimension: A Conversation between Herbert Marcuse and Larry Hartwick' in *Art and Liberation*; cited by Kellner in his

'Introduction' to that volume, p. 23 (first published, *Contemporary Literature*, XXII, 4, Fall 1981, pp. 416–24).
13. Marcuse, 'The Affirmative Character of Culture', p. 88.
14. Ibid., p. 91.
15. Ibid., p. 92.
16. Ibid., p. 94.
17. Ibid., p. 95.
18. See also R. Williams, *Keywords*, London, Fontana, 1976, pp. 76–82.
19. T.W. Adorno, 'The Schema of Mass Culture' in *The Culture Industry: Selected Essays on Mass Culture*, London, Routledge, 1991, pp. 53–84.
20. See J.B. Slater and A. Iles, *No Room to Move: Radical Art and the Regenerate City*, London, Mute, 2010, pp. 9–11.
21. Marcuse, 'The Affirmative Character of Culture', p. 95.
22. Ibid., p. 97.
23. Kellner, 'Introduction' to *Art and Liberation*, p. 25.
24. Marcuse, 'The Affirmative Character of Culture', p. 98.
25. Ibid., pp. 98–9.
26. Kellner, 'Introduction' to *Art and Liberation*, p. 21.
27. C. Reitz, *Art, Alienation and the Humanities: A Critical Engagement with Herbert Marcuse*, Albany NY, State University of New York Press, 2000, pp. 85–6.
28. H. Marcuse, *Counter-Revolution and Revolt*, Boston, Beacon Press, 1972, p. 97; cited in ibid., p. 197 (Reitz adds his own emphasis to certain words).
29. Marcuse, 'The Affirmative Character of Culture', p. 111.
30. Ibid.
31. Ibid., pp. 111–12.
32. Ibid., p. 115.
33. See J. Kristeva, *The Sense and Non-sense of Revolt: The Powers and Limits of Psychoanalysis*, New York, Columbia University Press, 2000, pp. 108–10.
34. Marcuse, 'The Affirmative Character of Culture', p. 115, see also p. 279, n. 33.
35. Ibid., see also p. 279, n. 35.
36. Ibid., pp. 115–16.
37. Marcuse, *Counter-Revolution and Revolt*, p. 102.
38. Ibid.
39. Marcuse, 'The Affirmative Character of Culture', p. 115.
40. Ibid., p. 118.
41. Ibid.
42. Ibid.
43. Ibid., p. 119.
44. H. Marcuse, *A Study on Authority*, London, Verso, 2008, p. 51 (first published as *Studien über Autorität und Familie*, Paris, Libraire Félix Alcan, 1936).
45. Marcuse, *The Aesthetic Dimension*, p. 55.
46. Ibid., p. 56.
47. Marcuse, 'The Affirmative Character of Culture', p. 125.
48. Ibid.
49. Ibid., p. 127; see also Reitz, *Art, Alienation, and the Humanities*, p. 89.
50. Marcuse, 'The Affirmative Character of Culture', p. 127.
51. E. Bloch, 'Inventory of Revolutionary Appearance' in *Heritage of Our Times*, Cambridge, Polity, 1991, p. 64.

52. Ibid., p. 65.
53. Ibid., p. 67.
54. E. Bloch, 'On the Original History of the Third Reich' in *Heritage of Our Times*, p. 117 (first published in *Internationale Literatur*, 1937).
55. E. Bloch, 'Amusement Co., Horror, Third Reich' in *Heritage of Our Times*, pp. 56–63.
56. S. Michalski, *Public Monuments: Art in Political Bondage 1870–1997*, London, Reaktion, 1998, p. 57.
57. Ibid., pp. 63–4.
58. Bloch, 'Amusement Co., Horror, Third Reich', p. 57.
59. Michalski, *Public Monuments*, p. 66.
60. Marcuse, 'The Affirmative Character of Culture', p. 125.
61. T. Benton, 'Exhibiting Modernity: The 1889 Universal Exposition and the Eiffel Tower' in P. Wood, ed., *The Challenge of the Avant-Garde*, New Haven, Yale, 1999, p. 163.
62. Marcuse, 'The Affirmative Character of Culture', p. 126.
63. Ibid., p. 129.
64. J. Willett, *The New Sobriety: Art and Politics in the Weimar Period, 1917–1933*, London, Thames and Hudson, 1978, p. 34.
65. Marcuse, 'Society as a Work of Art' in *Art and Liberation*, pp. 123–4 (source not given).
66. Ibid., p. 124.
67. Ibid., p. 125.
68. E. Bloch, 'Jugglers' Fair Beneath the Gallows' in *Heritage of Our Times*, p. 75.
69. Ibid., p. 77.
70. E. Bloch, 'Expressionism, Seen Now' in *Heritage of Our Times*, pp. 234–235.
71. Ibid., p. 240.
72. Ibid.
73. E. Bloch, 'Discussing Expressionism' in *Heritage of Our Times*, p. 242.
74. Marcuse, *A Study on Authority*, p. 73.

4   A LITERATURE OF INTIMACY

1. H. Marcuse, 'Some remarks on Aragon: Art and Politics in the Totalitarian Era' in *Technology, War and Fascism*, London, Routledge, 1998, pp. 199–215 (first published, *Theory, Culture & Society*, 10, 1993, pp. 181–95); see p. 200 n. 1.
2. Interview with J. Habermas, cited in D. Kellner, 'Introduction' to *Technology, War and Fascism*, p. 23 (first published, *Telos* 38, pp. 130–1, Winter 1978–79).
3. Kellner, 'Introduction' to *Technology, War and Fascism*, p. 15.
4. M. Horkheimer and T.W. Adorno, *Dialectic of Enlightenment*, London, Verso, 1997 (first published in German, New York, Social Studies Association, 1944; first English edition, New York, Herder & Herder, 1972).
5. V. Geoghegan, *Ernst Bloch*, London, Routledge, 1996, p. 19.
6. E. Leslie, *Walter Benjamin: Overpowering Conformism*, London, Pluto, 2000, pp. 130f; I use Leslie's translation of the title as more accurate than the standard English version: 'The Work of Art in the Age of Mechanical

Reproduction' in *Illuminations*, ed. H. Arendt, London, Fontana, 1973, pp. 219–54.

7. C. Greenberg, 'Avant-garde and Kitsch' in *The Collected Essays and Criticism: Perceptions and Judgments, 1939–1944'*, Chicago, University of Chicago Press, 1988, p. 22 (first published, New York, *Partisan Review*, Fall 1939; New York, *Horizon*, 1940).

8. Ibid.

9. J. O'Brian, 'Introduction' to Greenberg, *The Collected Essays and Criticism*, p. xx.

10. T.W. Adorno, Letter to Horkheimer, 30 August 1955, cited in D. Kellner, 'Introduction' to H. Marcuse, *Towards a Critical Theory of Society*, London, Routledge, 2001, p. 21.

11. H. Marcuse and F. Neumann, 'A History of the Doctrine of Social Change' in Marcuse, *Technology, War and Fascism*, pp. 95–104; see also in the same volume, Marcuse and Neumann, 'Theories of Social Change', pp. 105–37.

12. H. Marcuse, *A Study on Authority*, London, Verso, 2008 (first published as *Stüdien über Autorität und Familie*, Paris, Alcan, 1936).

13. Kellner, 'Introduction' to *Towards a Critical Theory of Society*, p. 11.

14. H. Marcuse, 'Philosophy and Critical Theory' in *Negations*, Harmondsworth, Penguin, 1968, pp. 134–58 (first published, *Zeitschrift für Sozialforschung*, VI, 1937); see also Kellner, 'Introduction' to *Towards a Critical Theory of Society*, p. 15.

15. B. Katz, *Herbert Marcuse and the Art of Liberation*, London, Verso, 1982, p. 95.

16. H. Marcuse, Letter to Max Horkheimer, 15 October 1941, in *Technology, War and Fascism*, p. 231.

17. Marcuse, cited in *Technology, War and Fascism*, p. 9.

18. H. Marcuse, 'The New German Mentality' in *Technology, War and Fascism*, pp. 139–90.

19. Ibid., p. 141.

20. Ibid., p. 167.

21. Ibid., p. 168.

22. Kellner, 'Introduction' to *Technology, War and Fascism*, p. 24.

23. H. Marcuse, *Soviet Marxism: A Critical Analysis*, Harmondsworth, Penguin, 1971 (first published, London, Routledge and Kegan Paul, 1958; republished, New York, Columbia University Press, 1985).

24. Kellner, 'Introduction' to *Technology, War and Fascism*, p. 29.

25. Marcuse, 'Some Remarks on Aragon', p. 201.

26. H. Marcuse, *The Aesthetic Dimension*, Boston, Beacon Press, 1978, p. 1.

27. Marcuse, 'Some Remarks on Aragon', p. 201.

28. H. Marcuse, 'Liberation from the Affluent Society' in D. Cooper, ed. *The Dialectics of Liberation*, Harmondsworth, Penguin, 1968, pp. 175–92; 'Society as a Work of Art' in Marcuse, *Art and Liberation*, pp. 123–9.

29. H. Marcuse, *An Essay on Liberation*, Harmondsworth, Penguin, 1969.

30. Ibid.

31. Marcuse, 'Some Remarks on Aragon', p. 201.

32. Ibid., p. 213.

33. Ibid.

34. Ibid., p. 201.

35. Ibid., p. 202.

36. Ibid., p. 201.
37. Ibid., p. 202.
38. Marcuse, 'Society as a Work of Art', pp. 126–7.
39. Marcuse, 'Some Remarks on Aragon', p. 202.
40. Ibid.
41. Ibid., p. 203.
42. Ibid.
43. Ibid.
44. Ibid.
45. Kellner gives the source as C. Baudelaire, 'Invitation au voyage' in *The Complete Verse*, London, Anvil Press, 1986. Marcuse used an earlier edition, presumably in the original French.
46. Marcuse, 'Some Remarks on Aragon', p. 204.
47. Ibid., p. 204 (source not given).
48. P. Éluard, *Selected Poems*, London, John Calder, 1987 p. 86 (my translation from French, not using the parallel English text).
49. Marcuse, 'Some Remarks on Aragon', p. 205.
50. See E. Bloch, *The Principle of Hope*, Cambridge MA, MIT, 1986, pp. 797–8 (first published as *Das Prinzip Hoffnung*, Frankfurt-am-Main, Suhrkamp, 1959).
51. P. Éluard, '*Les sept poèmes d'amour en guerre*; in *Selected Poems*, p. 78 (author's translation from French).
52. Marcuse, 'Some Remarks on Aragon', p. 205.
53. Éluard, '*Liberté*' in *Selected Poems,* pp. 72–7.
54. Marcuse, 'Some Remarks on Aragon', p. 206
55. Éluard, '*Liberté*', p. 76 (author's translation from French).
56. W. Benjamin, 'The Author as Producer' in *Understanding Brecht*, London, Verso, 1998, pp. 85–104 (first published as *Versuche über Brecht*, Frankfurt-am-Main, Suhrkamp, 1966).
57. Leslie, *Walter Benjamin*, p. 94.
58. Ibid., p. 102, citing L. Aragon, *Pour un réalisme socialiste*, Paris, Denoël, 1934.
59. V. Holmam, 'The Impact of War: British Publishers and French Publications 1940–1944', *Publishing History*, 48, 2000, p. 56.
60. Ibid., p. 44.
61. V. Holman, 'Air-Borne Culture: Propaganda Leaflets Over Occupied France in the Second world War' in J. Raven, ed., *Free Print and Non-Commercial Publishing since 1700*, Aldershot, Ashgate, 2000, p. 196.
62. P. Fouché, *L'edition Française sous l'Occupation 1940–1944*, Paris, University of Paris VII, 1987, vol. II, p. 35, cited in Holman, 'The Impact of War', p. 45.
63. 'Propaganda Policy, PWE: Notes on the Memorandum by the Minister of Economic Warfare', Public Records Office, FO 898/13, cited in Holman, 'Air-borne Culture', p. 197.
64. 'Note to Miss Tollenaer from Mr McMillan, 6 October 1941, Public Records Office FO 898/206, cited in Holman, 'Air-borne Culture', p. 198.
65. M-P Fouchet, *Un jour, je m'en souviens*, Paris, Mercure de France, 1968, p. 90, translated and cited by Holman, 'Air-borne Culture', p. 207.
66. Holman, 'Air-borne Culture', p. 208.
67. Ibid., pp. 209–10.

68. S. Kendall, *Paul Éluard, Love, Poetry*, Boston, Black Widow Press, 2007, p. 14.
69. Holman, 'Air-borne Culture', pp. 215–16, p. 208.
70. Marcuse, 'Some Remarks on Aragon', p. 208.
71. Ibid., p. 209.
72. Ibid.
73. L. Aragon, *Aurélien*, London, Pilot Press, 1946, p. 486 (first published Paris, Gallimard, 1945).
74. Ibid., p. 532.
75. Ibid., p. 557.
76. Ibid., p. 559.
77. Marcuse, 'Some Remarks on Aragon', p. 210.
78. Ibid.
79. Ibid., p. 211.
80. Ibid.
81. Ibid.
82. Aragon, *Aurélien*, p. 750.
83. Marcuse, 'Some Remarks on Aragon', p. 211.
84. Ibid.
85. Ibid.
86. Aragon, *Aurélien*, p.1.
87. Ibid., p. 129.
88. Marcuse, 'Some Remarks on Aragon', p. 213.
89. Ibid., p. 214.
90. W. Benjamin, 'Theses on the Philosophy of History, VIII' in *Illuminations*, p. 259.
91. Leslie, *Walter Benjamin*, p. 174.
92. Marcuse, 'Some Remarks on Aragon', p. 213.
93. R. Wolin, *Walter Benjamin: An Aesthetic of Redemption*, Berkeley, University of California Press, 1994, pp. 29–30.
94. Marcuse, 'Some Remarks on Aragon', p. 212.
95. Ibid.
96. J. Kristeva, *The Sense and Non-Sense of Revolt*, New York, Columbia University Press, 2000, p. 191.

5 SOCIETY AS A WORK OF ART

1. Marcuse was born on 19 July 1898. His 69th birthday occurred during his visit to Europe, speaking in Berlin before going to London for the Dialectics of Liberation Congress (which took place from July 15 to 30).
2. H. Marcuse, 'Liberation from the Affluent Society' in D. Cooper, ed., *The Dialectics of Liberation*, Harmondsworth, Penguin, 1968, pp. 175–92.
3. 3rd Humanismusgespricht (Conversation on Humanism), *Neues Forum*, vol. XIV, 167–8, pp. 863–8; published in English in H. Marcuse, *Art and Liberation*, London, Routledge, 2007, pp. 124–9.
4. D. Farber, 'The Intoxicated State/Illegal Nation: Drugs in the Sixties Counterculture' in P. Braunstein and M.W. Doyle, eds, *Imagine Nation*, New York, Routledge, 2002, p. 18.
5. J. McGuigan, *Cool Capitalism*, London, Pluto, 2009, p. 5.

6. Marcuse, 'Liberation from the Affluent Society', p. 185.
7. H. Marcuse, *Five Lectures* (Harmondsworth, Penguin, 1970) pp. 62–82.
8. H. Marcuse, *An Essay on Liberation*, Harmondsworth, Penguin, 1969.
9. H. Marcuse, *Eros and Civilization*, Boston, Beacon Press, 1955.
10. H. Marcuse, *One Dimensional Man*, Boston, Beacon Press, 1964.
11. A. Davies, *An Autobiography*, New York, International Publishers, 1974, pp. 113–14, cited in B. Katz, *Herbert Marcuse and the Art of Liberation*, London, Verso, 1982, p. 163.
12. Katz, *Herbert Marcuse and the Art of Liberation*, p. 169.
13. A. Feenberg, 'Remembering Marcuse' in H. Marcuse, *Philosophy, Psychoanalysis and Emancipation*, London, Routledge, 2011, p. 235.
14. Katz, *Herbert Marcuse and the Art of Liberation*, p. 173.
15. H. Marcuse, 'Varieties of Humanism: Herbert Marcuse Talks with Harry Wheeler', *The Center Magazine*, vol. 1, 5, 1968, p. 19, cited in ibid., p. 174.
16. D. Kellner, 'Introduction' to H. Marcuse, *The New Left and the 1960s*, London, Routledge, 2005, p. 2.
17. H. Marcuse, 'On the New Left' in M. Teodori, *The New Left: A Documentary History*, New York, Bobbs-Merrill, 1969, p. 469, cited in V. Geoghegan, *Reason and Eros: The Social Theory of Herbert Marcuse*, London, Pluto, 1981, p. 94; republished in *The New Left and the 1960s*, p. 122 (talk given 4 December 1968, for the 20th anniversary of *The Guardian*).
18. Marcuse, 'On the New Left' in *The New Left and the 1960s*, p. 123.
19. Ibid., p. 126.
20. J. Farrell, *The Spirit of the Sixties*, London, Routledge, 1997, p. 138, citing S. Evans, *Personal Politics: The Roots of Women's Liberation in the Civil Rights Movement and the New Left*, New York, Knopf, 1979.
21. B. Sweers, *Electric Folk: The Changing Face of English Traditional Music*, Oxford, Oxford University Press, 2005, pp. 25–6.
22. M. Brocken, *The British Folk Revival, 1944–2002*, Aldershot, Ashgate, 2003, pp. 49–55.
23. T. Merton, *The Hidden Ground of Love: The Letters of Thomas Merton on Religious Experience and Social Concerns*, ed. W.H. Shannon, San Diego, Harcourt Brace, 1985; *Ghandi on Nonviolence*, New York, New Directions, 1979; *Albert Camus' The Plague*, New York, Seabury, 1968.
24. Farrell, *The Spirit of the Sixties*, p. 144.
25. See H. Arendt, *Eichmann in Jerusalem: A Report on the Banality of Evil*, New York, Penguin, 1965.
26. H.F. Pitkin, *The Attack on the Blob: Hannah Arendt's Concept of the Social*, Chicago, University of Chicago Press, 1998, p. 206; 207.
27. Farrell, *The Spirit of the Sixties*, p. 144.
28. Ibid., p. 142.
29. Ibid., p. 149, citing C.W. Mills, *The Causes of World War Three*, New York, Ballantine, 1958, pp. 163–77; and Mills, *The Sixties: Art, Politics, and Media of Our Most Explosive Decade*, New York, Paragon House, 1991, pp. 76–77.
30. D. Rossinow, 'The Revolution Is About Our Lives: The New Left's Counterculture' in Braunstein and Doyle, eds, *Imagine Nation*, p. 99 (source of quote not given).
31. Ibid., p. 101.
32. Ibid., p. 117.
33. L. Sandercock, *Towards Cosmopolis*, Chichester, Wiley, 1998, pp. 107–25.

34. E. Bloch, *The Principle of Hope*, Cambridge MA, MIT, 1968, p. 591.
35. H. Marcuse, *One-Dimensional Man*, Boston, Beacon Press, 1964, p. ix.
36. Ibid., p. xv.
37. See J.R. Searle, *The Campus War*, Harmondsworth, Penguin 1972, pp. 44–60.
38. Farrell, *The Spirit of the Sixties*, p. 164.
39. Ibid., p. 166.
40. Kellner, 'Introduction' to *The New Left and the 1960s*, p. 17.
41. H. Marcuse, 'Marcuse Defines His New Left Line' in *The New Left and the 1960s*, p. 102.
42. Ibid.
43. K. Kesey, quoted in T. Wolfe, *The Electric Cool-Aid Acid Test*, New York, Bantam, 1968, p. 200, cited in Rossinow, 'The Revolution Is About Our Lives', p. 106; 122, n. 18.
44. Rossinow, 'The Revolution Is About Our Lives', p. 106, citing T. Gitlin, *The Sixties: Years of Hope, Days of Rage*, New York, Bantam, 1987, p. 225.
45. J. Didion, *Slouching Towards Bethlehem*, London, Flamingo, 2001, p. 72 (first published, New York, Farrar, Straus and Giroux, 1968).
46. E. Homberger, *The Art of the Real: Poetry in England and America since 1939*, London, Dent, 1977, p. 179.
47. A. Kaprow, *The Blurring of Art and Life*, ed. J. Kelley, Berkeley, University of California Press, 1993, pp. 66–80.
48. Farber, 'The Intoxicated State/Illegal Nation', p. 25.
49. From J. Sinclair, *Guitar Army*, New York, Douglas Books, 1972, pp. 22–3, cited in ibid., p. 26.
50. Farber, 'The Intoxicated State', p. 26.
51. T. Leary, *The Politics of Ecstasy*, London, Paladin, 1970, p. 55.
52. Ibid., p. 56.
53. Ibid., p. 53.
54. Ibid., p. 59.
55. Farber, 'The Intoxicated State', p. 27.
56. Farrell, *The Spirit of the Sixties*, p. 212.
57. Farber, 'The Intoxicated State', p. 30, quoting from an interview with Peter Coyote, 12 January 1989.
58. M.W. Doyle, 'Staging the Revolution: Guerilla Theatre as a Countercultural Practice' in Braunstein and Doyle, *Imagine Nation*, p. 72.
59. Ibid., p. 75.
60. Poster illustrated ibid., p. 77.
61. Didion, *Slouching Towards Bethlehem*, p. 107.
62. Ibid., p. 108.
63. Ibid., p. 106 (source of quote given).
64. Ibid., p. 105.
65. C. Coates, *Utopia Britannica*, London, Diggers and Dreamers Publications, 2001, pp. 21–5.
66. Doyle, 'Staging the Revolution', p. 79.
67. Farrell, *The Spirit of the Sixties*, p. 209.
68. Ibid.
69. Kellner, 'Introduction' to *The New Left and the 1960s*, p. 24.
70. H. Marcuse, 'The Problem of Violence and the Radical Opposition' in *Five Lectures*, p. 93, first two sentences quoted in Kellner, 'Introduction' to *The New Left and the 1960s*, p. 24.

71. Farrell, *The Spirit of the Sixties*, p. 220.
72. K. Ross, *May '68 and its Afterlives*, Chicago, University of Chicago Press, 2002, p. 191.
73. Kellner, 'Introduction' to *The New Left and the 1960s*, p. 17.
74. D. Cooper, 'Introduction' to *The Dialectics of Liberation*, Harmondsworth, Penguin, 1968, p. 7.
75. Ibid., pp. 9–10.
76. H. Marcuse, 'A Conversation with Marcuse: Revolutionary Eroticism, the Tactics of Terror, the Young, Psychotherapy, the Environment, Technology, Reich' in *Philosophy, Psychoanalysis and Emancipation*, pp. 193–4 (first published, *Psychology Today*, 1971, pp. 35–40; 60–6).
77. Kellner, 'Introduction' to *The New Left and the 1960s*, p. 19.
78. Marcuse, 'Liberation from the Affluent Society', p. 175.
79. Ibid.
80. Ibid., p. 176.
81. Ibid., pp. 176–7.
82. Ibid., p. 177.
83. L. Mumford, 'The Monastery and the Clock' in *The Human Prospect*, London, Secker and Warburg, 1956, pp. 5–6.
84. Kellner, 'Introduction' to *The New Left and the 1960s*, p. 19.
85. Marcuse, *Eros and Civilization*, p. 172.
86. Ibid., pp. 172–3.
87. K. Marx, 'Theses on Feuerbach' in K. Marx and F. Engels, *Selected Works in One Volume*, London, Lawrence and Wishart, 1968, p. 29.
88. R. King, *The Party of Eros: Radical Social Thought and the Realm of Freedom*, New York, Delta Books, 1973, p. 131 (first published, Chapel Hill, University of North Carolina Press, 1972).
89. V. Geoghegan, *Reason and Eros: The Social Thought of Herbert Marcuse*, London, Pluto, 1981, p. 52.
90. S. Carmichael, 'Black Power' in Cooper, ed., *The Dialectics of Liberation*, p. 172.
91. Marcuse, 'Liberation from the Affluent Society', p. 178.
92. Ibid., p. 179.
93. Ibid., p. 180.
94. Ibid., p. 181.
95. Ibid., pp. 181–2.
96. Ibid., p. 184.
97. Ibid., p. 185.
98. N.O. Brown, *Love's Body*, New York, Vintage, 1966, pp. 179, 180.
99. N.O. Brown, *Life Against Death: The Psychoanalytic Meaning of History*, London, Routledge and Kegan Paul, 1957, p. 317.
100. King, *The Party of Eros*, p. 154.
101. Marcuse, 'Liberation from the Affluent Society', p. 185.
102. Ibid., p. 186.
103. Ibid.
104. M. Miles, *Urban Utopias: The Built and Social Architectures of Alternative Settlements*, London, Routledge, 2008, Chapter 3.
105. E. Bloch, *The Principle of Hope*, Cambridge MA, MIT, 1986, p. 813.
106. V. Papanek, *Design for the Real World: Human Ecology and Social Change*, 2nd edition, London, Thames and Hudson, 1985.

107. Marcuse, 'Society as a Work of Art' in *Art and Liberation*, p. 125.
108. Ibid., p. 123.
109. Ibid., p. 124 (source not given).
110. Ibid.
111. Ibid., p. 125.
112. Ibid.
113. Ibid., p. 126.
114. Ibid.
115. Ibid.
116. Ibid.
117. T.W. Adorno, *Aesthetic Theory*, London, Athlone, 1997, pp. 29–30, 249–50 (first published as *Asthetische Theorie*, Frankfurt-am-Main, Suhrkamp, 1970).
118. Ibid.
119. Marcuse, 'Society as a Work of Art', p. 129.
120. Ibid.
121. Marcuse, *Five Lectures*, p. 88.
122. J. Kristeva, *Revolt, She Said*, Los Angeles, Semiotext(e), 2002, p. 18.

6 THE END OF UTOPIA

1. H. Marcuse, *An Essay on Liberation*, Harmondsworth, Penguin, 1969.
2. A. Gorz, *Farewell to the Working Class*, London, Pluto, 1982 (first published as *Adieux au Prolétariat*, Paris, Galilée, 1980).
3. R. Bahro, *The Alternative in Eastern Europe*, London, Verso, 1981 (first published in English, London, New Left Books, 1978).
4. H. Marcuse, 'The End of Utopia' in *Five Lectures*, Harmondsworth, Penguin, 1970, pp. 62–82.
5. G-H. Horn, *The Spirit of '68: Rebellion in Western Europe and North America, 1956–1976*, Oxford, Oxford University Press, 2007, p. 200.
6. J. Varon, *Bringing the War Home: The Weather Underground, the Red Army Faction, and Revolutionary Violence in the Sixties and Seventies*, Berkeley, University of California Press, 2004.
7. H. Marcuse, 'Critical Philosophy: A Personal Conversation with Dr Herbert Marcuse' (transcribed radio interview, April 1979) in *Philosophy, Psychoanalysis and Emancipation*, London, Routledge, 2011, pp. 232–3.
8. Ibid., p. 233.
9. E. Bloch, *The Principle of Hope*, Cambridge MA, MIT, 1986, p. 357n; 813 (first published as *Das Prinzip Hoffnung*, Frankfurt-am-Main, Suhrkamp, 1959).
10. Marcuse, 'The End of Utopia', p. 62.
11. Ibid., p. 64.
12. H. Marcuse, *One Dimensional Man*, Boston, Beacon Press, 1964, pp. 19–55.
13. Horn, *The Spirit of '68*, p. 147.
14. Marcuse, *One Dimensional Man*, p. 89.
15. E. Bloch, 'On the Original History of the Third Reich' in *Heritage of Our Times*, Cambridge, Polity, 1991, pp. 117–27.
16. Marcuse, 'The End of Utopia', p. 64.

17. E. Laclau, 'Beyond Emancipation' in *Emancipation(s)*, London, Verso, 1996, pp. 1–19.
18. H. Marcuse, 'The Problem of Violence and the Radical Opposition' in *Five Lectures*, p. 87.
19. Ibid., p. 89.
20. Ibid., p. 92.
21. E. Leslie, *Walter Benjamin: Overpowering Conformity*, London, Pluto, 2000, p. 203, citing C.L.R. James, *Notes on Dialectics: Hegel, Marx, Lenin*, London, Allison and Busby, 1980, p. 99.
22. Leslie, *Walter Benjamin*, p. 204.
23. W. Benjamin, 'Theses on the Philosophy of History' (XIV), in *Illuminations*, ed. H. Arendt, London, Fontana, 1973, p. 254, cited in Leslie, *Walter Benjamin*, p. 203.
24. B. Péret, *Le Déshonneur des poètes*, Paris, Pauvert, 1965, p. 65 (written 1945), cited in H. Marcuse, 'Society as a Work of Art' in *Art and Liberation*, London, Routledge, 2007, p. 125.
25. Marcuse, *An Essay on Liberation*, p. 40.
26. Ibid., pp. 41–2.
27. Marcuse, 'Art and Revolution' in *Art and Liberation*, p. 169.
28. Marcuse, 'The End of Utopia', p. 65.
29. Marcuse, 'The Problem of Violence and the Radical Opposition', p. 68.
30. Ibid., p. 80.
31. Ibid.
32. Ibid.
33. Marcuse, *An Essay on Liberation*, p. 36.
34. Ibid., p. 37.
35. Marcuse, 'The End of Utopia', p. 68.
36. Marcuse, *An Essay on Liberation*, p. 31.
37. Ibid., pp. 29–30.
38. Ibid., p. 30.
39. Ibid.
40. B. O'Donoghue, *The Courtly Love Tradition*, Manchester, Manchester University Press, 1982.
41. G. McKay, *Senseless Acts of Beauty: Cultures of Resistance Since the Sixties*, London, Verso, 1996, pp. 134–48.
42. D. Kellner, C. Pierce and T. Lewis, 'Introduction' to Marcuse, *Philosophy, Psychoanalysis and Emancipation*, p. 53, citing A. Johnston, 'A Blast from the Future: Freud, Lacan, Marcuse, and Snapping the Threads of the Past', *Umbr(a): Utopia*, 1, 2008, pp. 67–88.
43. C.F. Alford, 'Commentary' (on Marcuse's 'Ecology and the Critique of Modern Society') in Marcuse, *Philosophy, Psychoanalysis and Emancipation*, p. 221.
44. Ibid.
45. M. Miles, *Cities and Cultures*, London, Routledge, 2007, pp. 13–15; see also E.W. Burgess, 'The Growth of a City: Introduction to a Research Project' in R.T. Le Gates and F. Stout, eds, *The City Reader*, London, Routledge, 2003, 3rd edition, pp. 157–63.
46. E. Grosz, *The Nick of Time: Politics, Evolution, and the Untimely*, Durham NC, Duke University Press, 2004, pp. 17–39.

47. P. Corrigan, *The Sociology of Consumption*, London, Sage, 1997; D. Slater, *Consumer Culture and Modernity*, Cambridge, Polity, 1997; A. Tomlinson, ed., *Consumption, Identity and Style: Marketing, Meaning and the Packaging of Pleasure*, London, Routledge, 1990.
48. C. Lodziak, *The Myth of Consumerism*, London, Pluto, 2002, p. 91.
49. A. Gorz, *Strategy for Labour: A Radical Proposal*, Boston, Beacon Press, 1967, p. 71, cited in ibid., p. 92.
50. C. Lodziak and J. Tatman, *André Gorz: A Critical Introduction*, London, Pluto, 1997, p. 71.
51. Grosz, *The Nick of Time*, pp. 26–32.
52. Marcuse, *An Essay on Liberation*, pp. 31–2.
53. H. Marcuse, *Eros and Civilization*, London, Routledge and Kegan Paul, 1956.
54. S. Zukin, *The Cultures of Cities*, Oxford, Blackwell, 1995, p. 9.
55. J. McGuigan, *Cool Capitalism*, London, Pluto, 2009, p. 108.
56. J. Williamson, *Decoding Advertisements: Ideology and Meaning in Advertising*, London, Marion Boyars, 1978, p. 174, cited in McGuigan, *Cool Capitalism*, p. 108.
57. Marcuse, *An Essay on Liberation*, p. 57.
58. E. Wilson, *Bohemians: The Glamorous Outcasts*, London, I.B. Tauris, 2003, pp. 240–9.
59. Ibid., p. 240.
60. Ibid., p. 247.
61. Ibid.
62. Marcuse, *An Essay on Liberation*, pp. 57–8.
63. Ibid., p. 59.
64. Ibid., p. 63; see also K. Ross, *May '68 and its Afterlives*, Chicago, University of Chicago Press, 2002, p. 68.
65. Marcuse, *An Essay on Liberation*, p. 65.
66. Ibid., p. 82.
67. Ibid., p. 86.
68. Ibid., p. 90.
69. E. Bircham and J. Charlton, eds, *Anti-Capitalism: A Guide to the Movement*, London, Bookmakers Publications, 2001.
70. P.E. Wilson and B. Weinberg, eds, *Avant-Gardening: Ecological Struggle in the City and the World*, New York, Autonomedia, 1999.
71. T. Terranova, *Network Culture: Politics for the Information Age*, London, Pluto, 2004.
72. A. Roy, *Power Politics*, Cambridge MA, South End Press, 2001.
73. D. Kellner, 'Globalization, Technopolitics, and Revolution' in J. Foran, ed., *The Future of Revolutions: Rethinking Radical Change in the Age of Globalization*, London, Zed Books, 2003, pp. 180–94.
74. G. Cox and J. Krysa, eds, *Engineering Culture: On 'The Author as (Digital) Producer'*, New York, Autonomedia, 2005.
75. H. Marcuse, 'Conversation with Marcuse' in *Philosophy, Psychoanalysis and Emancipation*, p. 190 (first published, *Psychology Today*, 1971, pp. 35–40, 60–6).
76. Marcuse, *An Essay on Liberation*, p. 39.
77. Ibid., p. 55.
78. Ibid., p. 56.

79. R. King, *The Party of Eros: Radical Social Thought and the Realm of Freedom*, New York, Delta, 1973, p. 122 (first published, Chapel Hill, University of North Carolina Press, 1972).

80. Marcuse, *An Essay on Liberation*, p. 37.

81. Ibid.

82. Marcuse, 'The Problem of Violence and the Radical Opposition', p. 94.

83. M. Miles, *Urban Utopias: The Built and Social Architectures of Alternative Settlements*, London, Routledge, 2008, pp. 83–90; A.R. Buenfil, *Rainbow Nation Without Borders: Toward an Ecotopian Millennium*, Santa Fe, Bear, 1991.

84. Marcuse, 'The End of Utopia', p. 68.

85. Ibid.

86. Ibid., p. 69.

87. Kellner, Pierce and Lewis, 'Introduction' to *Philosophy, Psychoanalysis and Emancipation*, p. 14.

88. A. Gorz, *Capitalism, Socialism, Ecology*, London, Verso, 1994, p. 99, cited in Lodziak and Tatman, *André Gorz*, p. 55.

89. H. Marcuse, *Counter-Revolution and Revolt*, Boston, Beacon Press, 1972, pp. 33–4, cited in ibid., p. 55.

90. Gorz, *Farwell to the Working Class*, p. 88.

91. Ibid., p. 87.

92. R. Bahro, *The Alternative in Eastern Europe*, London, Verso, 1981, p. 260.

93. Ibid., p. 404, cited in Gorz, *Farwell to the Working Class*, p. 88.

94. Gorz, *Farwell to the Working Class*, p. 85, citing H. Marcuse, 'Marxisme et feminisme' in *Actuels*, Paris, Galilée, 1975 (page reference not given).

95. Gorz, *Farwell to the Working Class*, p. 75.

96. Ibid., p. 87.

97. I. Illich, *Tools for Conviviality*, London, Marion Boyars, 1990, p. 10 (first published 1973).

98. H. Marcuse, 'In Conversation with B. Moyers, 12 March 1974' in *The New Left and the 1960s*, London, Routledge, 2005, p. 154.

99. King, *The Party of Eros*, p. 153.

100. H. Marcuse, 'The Movement in a New Era of Repression' in *The New Left and the 1960s*, p. 150 (lecture at the University of California, Berkeley, 3 February 1971, first published in the *Berkeley Journal of Sociology*, Winter 1971–72, pp. 1–14).

101. Ibid.

102. Ibid., p. 151.

103. H. Lefebvre, *The Production of Space*, Oxford, Blackwell, 1991 (first published as *La production de l'espace*, Paris, Anthropos, 1974); my comment that the theory of moments is an earlier version of the theory of space derives from an informal conversation with Edward Soja at a conference, University of Wales, Aberystwyth, c. 2001.

104. Ross, *May '68 and its Afterlives*, p. 193.

105. A. Feenberg, 'Remembering Marcuse' in Marcuse, *Philosophy, Psychoanalysis and Emancipation*, p. 236.

106. Ibid.

107. H. Lefebvre, *Conversation avec Henri Lefebvre*, Paris, Messidor, 1991, p. 70, cited in A. Merrifield, *Henri Lefebvre: A Critical Introduction*, London, Routledge, 2006, p. 26.

108. H. Marcuse, 'The Paris Rebellion', *Peace News*, 28 June 1968, p. 6, cited in V. Geoghegan, *Reason and Eros: The Social Theory of Herbert Marcuse*, London, Pluto, 1981, p. 92.
109. Ross, *May '68 and its Afterlives*, p. 70.
110. Merrifield, *Henri Lefebvre*, p. 26.
111. H. Lefebvre, *La Somme et le reste*, Paris, La Nef de Paris, 1959.
112. Merrifield, *Henri Lefebvre*, p. 27.
113. Ibid., p. 28; see also R. Shields, *Lefebvre, Love and Struggle*, London, Routledge, 1999, pp. 58–63.
114. H. Lefebvre, *Critique of Everyday Life*, Vol. 1, London, Verso, 1991, pp. 33–4 (first published as *Critique de la vie quotidien I: Introduction*, Paris, Grasset, 1947).
115. Ibid., p. 35.
116. Ibid., p. 40.
117. Leslie, *Walter Benjamin*, p. 196.

7   THE AESTHETIC DIMENSION

1. H. Marcuse, *The Aesthetic Dimension*, Boston, Beacon Press, 1978.
2. T.W. Adorno, *Aesthetic Theory*, London, Athlone, 1997 (first published as *Asthetische Theorie*, Frankfurt-am-Main, Suhrkamp, 1970).
3. Marcuse, *The Aesthetic Dimension*, p. 73.
4. H. Marcuse, *Counter-revolution and Revolt*, Boston, Beacon Press, 1972.
5. Ibid., p. 1.
6. H. Marcuse, 'Ecology and the Critique of Modern Society' in *Philosophy, Psychoanalysis and Emancipation*, London, Routledge, 2011, pp. 206–13.
7. Marcuse, *The Aesthetic Dimension*, p. 1.
8. See B. Katz, *Herbert Marcuse and the Art of Liberation*, London, Verso, 1982, p. 188, n. 61.
9. D. Kellner, 'Introduction' to H. Marcuse, *The New Left and the 1960s*, London, Routledge, 2005, p. 21.
10. H. Marcuse, 'On the New Left' in *The New Left and the 1960s*, p. 126; cited by Kellner, 'Introduction' to the same volume, p. 27 (transcription of a talk, 4 December 1968, to mark the twentieth anniversary of *The Guardian*, first published in M. Teodori, ed., *The New Left: A Documentary History*, New York, Bobbs-Merrill, 1969, pp. 468–73).
11. Marcuse, 'On the New Left', p. 122.
12. Kellner, 'Introduction' to *The New Left and the 1960s*, p. 28.
13. Marcuse, *Counter-revolution and Revolt*, p. 16.
14. Ibid.
15. Ibid., p. 17.
16. H. Marcuse, 'Ecology and Revolution' in *The New Left and the 1960s*, pp. 173–7 (from a conference paper, first published in French in *Nouvel Observateur*, 397, 1972).
17. Marcuse, *Counter-revolution and Revolt*, p. 17.
18. Ibid., p. 31.
19. Ibid., p. 33.
20. Ibid., p. 37.
21. Ibid., p. 55.

22. R. Williams, *The Long Revolution*, London, Chatto and Windus, 1961.
23. R. Williams, 'On Reading Marcuse', *Cambridge Review*, 30 May 1969, p. 366, cited in A. O'Connor, *Raymond Williams: Writing, Culture, Politics*, Oxford, Blackwell, 1989, p. 26.
24. Marcuse, *Counter-revolution and Revolt*, p. 87.
25. Ibid.
26. Ibid., p. 89.
27. Ibid., p. 87.
28. Ibid., p. 105.
29. Ibid., p. 106; Marcuse cites A. Ferninger, quoted in R. Fernier, *Gustave Courbet*, Paris, Blibiothèque des Arts, 1969, p. 110, and in *Manifestos of Surrealism*, Ann Arbor, University of Michigan Press, 1969, p. 220.
30. Marcuse, *Counter-revolution and Revolt*, p. 116.
31. Ibid., p. 117.
32. Adorno, *Aesthetic Theory*, p. 31.
33. Ibid., p. 81.
34. Ibid., p. 250.
35. Marcuse, *Counter-revolution and Revolt*, pp. 121–2.
36. Ibid., p. 125.
37. H. Marcuse, 'Some Remarks on Aragon: Art and Politics in the Totalitarian Era' in *Technology, War and Fascism*, London, Routledge, 1998, pp. 199–214.
38. Marcuse, *The Aesthetic Dimension*, p. ix.
39. Ibid., p. 2.
40. Ibid., p. 5.
41. Ibid., p. xiii.
42. Ibid., p. 6.
43. Ibid., p. 7.
44. Ibid., p. 9.
45. Ibid., p. 72.
46. Ibid., p. 47.
47. e.g. Ibid., p. 44.
48. Ibid.
49. Ibid., p. 45.
50. Ibid., p. 46.
51. S. Beckett, *The Unnamable*, London, Calder and Boyars, 1975 (first published as *L'Innomable*, Paris, Editions de Minuit, 1952).
52. D. Bair, *Samuel Beckett*, London, Picador, 1980, p. 299, citing a quotation from a source wishing to remain anonymous (p. 578, n. 17).
53. Ibid., p. 262.
54. Adorno, *Aesthetic Theory*, p. 318.
55. Ibid., p. 224.
56. H. Marcuse, Letter to Samuel Beckett, 13 December 1978, in *Art and Liberation*, London, Routledge, 2007, p. 201.
57. Ibid.
58. H. Marcuse, 'Lyric Poetry after Auschwitz' in *Art and Liberation*, p. 211 (previously unpublished manuscript in English and German).
59. H. Marcuse, 'On The Aesthetic Dimension', conversation with Larry Harwick in *Art and Liberation*, p. 224 (first published, *Contemporary Literature*, vol. XXII, no. 4 (Fall) 1981, pp. 416–34).
60. Marcuse, *The Aesthetic Dimension*, p. 50.

61. Ibid., p. 53.
62. Ibid., p. 46.
63. Marcuse, 'Some Remarks on Aragon', p. 214.
64. Marcuse, *The Aesthetic Dimension*, p. 49.
65. Ibid., p. 53.
66. H. Marcuse, Letters to the Chicago Surrealists, in *Art and Liberation*, pp. 178–93.
67. Kellner, 'Introduction' to *Art and Liberation*, p. 61.
68. See H. Marcuse, *Soviet Marxism: A Critical Analysis*, London, Routledge and Kegan Paul, 1958.
69. Kellner, 'Introduction' to *Art and Liberation*, p. 54.
70. Marcuse, *The Aesthetic Dimension*, p. 14.
71. J. Reddick, 'Introduction' to G. Büchner, *Complete Plays, Lenz and Other Writings*, London, Penguin, 1993, p. xiv.
72. Marcuse, *The Aesthetic Dimension*, p. 54.
73. Ibid.
74. Ibid., p. 55, citing G.W.F. Hegel, 'Vorlesingen über die Aesthetic' in *The Philosophy of Fine Art*, London, Bell, 1920, p. 10.
75. Marcuse, *The Aesthetic Dimension*, p. 55.
76. Ibid., p. 56.
77. T.W. Adorno, 'Cultural Criticism and Society' in *Prisms*, Cambridge, MIT, 1983, p. 34.
78. Adorno, *Aesthetic Theory*, p. 152.
79. Marcuse, 'Lyric Poetry After Auschwitz', p. 212.
80. Ibid.
81. Ibid., p. 214.
82. Ibid., p. 216.
83. e.g. M. Bladek, 'Jewish-American Postgenerational Returns to Eastern and Central Europe'; S. Aloszko, 'The Culture of Remembrance and Memorialisation at Auschwitz', both in M. Miles and V. Azatyan, eds, *Cultural Memory: Reformations of the Past in the Present and the Present in the Past*, Plymouth, Plymouth University Press, 2010, pp. 126–37 and 96–109 respectively.
84. Marcuse, *The Aesthetic Dimension*, p. 56.
85. Ibid., p. 60.
86. Ibid., p. 64.
87. Büchner, *Complete Plays, Lenz and Other Writings*, p. 152.
88. M.B. Benn, *The Drama of Revolt: A Critical Study of Georg Büchner*, Cambridge, Cambridge University Press, 1976, p. 267.
89. Ibid., p. 268.
90. Marcuse, *The Aesthetic Dimension*, p. 67.
91. K. Marx, 'Theses on Feuerbach' in K. Marx and F. Engels, *Selected Works in One Volume*, London, Lawrence and Wishart, 1968, p. 29.
92. Marcuse, *The Aesthetic Dimension*, p. 69.
93. C. Becker, 'Herbert Marcuse and the Subversive Potential of Art' in C. Becker, ed., *The Subversive Imagination: Artists, Society, and Social Responsibility*, New York, Routledge, 1994, pp. 113–14.
94. Ibid., p. 114.
95. Ibid.
96. Ibid., p. 117.
97. Ibid.

98.   Ibid.
99.   Ibid., p. 119.
100. Ibid.
101. Ibid., p. 122.
102. Ibid.
103. Ibid., pp. 128–9.
104. P. Fuller, *Marches Past*, London, Hogarth Press, 1991, p. 29 (first published, London, Chatto and Windus, 1986).
105. P. Fuller, 'Where Was the Art of the Seventies?' in *Beyond the Crisis in Art*, London, Writers and Readers Publishing Cooperative, 1980, p. 32.
106. See also P. Fuller, 'Art and Biology' in J. Palmer and M. Dodson, eds, *Design and Aesthetics: A Reader*, London, Routledge, 1996, pp. 87–93.
107. Conversations with Peter Fuller around 1980 in London and Farnham.
108. In J. McDonald, ed., *Peter Fuller's Modern Painters: Reflections on British Art*, London, Methuen, 1993, p. xxix.
109. Marcuse, *The Aesthetic Dimension*, p. 134 (final sentence).

8   LEGACIES AND PRACTICES

1.   H. Marcuse, 'Children of Prometheus: 25 Theses on Technology and Society' in *Philosophy, Psychoanalysis and Emancipation*, London, Routledge, 2011, p. 224 (Thesis 13, from a translation by Charles Reitz, lecture notes revised as a position paper).
2.   Ibid. (Thesis 16.)
3.   H. Marcuse, *An Essay on Liberation*, Harmondsworth, Penguin, 1969.
4.   H. Marcuse, *Eros and Civilization*, London, Routledge and Kegan Paul, 1956.
5.   H. Marcuse, *The Aesthetic Dimension*, Boston, Beacon Press, 1978, p. 69.
6.   Quoted by J. Marabini in 'Derniers désirs', *Le Monde*, 3 August 1979, p. 12, cited in B. Katz, *Herbert Marcuse and the Art of Liberation*, London, Verso, 1982, p. 214.
7.   Katz, *Herbert Marcuse and the Art of Liberation*, p. 217.
8.   R. Bahro, *The Alternative in Eastern Europe*, London, Verso, 1981.
9.   C. Hilton, *The Wall: The People's Story*, Stroud, Sutton Publishing, 2003, p. 370.
10. S. Michalksi, *Public Monuments: Art in Political Bondage 1870–1997*, London, Reaktion, 1998, p. 150; see also M. Miles, *Urban Avant-Gardes: Art, Architecture and Change*, London, Routledge, 2004, pp. 96–7, 115, n. 13.
11. H. Marcuse, 'Cultural Revolution' in *Towards a Critical Theory of Society*, London, Routledge, 2001, p. 124 (previously unpublished manuscript, c.1970).
12. H. Marcuse, *One-Dimensional Man*, Boston, Beacon Press, 1964; T.W. Adorno, *The Culture Industry: Selected Essays on Mass Culture*, London, Routledge, 1991.
13. N. Power, *One-Dimensional Woman*, Ropley, Zero Books, 2009, p. 2.
14. Ibid., p. 29.
15. M. Rosler, 'Place, Position, Power, Politics' in C. Becker, ed., *The Subversive Imagination: Artists, Society, and Social Responsibility*, New York, Routledge, 1994, p. 57.

16. C. Doherty, 'The Institution is Dead! Long Live the Institution', *Engage*, 15, 2004, pp. 6–13.
17. V. Geoghegan, *Reason and Eros: The Social Theory of Herbert Marcuse*, London, Pluto, 1981, p. 102.
18. P. Bürger, *Theory of the Avant-Garde*, Minneapolis, University of Minnesota Press, 1984, p. 50 (first published as *Theorie der Avantgarde*, Frankfurt-am-Main, Suhrkamp, 1974).
19. M. Löwy and R. Sayre, *Romanticism Against the Tide of Modernity*, Durham, Duke University Press, 2001, p. 221.
20. Marcuse, *An Essay on Liberation*, p. 30.
21. M. Miles, *Urban Avant-Gardes: Art, Architecture and Change*, London, Routledge, 2004, pp. 195–203; 'Aesthetics in a Time of Emergency', *Third Text*, vol. 23, 4, issue 99, July 2009, pp. 421–34.
22. Marcuse, *An Essay on Liberation*, p. 72.
23. Ibid., p. 45.
24. P. Wood, 'Conclusion: For and Against the Avant-garde' in *The Challenge of the Avant-Garde*, New Haven, Yale, 1999, p. 267.
25. H. Marcuse, 'Some Remarks on Aragon: Art and Politics in the Totalitarian Era' in *Technology, War and Fascism*, London, Routledge, 1998, p. 201.
26. Ibid., p. 213.
27. Ibid., p. 207.
28. Wood, 'Conclusion: For and Against the Avant-garde', p. 268.
29. C. Duncan, *The Aesthetics of Power: Essays in Critical Art History*, Cambridge, Cambridge University Press, 1993, p. 96.
30. Ibid.
31. L. Nochlin, *Representing Women*, London, Thames and Hudson, 1999, p. 126.
32. B. Taylor, 'From Penitentiary to "Temple of Art": Early Metaphors of Improvement at the Millbank Tate' in M. Pointon, ed., *Art Apart: Art Institutions and Ideology Across England and North America*, Manchester, Manchester University Press, 1994, pp. 9–32.
33. C. Grunenberg, 'The Politics of Presentation: The Museum of Modern Art, New York' in Pointon, ed., *Art Apart*, pp. 192–211.
34. C. Duncan, *Civilizing Rituals: Inside Public Art Museums*, New York, Routledge, 1995, p. 107.
35. R. Krauss, 'No To ... Joseph Beuys' in C. Mesch and V. Michely, eds, *Joseph Beuys: The Reader*, Cambridge MA, MIT, 2007, p. 170.
36. From G. Adriani et al., *Joseph Beuys: Life and Works*, Woodbury, Barron's, 1979, p. 72; cited by Krauss in ibid., p. 170.
37. Krauss, 'No To ... Joseph Beuys', p. 171.
38. Ibid.
39. Ibid.
40. Ibid., p. 172.
41. Marcuse, *The Aesthetic Dimension*, p. 45.
42. Ibid.
43. A. Kaprow, 'Education of the Un-Artist, part III' in J. Kelley, ed., *The Blurring of Art and Life*, Berkeley, University of California Press, 1993, p. 132 (Kaprow dates the remark to 1973, but Documenta V took place in 1972); see also C. Bodenmann-Ritter, 'Every Man is an Artist: Talks at Documenta V' in Mesch and Michely, eds, *Joseph Beuys*, pp. 189–97.

44. Beuys, cited in Bodemann-Ritter, 'Talks at Documenta V by Joseph Beuys', p. 197.
45. B. Buchloch, 'Beuys: Twilight of the Idol' in Mesch and Michely, eds, *Joseph Beuys*, p. 110.
46. C. Tisdall, *Joseph Beuys* (catalogue essay), London, Anthony d'Offay Gallery, August 1980, n.p.
47. Beuys, cited in ibid., n.p.
48. Ibid.
49. S. Gablik, *The Reenchantment of Art*, London, Thames and Hudson, 1991.
50. D. Kuspit, *Signs of Psyche in Modern and Post-Modern Art*, Cambridge, Cambridge University Press, 1991, p. 127, citing D.W. Winnicott, 'Psycho-Neurosis in Childhood' in *Psycho-Analytic Explorations*, Cambridge MA, Harvard, 1989, p. 71.
51. T.W. Adorno and M. Horkheimer, *Dialectic of Enlightenment*, London, Verso, 1997, pp. 3–42 (first published as *Dialektik der Aufklarung*, New York, Social Studies association, 1944).
52. Beuys cited in Tisdall, *Joseph Beuys*, front cover.
53. Kuspit, *Signs of Psyche in Modern and Post-Modern Art*, p. 198.
54. H. Marcuse, 'Society as a Work of Art' in *Art and Liberation*, London, Routledge, 2007, p. 127.
55. E. Lucas, *Märzrevolution*, 1970, cited by C. Schäfer, email to author, 4 August 2010 (detail of source not given).
56. Schäfer, email to author, 4 August 2010.
57. Ibid.
58. P. Bianchi, 'What is the Art in Art?' in M. Landert, ed., *Miami Islet: Interactive Strategies in the Work of Jochen Gerz*, Zürich, Niggli, 2000, p. 127 (parallel German-English texts).
59. Ibid.
60. Ibid., p. 125.
61. Ibid., p. 139.
62. Ibid.
63. J. Gerz, text for *Mahnmal gegen Fascismus*, in *Jochen Gerz: Res Publica: The Public Works 1968–1999* (exhibition catalogue), Bolzano, Hatje Cantz, 1999, p. 54.
64. H.E. Nosack, *The End: Hamburg 1943*, Chicago, University of Chicago Press, 2004 (first published as *Der Untergang: Hamburg 1943*, Frankfurt-am-Main, Suhrkamp, 1948); W.G. Sebald, *On the Natural History of Destruction*, London, Penguin, 2003.
65. H. Prigann, in conversation with the author, Gelsenkirchen, 2002 (from memory).
66. J. Gerz, quoted in D. von Dräteln, 'Jochen Gerz's Visual Poetry', *Contemporaneo*, September, 1989, p. 47, cited in J.E. Young, *At Memory's Edge: After-Images of the Holocaust in Contemporary Art and Literature*, New Haven, Yale, 2000, p. 134.
67. Young, *At Memory's Edge*, p. 138.
68. Cited in M. Gibson, 'Hamburg: Sinking Feelings', *Art News*, Summer, 1987, p. 107, cited in ibid., p. 139.
69. Sebald, *On the Natural History of Destruction*, p. 28.
70. Ibid., p. 34.

71. J. Habermas, *The Structural Transformation of the Public Sphere: An Inquiry into a Category of Bourgeois Society*, Cambridge MA, MIT, 1991 (first published as *Strukturwandel der Offentlicheit*, Darmstadt, Luchterhand Verlag, 1962).
72. www.freee.org.uk/work/protestdriveshistory (accessed 17 March 2011).
73. L. Sandercock, 'Cosmopolitan Urbanism: A Love Song to Our Mongrel Cities' in J. Binnie, S. Holloway, S. Millington and C. Young, eds, *Cosmopolitan Urbanism*, London, Routledge, 2006, p. 47.
74. N. Papastergiadis, 'Small Gestures in Specific Places' in S. McQuire and N. Papastergiadis, eds, *Empire, Ruins and Networks: The Transcultural Agenda in Art*, London, River Oram Press, 2005, p. 291.
75. Interview in J.B. Slater and A. Iles, *No Room to Live: Radical Art and the Regenerate City*, London, Mute, 2010, p. 86.
76. A. Hewitt and M. Jordan, 'A Transformative Art Gallery – Thoughts in Relation to Futurology' in *Futurology*, Walsall, the New Art Gallery, 2009, p. 12.
77. *The Concept of the Public Sphere*, poster-work, Freee Art Collective, 2008.
78. Marcuse, 'Society as a Work of Art', p. 125.
79. H. Marcuse, 'Some Social Implications of Modern Technology' in *Technology, War and Fascism*, London, Routledge, 1998, p. 65 (first published in *Studies in Philosophy and Social Science*, vol. 9, no. 3, 1941, pp. 414–39).
80. Ibid.
81. Ibid.

Index

Abromeit, John 41
Adorno, Theodor W. 1, 2, 11, 40, 42, 43–4, 54, 68, 86, 104, 119, 126, 131–2, 137, 139, 147
  Aesthetic Theory 104, 126, 132
  Dialectic of Enlightenment 67, 68
Alexander II of Russia 28
Alford, C. Fred 113
Aragon, Louis 11, 12, 65–6, 74, 77, 79–84
  Aurélien 66
  Le Monde Réel 80
Arendt, Hannah 89

Bahro, Rudolf 106, 121–2, 145
Bair, Deirdre 135
Bandel, Joseph-Ernst von 60
Baron Haussmann 74
Bateson , Gregory 97
Baudelaire, Charles 12, 34, 65, 73, 74, 84, 133, 136
  Les Fleurs du mal 136
Bauer, Bruno 20, 23
Bauer, Edgar 23
Bauer, Heinrich 23
Becker, Carol 15, 126, 142–3
Beckett, Samuel 40, 104, 131–2, 135–6, 140, 146
  Endgame 132
  L'Expulsé 136
  The Unnamable 135, 140–1
  Waiting for Godot 131
Beech, Dave 147, 160, 161–2
Benjamin, Walter 1, 11, 13, 14, 15, 43, 67, 77, 84, 98, 109
Benn, Maurice 141
Berg, Peter 95
Beuys, Joseph 104, 147, 152–5, 157
Bianchi, Paolo 156–7
Bloch, Ernst 2, 9, 15, 16, 40, 46, 59–60, 61, 62–4, 67, 86, 90–1, 111, 116
  The Principle of Hope 16, 111

Boulez, Pierre 131
Brecht, Berthold 12–13, 67, 133
  The Beggar's Opera 67
Breton, André 36, 40, 131
Brown, Norman O. 7–8, 100
  Life Against Death 7, 100
  Love's Body 8
Bruller, Jean 79
  Le Silence de la mer 79
Buchloch, Benjamin 154
Büchner, Georg 138, 140
  The Death of Danton 138
  Lenz 140
Bürger, Peter 148

Cage, John 131
Carmichael, Stokely 97, 99
Castro, Fidel 90, 118
Celan, Paul 139
Chernyshevsky, Nikolay 29
  What Is To Be Done? 29
Colère, François la, *see* Aragon
Cooper, David 97
Cornelius, Peter 19
Courbet, Gustave 13, 131, 151
Coyote, Peter 94

Darwin, Charles 113–14, 115
Davies, Angela 5, 6, 43, 87, 88
Defregger, Franz von 62
Deineka, Alexander 17
Didion, Joan 92–3, 94–5
Dix, Otto 30, 47
Dostoevsky, Fyodor 29
  The Little Hero 29
Doyle, Michael 94
Duncan, Carol 151, 152
Dürer, Albrecht 14
Dutschke, Rudi 96, 123, 129
Dylan, Bob 90, 137

Eichmann, Adolph 89
Eiffel, Alexandre Gustave 22

Eisner, Kurt 31
Éluard, Paul 11, 65, 70, 71, 74–7, 78, 79–80, 136, 151
 Poésie et vérité 76
Engels, Friedrich 14, 18, 23, 28
 The Communist Manifesto 18, 28
 The Dialectics of Nature 14
Evans, Sara 90

Farber, David 86, 93, 94
Farrell, James 89, 90
Feenberg, Andrew 2, 87–8
Feuerbach, Ludwig 23–4, 99, 141, 142
 Essence of Christianity 23
Fouchet, Max-Pol 78, 135
Fourier, Charles 22, 102, 120, 128, 146
Franco, Francisco 71
Freud, Sigmund 68, 98, 99, 110, 142
Friedrich Barbarossa 60–1, 62
Friedrich Wilhelm IV 19, 21
Fuller, Peter 8–9, 22, 126, 143–4

Gablik, Suzi 154
 The Reenchantment of Art 154
Garcia, Jerry 93
Gauguin, Paul 63, 84–5
Geoghegan, Vincent 16, 17, 88, 99, 148
Gerasimov, Alexander 17
Gerz, Jochen 147, 156–9
Ginsberg, Allen 93, 97
Gitlin, Todd 92
Goering, Herman 64, 156
Goethe, Johann Wolfgang 33, 37, 44, 55–6
 Faust 55–6
 The Sorrows of the Young Werther 38
 Wilhelm Meisters Lehrjahre 37
Gogh, Vincent van 63
Goldmann, Lucien 11, 97
Gorky, Arshile 155
Gorky, Maxim 29
 The Children of the Sun 29
Gorz, André 106, 114, 121–2
 Farewell to the Working Class 106, 121–2
Greenberg, Clement 16–17, 67–8, 143
Grosz, Elizabeth 114

Grosz, George 47
Grützner, Eduard 62

Habermas, Jürgen 145, 159
Hausmann, Raoul 103
Heartfield, John 47, 59, 64
Hegel, G.W.F. 20, 40, 41, 42, 44, 109, 138
 Phenomenology of Spirit 41
 Science of Logic 41, 109
Heidegger, Martin 32, 41, 42, 48
 Being and Time 41
Heine, Heinrich 19, 20, 21
Hewitt, Andy 147, 160, 161–2
Hitler, Adolf 62, 63, 67, 68
Holman, Valerie 77–8, 79
Homberger, Eric 93
Horkheimer, Max 42, 43–4, 67, 68
 Dialectic of Enlightenment, 67, 68
Horn, Gerd-Rainer 108
Hugo, Victor 112
 Les Misérables 112
Hunt, Holman 19

Illich, Ivan 122

Johnston, Adrian 113
Jordan, Mel 147, 160, 161–2
Joyce, James 40
Jung, Franz 39
 The Red Week 39

Kandinsky, Wassily 37, 59, 63, 64
 Concerning the Spiritual in Art 37
Kant, Immanuel 57
Kaprow, Allan 153–4
Katz, Barry 27, 29, 31, 32, 34, 38, 40, 41, 48–9, 68–9, 88
Keller, Gottfried 33, 37
Kellner, Douglas 1, 4, 11–12, 24, 27, 33, 35, 37, 39, 41–2, 43–4, 47, 48–9, 50, 51, 53, 54, 68, 70–1, 97, 113, 120, 127, 137
Kendall, Stuart 79
Kerouac, Jack 90
Kesey, Ken 92
Khrushchev, Nikita 17
King, Richard 99, 101, 119 ,122
Klee, Paul 16, 37, 63
Kooning, Willem de 155

Krauss, Rosalind 152–3
Kristeva, Julia 84, 104
Kuspit, Donald 155

Laclau, Ernesto 108
Laing, R.D. 97
Landauer, Gustav 31
Leary, Timothy 93–4
Lefebvre, Henri 107, 123–5
   Critique of Everyday Life 124
Léger, Fernand 77
Lenin, Vladimir 109
Leonardo da Vinci 14
Leslie, Esther 77, 109, 125
Levitas, Ruth 11, 17
Lewis, Tyson 113, 120
Liebknecht, Karl 29–30, 31
Lodziak, Conrad 114–15, 116, 121, 125
Lowell, Robert 93
Löwenthal, Leo 42, 43, 50
Löwy, Michael 148–9
Lukács, Georg 11, 16, 39–40, 59, 62, 63
Luxemburg, Rosa 29–30, 31, 146
Lynd, Robert 69

Madame Blavatsky 64
Mallarmé, Stéphane 84–5, 124
Mann, Thomas 6, 33, 37–8, 39, 40, 49, 145
   Death in Venice 6, 37, 38, 39
Marabini, Jean 145
Marc, Franz 59, 63, 64, 103
Marcuse, Herbert 1–2, 3–9, 10–26, 27–45, 46–64, 65–85, 86–105, 106–25, 126–44, 145–64
   The Aesthetic Dimension 2, 3, 8, 10, 11, 12, 16, 22, 51, 57, 71, 126, 127, 129, 131, 132–4, 137, 138, 140, 142, 144, 145, 153
   Art and Liberation 4, 6, 47
   Collected Papers 1, 6, 7, 47, 113
   Counter-Revolution and Revolt 7, 54, 56, 126–7, 128, 129
   Eros and Civilisation 7, 38, 40, 68, 87, 92, 98, 115, 142, 145
   An Essay on Liberation 2, 7, 8, 11, 36, 71, 87, 100, 106, 110, 111, 119, 122, 128, 130, 132, 145

   Hegel's Ontology and the Theory of Historicity 41
   One Dimensional Man 87, 91, 108, 147
   Soviet Marxism: A Critical Analysis 13
Marcuse, Peter 1
Marx, Karl 3, 8, 14, 16, 18–26, 28, 36, 40, 41, 42, 44, 48, 52, 66, 99, 101, 109, 112, 114, 117, 138, 142, 146
   The Communist Manifesto 18, 28
   Economic and Philosophical Manuscripts of 1844 41
   Grundrisse 21
   Theses on Feuerbach 22, 66, 99
Matisse, Henri 16
McGuigan, Jim 86, 116
McKay, George 88
Mendelsohn, Erich 30
Merleau-Ponty, Maurice 41
Merrifield, Andy 124
Merton, Thomas 89
Michalski, Sergiusz 60–1
Mills, C. Wright 90
Mitchell, Adrian 146
Monet, Claude 81, 82
Moyers, Bill 122
Mumford, Lewis 98

Napoleon, Bonaparte 61
Napoleon III 74
Negri, Antonio 145
Neumann, Franz 69
Nicholas II of Russia 28–9
Nietzsche, Friedrich 38, 55
Nochlin, Linda 151
Nolde, Emil 63

Otto, Louise 91

Papanek, Victor 102
   Design for the Real World 102
Papastergiadis, Nikos 161
Péret, Benjamin 109
Picasso, Pablo 16, 71–3, 147, 149–51
Pierce, Clayton 113, 120
Pitkin, Hannah 89
Pollock, Friedrich 42, 155

Pollock, Jackson 34
Prigann, Hermann 158

Racine, Jean 83
Radek, Karl 30
Reason, David 9
Reddick, John 138
Reitz, Charles 4, 30, 41–2, 54, 58
Repin, Ilya 16
Rilke, Rainer Maria 31
Rimbaud, Arthur 55, 131, 133
Rose, Margaret 19, 20–1, 23
    Marx's Lost Aesthetic 19
Rosler, Martha 147
Ross, Kristin 124
Rossinow, Doug 90, 92
Rothko, Mark 155
Rousseau, Jean-Jacques 18
Ruskin, John 8

Saint-Simon, Claude Henri de 20, 21
Sandercock, Leonie 90, 161
Sartre, Jean-Paul 11, 41
Sayre, Robert 148–9
Schäfer, Christoph 155–6
Schiller, Friedrich 57
Schmitz, Bruno 61
Sebald, W.G. 159
Seidemann, Alfred 41
Shalev, Esther 157–9
Sim, Stuart 17–18
Smith Patti 55

Stalin, Joseph 67
Stepanova, Varvara 22
Stockhausen, Karl-Heinz 131
Strauss, David 23

Tatlin, Vladimir 22
Tatman, Jeremy 114–15, 121
Tisdall, Caroline 154
Toller, Ernst 31
Tomsky, Nikolai 146
Tretyakov, Sergey 14

Vercors, *see* Bruller
Verlaine, Paul 55

Wagner, Richard 60
Watteau, Antione 74
Weber, Max 27
Wilhelm I 61
Willett, John 30, 39
Williams, Raymond 129
Williamson, Judith 116
    Decoding Advertisements 116
Wilson, Elizabeth 117
Wodiczko, Krzysztof 146, 156
Wolin, Richard 84
Wood, Paul 151
Wörringer, Wilhelm 37, 63

Young, James 158

Zukin, Sharon 115–16